Strategies for Cultural Change

For Wendy, Steve and Chris

Strategies for Cultural Change

Paul Bate
Director,
Centre for the Study of Organizational Change,
University of Bath

Butterworth-Heinemann Ltd
Linacre House, Jordan Hill, Oxford OX2 8DP

A MEMBER OF THE REED ELSEVIER GROUP

OXFORD   LONDON   BOSTON
MUNICH   NEW DELHI   SINGAPORE   SYDNEY
TOKYO   TORONTO   WELLINGTON

First published 1994

© Stuart P. Bate 1994

British Library Cataloguing in Publication Data

Bate, Paul
    Strategies for Cultural Change
    I. Title
    658

ISBN 0 7506 0519 7

Typeset and Illustrated by TecSet Ltd, Wallington, Surrey
Printed and bound in Great Britain by Clays, St Ives plc

Contents

Acknowledgements

Paul Valéry once said that works are never finished, only abandoned. This book would have been abandoned a good deal sooner – indeed would probably never have got started – had it not been for the following people: my students in the School of Management at the University of Bath, especially the final year undergraduates in my organization analysis and development class and the MBA students in my organization behaviour class; my colleagues and clients in industry, especially those in British Rail whose struggles to bring about cultural change provided the inspiration and leitmotiv for the present book; my fellow 'warriors' in SCOS who have done so much to put 'culture' on the map (generating a lot of energy and insanity in the process); my publishers who encouraged this project in the first place – and no doubt regretted it as deadlines passed unmet; my own university for granting me a year's sabbatical leave which enabled me to devote myself to writing; the College of Business Administration at the University of Massachusetts and the Norwegian School of Management for allowing me to spend this period in truly delightful company and lovely surroundings. To them all I express my deepest thanks.

A book that goes into the world with such a heavy load of gratitude is almost a community venture, and I suppose this is how it should be with a book on culture. However, cultures are also made up of individuals, and there are particular individuals whom I would like to take this opportunity to thank – for their practical help, support and friendship: Alan Savage, Bjørn Hennestad, John Barker, Ian Colville, Linda Smircich, Marta Calás, Suzanne Wilson Higgins, Alison Boyd, Paul Hills, Marc Chapman, Pete Huskinson, the consulting staff of A.I.M. in Oslo, and my colleagues in the School of Management and the Centre for the Study of Organizational Change. And finally there are thanks to those whom I have never met, the great scholars whose writings profoundly affected my thinking, indeed my whole being: Georg Simmel, Susanne Langer, Clifford Geertz, Hermann Hesse, Paul Watzlawick, Pitirim Sorokin and Morse Peckham. I take this opportunity of apologizing to them for my own less worthy efforts.

Every effort has been made to locate the original copyright holders of material used and the author would like to thank the following for *viii   Acknowledgements*

granting permission to include material copyrighted to them in the book: Geertz C. (1973) *The Interpretation of Cultures*. Selected excerpts. Copyright © 1973 by BasicBooks Inc. Reprinted by permission of HarperCollins, Publishers, Inc; Geertz C. (1974) From the native's point of view. On the nature of anthropological understanding. Reprinted by permission of the American Academy of Arts and Sciences, from the *Bulletin of the American Academy of Arts and Sciences*, **28** (1); Gilot F. and Lake C. (1964) *Life with Picasso*, McGraw-Hill, New York. Reprinted with the permission of the publisher; Green S. (1988) Strategy, organizational culture and symbolism. *Long Range Planning*, **21** (4), 121–9, with kind permission from Pergamon Press Ltd, Headington Hill Hall, Oxford OX3 OBW; Fox A. (1966) Industrial sociology and industrial relations. Royal Commission on Trade Unions and Employers' Associations 1965–1968, Research Paper No. 3, reproduced with the permission of the Controller of Her Majesty's Stationery Office; Kundera M. (1980) *The Book of Laughter and Forgetting*, trans, Michael Heim. English translation copyright © 1980 by Alfred A. Knopf, Inc. Reprinted by permission of the publisher; Langer S. K. (1953) *Feeling and Form*. Reprinted with permission of Macmillan College Publishing Company. Copyright 1953 Charles Scribner's Sons; copyright renewed © 1981 Susanne K. Langer; Laurent A. (1989) A cultural view of organizational change. In *Human Resource Management in International Firms. Change, Globalization, Innovation* (eds P. Evans, Y. Doz and A. Laurent). Reprinted with permission of Macmillan Ltd, London and St Martin's Press, Inc; Masuch M. (1985) Vicious circles in organizations. *Administrative Science Quarterly*, 30, 14–33. Reprinted by permission of Administrative Science Quarterly; Rosen C. and Zerner H. (1984) *Romanticism and Realism*. Copyright © by Charles Rosen and Henri Zerner. Used by permission of Viking Penguin, a division of Penguin Books USA Inc; Solomon R. C. (1976) *The Passions*, Anchor Press Doubleday, New York. Reissued (1993) as *The Passions, Emotions and the Meaning of Life*. Hackett, Indianapolis. Reprinted with the permission of the author.

Then there are the most important thanks of all. First to my children, Steve and Chris, who steadfastly refused to accept a closed study door as a sign to 'keep out', and whose very presence has kept this whole venture in a proper perspective. Their wit, intelligence and unselfish love have kept me sane. And then to my wife and closest friend, Wendy, who despite the huge demands of her own work has given an inordinate amount of time to this project, reading and correcting various drafts, and discussing and clarifying ideas – while at the same time managing to keep house and home together. Wendy, I wish I had half your intellect, humanity, energy and application. This book is dedicated to the three of you.

Part One Frameworks for Thinking about Cultural Change

1   Turtles all the way down

Introduction

Writing a book about cultural change is a daunting task. One cannot simply take the advice of the storyteller or policeman and 'begin at the beginning', and tell it 'how it happened'. In matters of change there is rarely a clear beginning – nor, for that matter, a discernible middle or end, and few people ever agree on what 'really happened', or if indeed anything happened at all. Even fewer will be able to say with any certainty what change is, or precisely what has changed, especially where matters of cultural change are involved. And, as we are well aware, the concept of culture is itself surrounded by a myriad of problems relating to meaning and definition. Therefore, put 'culture' and 'change' together and the chance of anything coherent emerging becomes all the more unlikely.

Change, as writers have pointed out on many previous occasions, is a highly complex business, difficult to understand, and because of its non-linear nature almost impossible to deal with systematically, or to write about convincingly. Pettigrew, for example, invites us to 'observe other men consciously attempting to move large and small systems in different directions, or attempt it yourself, and one sees what a difficult and complicated human process change is' (1985: 1). Certainly, if one's ambition is to tell it 'how it really is' – or was – the result is almost certain to be a story as labyrinthine and multilayered as an Agatha Christie whodunnit. Things, as they say, are going to take a whole lot of explaining.

Talking of stories, Clifford Geertz's story of the elephant captures perfectly the many difficulties and frustrations one experiences when trying to work with the concept of culture:

> There is an Indian story – at least I heard it as an Indian story – about an Englishman who, having been told that the world rested on a platform which rested on the back of an elephant which rested in turn on the back of a

turtle, asked . . . what did the turtle rest on? Another turtle. And that turtle?
'Ah, Sahib, after that it is turtles all the way down'.   (Geertz, 1973: 29)

In matters of culture it is nearly always a case of 'turtles all the way down': one just never seems to get to the bottom of things. As Geertz says, cultural analysis is intrinsically incomplete: 'And, worse than that, the more deeply it goes the less complete it is' (p. 29). Working with culture, one is constantly being reminded of the Chinese saying that the more you know the more confused you become, or the theoretical physicist John Wheeler's comment that 'The greater the island of knowledge grows, the greater becomes the shoreline of the unknown' (1980: 9). The question 'why bother?' is therefore never far from one's mind. Nor can one ever be sure that things will all come right in the end.

Working with complexity

cultural analysis runs counter to the preference for simplification that is prevalent in social science research. A greater tolerance for complexity, however, will reward investigators with a deeper understanding of the phenomena they are studying and a firmer basis for interpreting the data they collect.   (LeVine, 1984: 84)

At a moment when the authors of best-selling business books are exhorting us to keep things simple, follow what our commonsense tells us, and practise the 'technology of the obvious', one is conscious of the risks involved in drawing attention to complexity – especially in proposing that we, in fact, need to confront complexity head on, recognize it for what it is, and learn to work with it. The danger of advocating this kind of philosophy is that one exposes oneself to accusations of over-complicating the issues, using mystifying jargon, being over-theoretical and anti-practical, and generally refusing to 'come clean' on the straightforward answers that people in the real world are seeking. Borrowing a phrase used by Renfrew (1979: 4) when he found himself in a similar corner, my response would be that if the concepts in the book are sometimes difficult, so undoubtedly is the task.

Nevertheless, we cannot escape the fact that the siren-call of the simplifiers is extremely seductive, promising things far beyond the reach of our heavy-footed, land-locked complicators. Who, after all, could resist the song which says

'everything is what it is and not another thing'. . .The world is what the wide-awake, uncomplicated person takes it to be. Sobriety, not subtlety, realism, not imagination are the keys to wisdom; the really important facts of life lie scattered openly along its surface, not cunningly secreted in its depths. There is no need, indeed it is a fatal mistake, to deny, as poets, intellectuals, priests, and other professional complicators of the world so often do, the obviousness of the obvious. Truth is as plain, as the Dutch proverb has it, as a pikestaff over water. (Geertz, 1974: 89)

Given this highly attractive alternative, one might well ask what would induce anyone (practitioners especially) to read a book that promises no 'keys', no 'solutions', no 'simple secrets', not even an eight-point guide to 'excellence' or a single two-by-two matrix of strategic options for change! My reply would be to invite the reader seriously to consider how far the 'paradigm of simplicity' accords with his or her actual *experience* of organizational life. I believe the answer for the great majority would be that there is little correspondence: we all want things to be simple, but we know they rarely are; we all want the 'solution' but we know it will not always present itself, or that when it does it may not actually achieve the desired effect. It may be that the 'keep it simple' philosophy has a role in expressing some kind of ideal-world position, or even in providing a not unwelcome form of escapism or reverie for the user, but as a philosophy for action it is woefully inadequate. The thrust of my argument is that one ends up 'working with complexity' not out of choice or preference but because reality dictates that it cannot be otherwise. In saying this, one does not rule out the possibility in the end of having to make simplifications (which is arguably an essential part of the process of taking action), but that, of course, is very different from beginning with them.

The guiding maxim of the philosophy being proposed is that one should meet complexity with complexity, that is develop a framework sufficiently complex to embrace the complexity within the subject matter it is seeking to describe, but not so complex and lifesize as to be as confusing as the 'real thing'. Unfortunately, it is here at the very first stage of conceptualization that one encounters a major problem: there are apparently no frameworks like this available! Kennedy (1985: 325) writes: 'we don't even seem to have a reasonable way, i.e., a conceptual framework, for thinking about change'. As it stands the statement is probably incorrect – most researchers would probably agree that there is no shortage of frameworks for thinking about change (and culture) – but where *cultural change* is concerned it is unfortunately probably true. The implication for this particular 'story' is that one does not have the luxury of beginning at the beginning, using a framework that is already available, but needs to take several steps backwards in order to work on putting one together. This is where this first chapter finds itself.

Developing a conceptual framework is like learning a language. This book is based on this idea. First we need the vocabulary – the concepts –

and then we need the grammar – the thinking structures – and finally we need the 'oral' practice – the applications.

> As Simmel says, frameworks are

> languages into which the world or aspects of it may be translated. These languages may be conceived as general schemata which constitute conditions for the intelligibility of the world as a whole or specific aspects of it.
>
> (Oakes, 1980: 10)

The overall aim of this book is to create one such 'language', albeit a fairly rudimentary one, for the world of cultural change.

Asking good questions

> Our ignorance grows with our knowledge . . . We will always have more questions than answers.   (K. Popper, *Conjectures and Refutations,* 1963)

Thinking conceptually, whether it be for analytical, strategic or action purposes, is itself a complex business. What it all seems to boil down to in the end, however, is the knack of being able to ask 'good' questions. The stress is on questions rather than answers since the answers you get depend on the questions you ask. Contrary to the normal way of thinking, 'answers' are not independent phenomena that are in some way unlocked or 'released' by questions, but phenomena that are actually created by them. The form of the original question is therefore absolutely crucial because it frames one's entire perspective on this or that issue. And perspective, as the artist is constantly reminding us, is everything. The point I am making has been summed up as follows:

> It is vital to recognize this 'correlativity' of questions and answers . . . An answer assumes all that the question presupposes.   (Crick, 1976: 131)

If we are to take this point seriously, it means that we need to exercise special care in our selection of the main questions – the primary form of interrogative – for our framework on cultural change. This choice will determine what the shape of the framework will be (structure), what we subsequently 'see' and do not see (perspective and focus of attention), and where we finally stand on the subject (judgement).

The definition of what constitutes a 'good' question will obviously vary, depending on our reasons for asking it in the first place, but I believe one of the more important requirements is that it addresses and, where necessary, challenges the fundamental and 'taken for granted' views that may have grown up around a subject or in our own minds. A question must truly 'question' something: this idea is part of that larger (originally Greek) philosophy of scepticism which says that learning proceeds as the result of constantly challenging the prevailing views and conventions of the time. Asking questions provides an effective safeguard against dogmatism – that closed frame of mind which foolishly claims to know how things actually are, and which is always discouraging us from looking further. There is always the temptation in management, as no doubt in other commercially influenced subjects, to give the client what he or she 'wants to hear', the unfortunate consequence being that prejudices, whims and dogmas are reinforced, and a cosy, self-congratulatory atmosphere created. My position is that while not averse to pleasing (who would want to be accused of being a spoil-sport and not joining in?), I would always reserve the right to ask questions that may be disturbing.

The questions below form the organizing framework for this book. They are all directed towards certain 'taken for granteds' that have grown up in the field. They are summarized here, and will be discussed in detail as the book unfolds:

Why change culture?

A functional, 'so what?' question which examines the grounds upon which we might assume or believe that a strategy for cultural change would serve any useful function or purpose, or offer anything of value or interest. The question is really twofold: why change, and why culture?

Is planned cultural change possible?

A question which asks what potential, if any, there exists for conscious and deliberately planned intervention in an organization's cultural change processes. If there is such potential, the question is intervention by whom, in what way, and for what purpose? If culture cannot be changed by deliberate human agency, why bother to try?

What kind of cultural change is envisaged?

Questions relating to the scale or level of cultural change: change 'what' precisely, and to what end? Questions about what is supposedly in line to be changed draw us away from generalized views about the subject and towards consideration of the different types and 'orders' of cultural change that exist, and the different change strategies that each may require.

How does cultural change occur?

The factual question for which sadly there seem to be few available 'facts'. An assumption seems to have grown up that an understanding of the cultural process is not absolutely necessary before an attempt is made to change it (which may explain why so little is known about the cultural change process in organizations). The question here signifies a departure from this view, being prompted by the opposite argument that any theory of (and strategy for) cultural change needs to grow from a thorough understanding of the processes that produce and maintain cultural order, and the processes that transform it.

So much for the point about 'asking good questions'. Another point – a twist on this one – is that 'asking questions is good'. It suspends our certainties and puts us in a healthily doubtful (and fumbling) frame of mind. To use Ott's phrase (1984), it turns us from self-satisfied know-alls into 'honest grapplers' after truth. A questioning frame of mind suspends our assumptions about the existence of 'one reality' and puts us in an interpretive (multiperspectival) frame of mind; and it frees us from the world of 'facts', enabling us to engage in the fruitful process of 'imaginative abstraction' (Geertz, 1973: 24). With this in mind, 'progress' has to be redefined, being 'marked less by perfection of consensus than by a refinement of debate. What gets better is the precision with which we vex each other' (1973: 29).

You can't judge a book by its cover

Still on the subject of questions, we might begin by questioning the title of the book itself: 'Strategies for Cultural Change (in Organizations)'. On the face of it, the title seems fairly innocuous and straightforward, and it does trip rather easily off the tongue. Yet the more we think about it the more we need to avoid being taken in by it! The truth of the matter is that any book with this title – which is too sensible and managerial by half – could easily end up glossing over problems, and perpetuating the very misconceptions that need to be challenged. Drawing critical attention to the title of one's own book may sound rather like shooting oneself through the foot. Nevertheless, this will be a small price to pay if it succeeds in highlighting some of the common fallacies about 'changing culture', and enables us to consider the possibility of an alternative perspective.

The title implies four key concepts:

- Strategy
- Culture
- Change
- Organization

The four phenomena are conventionally presumed to be different, otherwise why would they go by different names? Linguistic logic apart, common sense tells us that strategy is different from culture, culture is different from organization, and so on. But is this really the case? The reader is invited to reflect on and reconsider these assumptions because they have, in my view, created a false frame within which to consider the subject. I therefore wish to propose a perspective on cultural change that makes:

- 'culture' synonymous with 'organization';
- 'strategy' synonymous with 'culture'.

Anticipating the 'so what?' question, I would point out that the way people choose to define root concepts such as these bears directly upon what they do with them. In short, definitions determine actions. And thoughts and perceptions as well: 'What we notice and experience as cultural change depends directly on how we conceptualize culture' (Meyerson and Martin, 1987: 623). There is another point too, relating to my earlier comments about developing a 'language' for the world of cultural change. There is a line in an ancient Sanskrit poem:

Names. The first principle of language.

Labels – names – are the basis of any language, the 'language of culture' included. They structure language. Therefore, to put it crudely, if we are to get the language right, we need to get the labels right. Furthermore, to the extent that labels structure language, they can also be said to structure thought itself. For as Vico (1668-1744) once said,

Minds are formed by the character of language, not language by the minds of those who speak it.   (Quoted in Berlin, 1980: 42)

Culture as organization, organization as culture

Many organization writers, and probably the majority of organization practitioners, have opted for a 'scientific' rather than 'anthropological' view of culture. This involves conceiving of culture as

- An object or 'thing'
- A part of a bigger 'thing' (i.e. an organization).

The scientific rationalists' view of culture is that it is something that an organization 'has': culture is designated as a 'component' of organization, no different in status from any of its other 'components' – 'structure', 'strategy', 'systems' and so on. See, for example, the well-known McKinsey 7-S framework, which puts culture ('shared values') into a 'happy atom' alongside (in fact, in the middle of) structure, strategy, skills, staff, style and systems (Peters and Waterman, 1982: 10).

Like the other S's in the atom, this 'thing' is treated as a variable or sub-system which affects the overall functioning and effectiveness of the

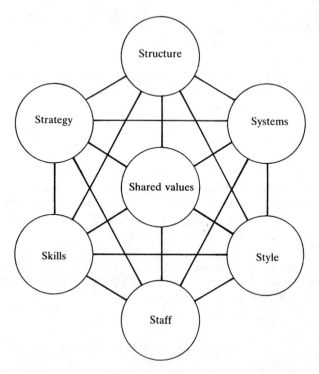

Figure 1.1   McKinsey 7-S framework. (Reproduced by permission of Harper Collins)

organizational system. Effectiveness of 'the' culture of 'the' organization (note the way both have been objectified by use of the definite article) is seen to depend on two factors:

1 How 'strong' the culture is: the idea of a culture being like a strong heart or pair of lungs – basically the stronger the better.

In this regard there are writers who have claimed that the effects of a good 'strong culture' can actually be measured – Deal and Kennedy, for example:

> The impact of a strong culture on productivity is amazing. In the extreme, we estimate that a company can gain as much as one or two hours of productive work per employee per day.   (1982: 15)

There are others, of course, who have taken the opposite view

> Culture can be a brake on change. Strong cultures seem to be like powerful inertial systems. Changing direction demands enormous energy . . .
> (Thomas, 1985: 24)

But what they all have in common is a shared conception of culture as an object – a benevolent or malevolent object, but an object all the same.

2 How well culture is 'aligned' with the other organs of the 'body' (e.g. the strategy-culture fit): the idea, similar to the one found in holistic medicine, of systemic health and balance; of synergy arising from functional integration of the parts.

Hence one finds comments like

> Strategy, and structure, and culture are part of the same package, and require simultaneous attention.   (Dalmau and Dick, 1991: 4)

And

> The concepts of strategy, culture and communication are hardly foreign to managers today. However, many of the organizations that I have evaluated over the past five years are ineffective at aligning these three components to achieve their goals.   (Schiemann, 1989)

How does this perspective impact on conceptions of cultural change? 'Changing culture' tends to be seen as a modular, design-and-build activity, not dissimilar in conception from replacing a faulty component in a television set or trading in an old cooker for a new one. There is no process as such, merely the physical task of 'unbolting' the old component and 'bolting' on a new one. The language used by people who subscribe to this view is often quite revealing: they talk about 'overhauling' , 'renewing' or 'renovating' the corporate culture (as one might overhaul one's car or trade it in for a new one, or renovate one's house), and 'getting a handle on culture' or using it as a 'lever' to raise organizational performance:

> a strong culture is a powerful lever for guiding behaviour.
>
> (Deal and Kennedy, 1982: 15)

From this perspective, cultural change is essentially 'cultural engineering', a rational, technical, physical and scientific activity directed towards the control and manipulation of this 'thing' we call culture. Such a perspective turns cultural change into a push-button affair.

The anthropologists' conception of culture is quite different from this. They remind us that we do not think of societies as *having* cultures in an object sense. Societies *are* cultures. So why should we think of organizations as being any different? They are, after all, only society 'writ small' (Silverman, 1970). Thus, a hospital *is* a culture, as is a salted crisp manufacturer, soccer club, or school. The point is that culture is not something an organization has but something an organization *is* (Smircich, 1983: 347). It is a label or metaphor *for*, not a component *of*, the total work organization. People of this persuasion are prone to accuse scientists and engineers of having committed the mortal sin of reifying culture (Berger and Luckmann, 1966: 106), turning an immaterial phenomenon that exists only in people's 'hearts and minds' into an external non-human factity, a self-contained 'super-organic' reality with forces and purposes of its own (Geertz, 1973: 11). They accuse them of taking the essential human-ness and subjectivity out of culture and making it into 'something out there and very large' (D'Andrade, 1984: 7). In effect, making something out of nothing.

The anthropological view (and the view of most academic writers today) is therefore that culture is

- Synonymous with organization (organizations are cultures).
- A particular way of viewing and thinking about organization; a paradigm (Sheldon, 1980) for interpreting organizational life processes; a perspective if you like.

The first point about 'culture' being interchangeable with 'organization' finds considerable support when we examine some of the current definitions of culture. For example, the layperson's definition might be 'the way we do things around here', and few of us would probably object to using this as a layperson's definition of organization. The picture is very much the same at the expert level. Schein (1983), for example, writes that

> Organization culture is the pattern of basic assumptions which a given group has invented, discovered or developed in learning to cope with its problems of external adaptation and internal integration.

But omission of the word 'culture' from the first line would make it an equally respectable (and probably for most people, acceptable) definition of organization. Schein's framework showing the three 'levels' of culture (deepest level: 'basic assumptions'; middle level: 'values'; surface level: 'artifacts and creations') has become the standard benchmark for defining organization culture. The framework is all-inclusive, referring to every kind of phenomenon imaginable (physical, behavioural, normative, cognitive and affective) and to every conceivable kind of process (thinking, acting, perceiving, believing and judging). Not a single stone has been left unturned, and not a single thing has been left out. The author (quite rightly) has left us with no way of discriminating between a culture and an organization.

My point is that, when we get down to it – doing what Louis and Sutton (1989) describe as 'switching cognitive gears' from an 'automatic' habit of mind to 'active', conscious reflection – it is difficult, if not impossible, to see the difference between the two concepts. The reason, say the anthropologists, is that there isn't any. If there is, it is in our own minds. The problem is historical. The 'organization' concept, as it were, got in there before 'culture'. When culture finally arrived (in the early 1980s), it became popular and influential, but it was never able to replace the traditional conception of 'organization' as it then existed. Culture and organization became co-existent conceptual entities, with culture occupying secondary status as a component of organization. Effectively, culture was deprived of the opportunity of providing a relacement concept and an alternative paradigm. Since then, organization anthropologists have been committed to rectification of this situation, seeing their task as one of liberating culture from the traditional paradigm, and campaigning for the cultural framework to be used in a less restricted conceptual environment.

How does this discussion relate to core conceptions about cultural change? There are two key conclusions to be drawn here:

1   If organizations are indeed cultures, no conceptual distinction should be made between a 'strategy for cultural change' and a 'strategy for organizational change': cultural change *is* organizational change. As Morgan puts it, 'since organization ultimately resides in the heads of the people involved, effective organizational change implies cultural change' (1986:138). Anyone engaged in cultural change should see themselves as involved in organizational change (the reverse is also true: people engaged in organization development (OD) should also see themselves as being engaged in cultural development). Strategies aimed exclusively at changing the culture of an organization are based on the false notion of culture as a 'thing' and should be avoided on account of the fact that they are, in effect, strategies for something that does not actually exist – mythical strategies for a mythical entity.

2   In strategic terms we need to think about organizations as being cultures rather than having cultures. It is the conception of organization rather than the object of study that makes the culture perspective unique. The important point, therefore, is not *what* we study, but the different *way* we look at the organization: the task for the culture strategist is not to think *about* culture but to *think culturally*.

A strategy for managing or changing culture is not therefore a 'tool' or 'method' – tools need something more concrete than culture to work on – but a *way of thinking* about organization. In short, a paradigm. Dalmau and Dick (1991) put it this way: 'What seems more important [than finding the tools of change] is that [change strategists] peer through the eyes of a cultural perspective at those things already available to them. To put the extreme case: culture does not exist as a reality, it exists as a framework of attention in the eye of the beholder (p. 8).

If a strategy for cultural change is to be based on the notion of 'thinking culturally', one needs to be clear from the outset about what this involves. Broadly speaking, thinking culturally is thinking about organizations in a non-concrete, non-objective way – as social constructions rather than physical, 'bricks-and-mortar' type constructions:

> they have no external reality but are merely social creations and constructions emerging from actors making sense out of ongoing streams of actions and interactions.   (Allaire and Firsirotu, 1984: 208)

Thinking culturally involves adopting an anthropological outlook on organizational life:

Works in the anthropological tradition of the study of culture invariably focus (save for the most materialist efforts) on this social constructedness, on the shared transactions simultaneously constituting and shaping the meanings underlying people's lives.   (Rosen, 1991: 6)

As Davis (1984: 12) has pointed out in this regard, searching for corporate culture is not unlike an anthropological expedition.

Breaking down the concept of 'social construction' further, we can say that thinking culturally is

● Thinking of organizations as *social* worlds.

The culture perspective focuses on the 'human-ness' of organizations, regarding them as social rather than physical entities, made up of people talking, acting, interacting and transacting with each other. Hence the idea that culture exists not so much 'inside' or 'outside' people as 'between' people. This conception helps us to see a cultural change effort as a form of social intervention aimed at altering the quality of this 'between-ness' in some way or other. As Meyerson and Martin put it, 'Any change among and between individuals, among the pattern of connections and interpretations, *is* cultural change' (1987: 639).

● Thinking of organizations as *constructed* worlds.

fiction is not a little tiny corner of the world . . . fiction is a mode natural to all of us, as we are all story-tellers. (Iris Murdoch, quoted in Bayley, 1980)

When people get together they 'make things up'. This is what organization is: a 'made up' or constructed world; a profusion of theories, explanations and interpretations that people devise in order to cope with the exigencies of their everyday lives. Every one of them is 'man-made' and every one is a fiction – fiction in the sense that they are 'something made,' 'something fashioned' – the original meaning of *fictio* (Geertz, 1973: 15). Decisions to move from a 'production facing' to a 'customer facing' culture, for example, or from a 'volume' to a 'quality' culture are all made up – fictions designed for a purpose.

In this sense, cultural change is, in the words of the old lampseller in Aladdin, a matter of exchanging 'new fictions for old'. In terms of the original phrase, it is the 'deconstruction' of something that already exists and the 'reconstruction' of something new or different to take its place. The concept of strategy relates simply to the manner in which this is done – the 'how' of exchange, e.g. simultaneously or sequentially, coercively or participatively, instantaneously or gradually, and so on.

A point to emphasize here is that social constructions (as the term implies) have both shape and form, this being provided by the language, symbol systems, myths, stories, rites and rituals in which they are situated and embedded, i.e. structured. A strategy for cultural change will therefore always involve finding ways of working with 'form' (which is what links the cultural strategist with the artist. More on this later). This itself may end up taking a number of different forms. For example, there are

- Conforming strategies – strategies aimed at adapting, improving, or perpetuating existing social constructions.
- Deforming strategies – strategies aimed at perverting or subverting existing social constructions.
- Reforming strategies – strategies aimed at abandoning or removing existing social constructions.
- Transforming strategies – strategies aimed at moving across from one form of social construction to another, i.e form- or frame-breaking.

Such strategies for cultural change may involve intervention in any of the following social forms or constructions:

Knowledge structures
Moral systems
Truth systems
Interpretive schema
Systems of ideas
Ideological systems
Value systems
Belief systems
Collective assumptions
Language games (scripts)
Common sense systems
Symbolic systems
Expressive systems
Folk theories and logic
Aesthetic systems

(Note that not one of these has concrete or physical attributes which would justify the scientists' reference to culture as a 'thing'.)

To summarize, 'thinking culturally' is a very different strategic outlook from 'thinking about culture'. It resists the natural temptation to reify culture into an object or thing, and chooses instead to define it as a way of thinking about organization – the notion of culture as a metaphor, frame of reference, schema or paradigm. 'Thinking culturally' uncovers the human, expressive, symbolic texture of organization life (as in the list above), qualities that the more factual, objective 'thinking about culture' school might easily miss or misconstrue.

But 'thinking culturally' is not just a perspective; it is also a philosophy about organizations and organization analysis. It puts itself forward as the antidote to the 'keep it simple' philosophies that have been emerging from various quarters in recent years. It represents the view that organization (and by that token, cultural) analysis and development must expect complexity, ambiguity, abstraction, and – above all – intangibility in its subject matter, and must at the same time learn to live and work with these qualities. One just cannot escape them. In the words of the Indian story, it is 'turtles all the way down.'

Culture as strategy, strategy as culture

Another commonsense view I wish to challenge is the traditional distinction between the concepts of 'culture' and 'strategy'. Again, those with more scientific leanings have chosen to regard culture and strategy as two separate variables or entities – two pieces of a jigsaw that need to be carefully cut and then fitted together in order to achieve organizational effectiveness. This has given rise to statements like the following:

> Good strategy only equals success when we possess an appropriate culture.
> (DeLisi, 1990: 4)

> In figuring out what to do, management has a number of choices. They can ignore the culture. They can manage around the culture by changing the implementation plan. They can change the strategy to fit the culture, perhaps by reducing performance expectations. Or they can try to change the culture to fit the strategy.   (Davis, 1984: 88)

This is not the perspective that I wish to advance. Once again, I would invite the reader to consider whether this kind of conceptual distinction is as real and obvious as it first appears, and whether the alternative conception, of making either of the concepts substitutable for the other, might not be preferable. Fortunately, while in the minority, I am not alone in advancing this view. Both Weick (1985) and Hennestad (1991) have argued similarly.

Weick offers a fun way into the argument in the form of a quiz (see Box 1). The reader is invited to complete this before proceeding.

Box 1.1 Weick's Culture Quiz (*Source:* Weick, 1985)

Listed below are four statements extracted verbatim from published articles. The first word in each statement has been deleted. The reader is asked to decide whether the first word in each statement should be 'strategy' or 'culture'.

- _ _ _ _ _ _ _ _ evolves from inside the organization – not from its future environment.

- _ _ _ _ _ _ _ _ is a deeply ingrained and continuing pattern of management behaviour that gives direction to the organization – not a manipulable and controllable mechanism that can be easily changed from one year to the next.

- _ _ _ _ _ _ _ _ is a non-rational concept stemming from the informal values, traditions, and norms of behaviour held by the firm's managers and employees – not a rational, formal, logical, conscious, and predetermined thought process engaged in by top executives.

- _ _ _ _ _ _ _ _ emerges out of the cumulative effect of many informed actions and decisions taken daily and over years by many employees – not a 'one-shot' statement developed exclusively by top management for distribution to the organization.

Those already turning to the back of the book for the answers should stop. There aren't any! The quiz is a trick (as one might have expected from Weick). The answer is 'either' (or 'both') to all questions. Although all four statements were originally made in an article on strategy, Weick had been able to find almost identical statements in the book for which he was then writing – statements relating to culture not strategy. He remarks,

> What I find striking is the plausibility of either term in each sentence. It is as if there were a common set of issues in organizations that some of us choose to call culture and others choose to call strategy.   (Weick, 1985: 382)

Weick's point is that culture and strategy are substitutable for one another – a kind of Oscar Wilde upside-down of 'one nation (a common set of ideas) divided by two languages' (paradigms) – the language of strategy and the language of culture.

In a second 'experiment', in which he compares two definitions of culture with one of corporate strategy (which are too long to be reproduced here), Weick uncovers a number of things that they have in common. These are listed in Box 1.2.

Box 1.2   What definitions of culture and strategy have in common
(Source: Weick, 1985)

- Their objects are theories rather than facts.
- They guide both expression and interpretation.
- They are retrospective, summarizing patterns in past decisions and actions.
- They are embodied in actions of judging, creating, justifying, affirming, and sanctioning.
- They summarize past achievements and practices that work.
- They provide continuity, identity and a consistent way of ordering the world (i.e. they resemble a code or cosmology).
- They are social, summarizing what is necessary to mesh one's own actions with those of others.
- They are often neither completely explicit nor completely articulated, which means that expressions of culture and strategy may vary in specifics.
- Their substance is seen most clearly when people confront unfamiliar situations where the routine application of existing understanding is not possible.
- They are tenacious understandings that resist change and that are unlikely to change.

In Box 1.3 I have randomly listed snatches of definitions of culture that I have come across in my own readings on the subject. Like Weick I believe that, although this was not the original intention, these would serve equally well as definitions of strategy.

To be clear here, I am not suggesting that culture is *like* strategy (and vice versa), nor am I saying that culture and strategy are closely *related* (as are Weick and others when they talk about the one being an 'outgrowth', 'offshoot' or 'dimension' of the other). What I am saying is that the one *is* the other: culture is a strategic phenomenon; strategy is a cultural phenomenon. When, for example, Sir Robert ('Bob') Reid declared in the early 1980s that he wanted to change the culture of British

Rail from being 'production-led' to 'marketing-led', this was a cultural statement and a strategic statement rolled into one; cultural change implied strategic change, and vice versa (Bate, 1990). One cannot possibly conceive of one without the other.

Box 1.3 Definitions of culture

- Directions for performance ('Directives')
- Guiding beliefs and philosophies
- Recipes
- A design for living
- Coded instructions
- 'This is the way things are; and this is why they ought to be as they are'
- A set of means for achieving designated ends
- A system of meanings
- 'It shapes the way we organize our experiences and choose our actions' (dispositions to action)
- A collective orientation\positioning
- A set of limits – prescriptions and proscriptions of conduct
- Propositional knowledge
- A set of interpretations and propositions
- Signposts
- Conventionalizing signals
- An historically emergent set of ideas
- A prevailing logic
- A framework governing behaviour
- A framework giving order and coherence to our lives
- A way of thinking
- A way of proceeding

This proposition can be expressed functionally or structurally:

1 Functionally: 'Cultural forms provide a strategic function.'

For example, Sir Bob's declaration may be described in the language of culture as a 'myth' (one of the cultural forms listed earlier), i.e. something he and his senior colleagues 'made up' – a fiction with a purpose. Myths like his fulfil a number of strategic functions (Bate, 1993). For example, they

- Categorize   ('BR will be divided into five sectors: Intercity, Provincial, Network South East, Freight and Parcels.')
- Dramatize   ('Unless we move to this BR's future will be far from secure.')
- Energize   ('We need to focus our efforts on ...')
- Enfranchise ('Authority will be devolved to the sectors.')
- Legitimize   ('The organization will be sector-led')
- Disguise   ('The organization will operate as a matrix – a partner-ship of equals': in practice, however, BR remained hier-archical with the sector directors very much in charge.)
- Moralize   ('Our duty is to provide a first class service for all our passengers.')
- Symbolize   ('Sectors stand for quality, reliability and service to the travelling customer.)
- Synthesize   ('With this strategy we are able to bring revenues and costs together for the first time.')

2   Structurally: 'Strategies are cultural forms.'

An organization's 'strategy' may be regarded as a cultural form or forms, in so far as it comprises a set of truths, a linguistic structure and a system of ideas, values and beliefs (see above for full list). Strategies, like Sir Bob's sectorization strategy, are also myths. This has been noted by people like Van Buskirk (1989: 255), who writes: 'Corporate strategies themselves have a 'mythic quality' which provides hopeful images of the future and self esteem for the strategists.' Again, the following definitions of myths from a wide variety of sources would do equally well as definitions of strategy (indeed they give a textural quality to strategy that rational-scientific accounts often miss). Implicit in this is the notion that good myths probably make good strategies!

- 'Myths are a body of likely stories which emerge from the life of any group and which enable a group to understand its past and present and thereby its future.'
- Myths are the structural categories within which people think; they are systematic ways of seeing, understanding and reacting to the world.
- Myths are the concrete expression of the collective imagination.
- Myths are collectively valued purposes.
- Myths define the realm of possibility.
- 'The myth is the story that we tell to explain the nature of our reality.'
- Myths are shaping visions, and symbolic scenarios.

- Myths are carrying mechanisms of the intangible.
- 'A myth is a good story that grips you, creates a world, and, to some significant degree, transforms and interprets the "real world".'
- Myths are 'commanding forms' (NB the suitability of such a phrase to the military origins of the strategy concept).
- Myths provide charters for institutions and rationalizations of social privilege.
- Myths are propaganda: presentations in analogical or symbolic form of what are claimed to be super-rational truths; socially-sanctioned palliatives.
- Myths are formulated feelings and judgements.
- Myths are simplifications, messages stripped down to the bare essentials.
- 'Myths are stories of a group's culture which describe its beginning, continuance, and ultimate goals.'

If we accept that culture and strategy are substitutable for one another, we need next to consider what implications this will have for the way that we view cultural change. Broadly speaking, there are two propositions that can be made, these being two sides of the same coin:

1 Strategy formulation of any kind is a cultural activity (the development of strategy is cultural development). Whether they see it this way or not, strategists are, in fact, engaging in a process of cultural change, and should therefore acquire greater familiarity with the culture paradigm. This is what Johnson (1990:183) seemed to be getting at when he wrote, 'There is a growing awareness that the problems and mechanisms of managing strategic change in organizations need to be explained and considered, not so much in terms of traditional rational planning models of strategic management, but in terms of the cognitive, cultural and political context and constraints in organizations and managerial action which [address] these.' I would interpret this as a plea to strategists to 'think culturally' about strategy and strategic change.
   The 'interpretive approach' to which Johnson is referring 'leads us to view strategy as a distinct phase in the cultural process whereby certain groups of people attempt to create symbols which drive people in certain directions and influence their interpretation of situations and of past and present events'.   (Green, 1988: 128)

2 Cultural change is strategic change. Avoid treating culture and strategy as two separate entities, requiring two separate processes, and learn to see them as one. The idea of setting up a separate programme for 'changing culture' is a nonsense; cultural change is already occurring within formal and informal strategic processes. Since there is no distinction in practice, there should be no distinction in conception. 'Culture' cannot be changed in the abstract. You do not deliberately set out to change 'the culture'.

Cultural change may therefore be simply defined as the movement from one strategy (*S*) to another over time: $S1 \rightarrow S2$.

We have to be very precise here in the way we define strategy, being particularly careful to avoid the narrow, formalistic and concrete meaning that some writers have attached to it. S as I am referring to it represents the 'strategy in use' (this term doubling-up very nicely as a definition of culture). The 'strategy in use' (Mintzberg, 1978) is the actual rather than desired, the real rather than espoused, the current rather than ideal, the informal rather than formal, strategy. It is a 'mundane' system of logic and reason (Pollner, 1987) that everyday folk in everyday places bring to the everyday objects and concerns in their everyday lives:

> An important point to make is that the organization culture constitutes the existing strategy or the *strategy in use* (or realized strategy). It constitutes the prevailing business and work logic of the organization. The members of an organization do in fact to a large extent act logically within this frame. (Hennestad, 1991: 30, original emphasis)

Cultural change can therefore be conceived as change 'of' and 'in' the strategy in use – a displacement of one set of 'operational myths' (Stephens & Eisen, 1984; see list above) by another. This change occurs through a process consisting of:

- *Mutations* of the strategy in use: where $S1$ changes at irregular intervals but retains its basic form (i.e., $S1a$, $S1b$, $S1c$, etc.). This is a change IN strategy, in which the 'shape' of the strategy changes but not its underlying properties (invariance); in other words there is continuity and an unbroken trajectory through time:
  $$S1a \rightarrow S1b \rightarrow S1c \rightarrow S1d \text{ etc.}$$
- *Transformations* of the strategy in use: where the process is interrupted by a frame-switch from one type of strategy to another ($S1$ to $S2$ below); the evolutionary chain is broken; there is discontinuity and variance of form. This may be described as a change OF strategy:
  $$S1a \rightarrow S1b \rightarrow S1c \setminus\setminus S2a \text{ etc.}$$

Examples of transformations:

'From'	'To'
Production-orientated	Customer-orientated
Volume-driven	Quality-driven
(hard selling)	(soft selling)
Top-down approach to	Devolved\participative
decision-making	

One could, of course, reverse all this and talk about strategic change as change 'of' or 'in' the 'culture in use' (C1 to C2). It all depends on whether one prefers to work with the concept of culture or the concept of strategy. In a way it does not really matter. What matters is that we have dispensed with some of the artificial distinctions created by the scientific approach to culture, and have begun working on the issue of change from a different perspective – a perspective that abandons 'thinking about culture' in favour of 'thinking culturally'. On the face of it, all we have done is change a couple of labels and tinker around with the language a little bit. However, there is a good deal more to word-games than this. As Kenny (1989) has pointed out, the struggle for words is a struggle for meaning. We rebel against words not for themselves but for the reality which lies behind them: they are the gatekeepers of that reality.

> Language exercises a tyranny, a bewitchment over us. We can only extricate ourselves from this by rebelling against language, fighting the urgent temptation to misrepresent to ourselves the way in which we really use words.   (1989)

2 Thinking culturally

If the first chapter was the 'vocabulary' for this book on culture, this chapter is its 'grammar': individual concepts will be combined into larger structures and frameworks to enable readers to think culturally about change, and strategically about culture – all of this leading, we hope, to the acquisition of a 'language' which has the potential for practical usage in the organizational setting.

This chapter focuses on the first of the four questions mentioned in the previous chapter: why change culture? I shall not be attempting to give a categorical answer to this, which frankly would be an impossible task. The 'right' answer obviously depends upon who you are and where you stand, and no single work could ever account for all the different positions that might be taken up on matters of change. Rather than fall into the trap of offering glib or inappropriate generalizations, I have concentrated instead on developing 'thinking frameworks' that readers can apply to their own situation, and adapt for their own purposes. This is very much in keeping with modern writings on strategy (cf. O'Farrell et al., 1991: 54) which take the view that the cognitive aspects of strategy (conceptual formulation) are just as important, if not more so, than the action components (mode of implementation).

Readers still need to beware, however. Some of the 'boards' in this exposition are very loose indeed, and cannot be relied upon to take much weight. But then, one wonders how it could be otherwise: as I have said before, framework development in the area of cultural change is not very far advanced; most of the conceptual materials from which they have been constructed come to us second hand from the natural sciences, and are of questionable relevance to human phenomena. The temptation to remove these loose boards has, nevertheless, been resisted. At least if they are left down, readers can jump up and down on them at will, even replace them if they so desire. Alternatively, they might care to use them as a springboard for their own ideas.

Why Change Culture?

As a result of my discussion about synonyms, this question may now be considered from a wider angle than was possible when it was first raised. Clearly, the question 'why change culture?' is the same as asking 'Why change organizations?' or 'Why change strategy?' There is no difference between them (other than one of language and perspective), and therefore no exceptional or additional case to be made for changing (or not changing) culture. The point that needs to be grasped is that structure, strategy and 'organization' are all implicit in the culture concept; when we change culture, we are, in effect, changing strategy, structure and organization. Despite the natural inclination to regard them as conceptually *independent* entities, they are, from the viewpoint of the culture perspective, conceptually *interdependent* dimensions of the same phenomenon, and should be treated as such.

Therefore, to the question 'Why change culture?', the short answer might well be

- To change structure
- To change strategy

and wider still,

- To change organization.

This is not the impression that has been conveyed in many of the popular business books. Their authors would have us believe that cultural change is quite different from strategic or structural change, and inspired by entirely different purposes; these three are treated as separate classes or types of change, each with its own distinctive rationale. And not only that: it is then assumed quite naturally that we have a choice between the three types and can select the one most appropriate to our situation. For example, if it is a change of 'software' (values, meanings, symbols) or 'something deeper' than the normal, run-of-the-mill change programme that you want, then 'culture' is your best bet. If, on the other hand, you want to change the 'hardware' (roles, relationships, behaviour) – the 'boxes' rather than the 'bubbles' (Hurst, 1984), the 'quantity' rather than the 'quality' aspects of organizational life – then a change of strategy or structure is probably what you need. While these distinctions may appear sensible, they are, in my opinion, both misleading and unfortunate.

I do not believe we should be thinking about culture (or the other concepts for that matter) in this hole-and-corner way. The fact of the matter is that culture has (or is) form and it has (or is) purpose (structure and strategy, if you prefer). These are intrinsic qualities or aspects of culture, not something that can be separated from it and parcelled off to be dealt with by some other perspective. The tendency to do this must be resisted. In all aspects of cultural production (process), whether it be creating a work of art or changing an organization, forms (structures) are constantly being developed in order to realize certain purposes (strategies). 'Form-making' and 'strategy-making' are therefore the very essence of the cultural process, and it would be as wrong to ignore them in an organization setting as it would be to do so in an artistic setting. By the same token, it is also quite impossible to conceive of being able to change culture without also changing structure and strategy in some way (and vice versa).

This observation has important implications for practitioners. It means that cultural change programmes not only require the services of organization 'development' people to attend to the process of change, they also need organization 'strategists' and organization 'designers' to help plan, formulate and reformulate that process. It requires a truly concerted activity where people who in the past may have operated quite independently from each other now come together and manage the change process as a developing whole. Better still, it needs people who, like artists, are able to appreciate form, function and process simultaneously, arranging, synthesizing and harmonizing them in pleasing and effective ways. What makes the culture paradigm distinctive in relation to other organizational paradigms is the stress it places on the multifaceted (structure, strategy, process) and multi-disciplinary (designers, strategists, developers) nature of organizational change. Certainly, it marks a departure from the segmented way in which the change process is normally conceived, led and managed.

This is a practical point to which I will return later. The conceptual point, which is more relevant here, is that 'thinking culturally' obliges us to abandon the 'either-or' kind of thinking that has bedevilled many previous approaches to change, in favour of a more holistic 'both-and' kind – a single, integrated frame of reference that is capable of embracing soft *and* hard, structure *and* process, order *and* change. This is a conversion that Thomas Quick (1989: xi), for one, would strongly approve of. Writing about his own experiences as a manager and consultant, he has this to say:

> I came to understand that either-or, which characterizes many managerial decisions, is a trap because you have only two boxes in which the whole world must fit. Sometimes, it occurred to me, reality was best defined by both-and. I further discovered that the more options I had, the more

possibilities I discovered, and the more successful I was in deciding and solving. And the more fun managing was.

While 'success' and 'fun' are probably not the first words I would reach for to describe the management of cultural change – and frankly neither of these can be guaranteed in this line of work – Quick's concept of 'both-and' thinking remains extremely useful as far as our emerging conceptual framework is concerned.

First, it serves as a warning that change is never going to be 'one or the other': evolutionary or revolutionary, continuous or discontinuous, planned or unplanned, top-down or bottom-up, transitional or transformational, conflictual or cooperative (the list is endless) – popular dualisms which show how pervasive 'either-or' thinking has become in the organizational change literature; instead it will involve combinations or sequences of some or all of these different types (this being a major source of the complexity referred to in the first chapter).

Secondly, it offers a general invitation for people to open up their minds to new ways of perceiving in their organizations (looking through two 'eyes' not one), and possibly to experience something quite new and different about 'change' and the roles they can play in relation to it. For example, Peters and Waterman's (1982: 319) 'both-and' invitation to us to think in terms of 'soft is hard, hard is soft' may sound clichéd, but if it were heeded, it would probably have some quite profound effects on our normal orientation towards organizational life and change. Thinking about structure as culture, culture as structure, strategy as culture and so on, might have similar mind-widening effects. We will return to these two points later.

Changing culture to change structure

First we must examine a different idea, namely that the culture perspective reveals the close affinity that exists between the world of the arts and the world of organizations. The word 'culture', which has always figured prominently in the language of music and art, provides a natural connection. The link is, in my view, highly propitious, opening up a side to organizations that the 'science of management' might never have noticed. Artists, for example, would not dream of separating the concepts of structure and culture in the way that organization scientists and practitioners have done in the past ('art is concerned with structure', Shelley, 1980: ix; see also books like Burnham's *The Structure of Art*, 1971). According to their paradigm it is simply a case of 'no form no culture, no culture no form'. Art is referred to as a *cultural form*. In other words, culture has structure, indeed culture is structure. Here is exactly the kind of 'both-and' thinking that needs to be adopted in organizational settings – a form of thinking that welds together the two concepts of structure and culture into one: the concept of organization as a *cultural form*.

I mention all this because it has a direct bearing on the way we conceptualize cultural change: gone is the traditionalists' notion of structural *or* cultural change, and in its place is the artists' notion of cultural change *as being* (among other things), a change of structure – a transformation: literally a change from one cultural form or structure to another. From the viewpoint of the artist, cultural production is defined simply and effectively as *the process of giving an idea form*, form being an integral part of that process, in fact the main purpose of it. This definition will also do nicely as a basic description of the cultural change\production process in organizations.

Another advantage of comparing organizations with the arts is that it stretches the conventional organizational definition of structure, and hence broadens and deepens our conception – and in turn our practices – of organization design. Art distinguishes between 'visible structure' and 'invisible structure' (Bayley, 1980: 87). Visible structure, as the term suggests, is that which you can see and touch – the picture, the sculpture and so on. It is a 'composition' – an artifact – consisting of different elements arranged in a pattern of spatial relationships. The equivalent in the organizational world would be the 'organization chart': this, too, is a picture, consisting of 'boxes' (elements) joined by various 'lines' and 'arrows' (relationships). I would argue that it is at this level of visible structure that the majority of organization designers tend to operate, as craftsmen (draughtsmen?) rather than artists, employing technical rather than creative skills in the execution of their work, and making reproductions or copies of old designs rather than 'originals'.

Visible structures do not need artists to produce them (anyone with good basic training in art technique could copy Van Gogh's *Sunflowers*); nor are they what makes art 'art'. Art is all to do with the 'invisible structures' that lie submerged beneath them. You cannot see them, you cannot touch them, you cannot measure them and you certainly cannot define them. And yet you know they are 'there' – as a 'quality' of the work – as 'art'.

In contrast [to the form of structure like the pattern of rhymes in a sonnet] there is something to me inherently mysterious about structure in a successful work of art. We recognize its presence but we cannot account for it or define it except in terms of its own absoluteness of being. Such structure, seen for instance in a Greek archaic statue, or a Chinese jar or a poem, seems – like the structures of flowers or snow-flakes – to have become detached from anything related to the purposive. Such a structure is not of course a natural thing because it is a work of art, but its ground of being as a given thing seems to have much in common with structures in the natural world. It has, or seems to have, the inherent stability which we attach to the idea of form; the permanence which Wordsworth referred to in the movement of a stream,

> 'I see what is and was, and shall abide. Still glides the stream and shall forever glide. The form remains, the function never dies.'
>
> (Bayley, 1980: 87-88)

Modelling itself on the arts, the organization culture perspective takes the view that there are similar 'invisible structures' to be found (though never to be seen) in organizations, and it is these which give organizations any form and enduring stability that they may possess. We shall look at some examples later. In relation to our original question, 'Why change culture?', this discussion now provides us with yet another possible answer: 'To change the "deep form" or "invisible structure" of organization' – the immaterial symbolic, spiritual and semantic structures that lie beneath a constantly moving, and often turbulent, surface; the 'webs of meaning' (Geertz, 1973) that give an organization shape, character, meaning and identity.

An interest in invisible, immaterial forms lies at the very heart of the culture perspective. Indeed, it was this interest, combined with the recognition that traditional organizational paradigms had no adequate way of dealing with these kind of phenomena, that led researchers to the culture perspective in the first place:

> When we speak of organizational cultural literature, we refer to the intellectual product of those scholars who – dissatisfied with the rationalistic and reductive paradigm which dominated organizational science up to the end of the 1970s - began looking at organizations as expressive forms and as systems of meaning, to be analyzed not merely in their instrumental, economic and material aspects, but also in their ideational and symbolic features.   (Gagliardi, 1990: 8)

What is significant is the way the 'cultural-artistic' conception of organization structure and design that I have been outlining here differs from the traditional, rational, 'scientific-engineering' conception found in (most?) organization planning departments today. In broad terms, the alternative conception of design as an art rather than a science suggests that

● Organization design is as much about 'meaning making' as 'relationship making', about consciousness as much as connections. The design is an interpretive scheme which helps people to understand what is happening. The designer creates semantic structures or patterns of meaning: 'These patterns of meaning and formation of meaning produce the organization's legitimacy for its members and its environment' (Frissen, 1989: 5). In place of the traditional organization chart, there might therefore conceivably be a cognitive map showing the logical connections between a set of complex ideas, or a painting symbolizing a desired way of working, or a set of cartoons caricaturing 'typical' problems. The range of possible art forms is infinite, but as yet unexplored in the organization context.

- Organization design needs artists as much as it needs engineers or craftstmen – people who deal as naturally with semantic structures as the latter do with physical structures. There is no hierarchy between them: the 'deep down' is useless without a surface carrier to communicate it: so too is the surface structure if it does not capture some deeper sentiment or idea. 'Good' art is when an invisible structure expresses itself as visible structure, 'remaining out of sight, though not necessarily beyond our powers of apprehension'

(Bayley, 1980: 93).

- Organization design should be elevated to an art form, its aim being to achieve what any work of art would be broadly seeking to do, i.e. symbolically represent reality, capturing and freezing a message or idea in structural form, and creating an 'illusion' of life – a truth rather than the truth. It should communicate more than just facts, for example qualites such as style and sensibility, enthusiasm and interest, appreciation and understanding. The aim of organization design should be to produce a work of art. It should be possible to judge any organizational form in terms of 'good' art or 'bad' art, e.g. how successfully it represents reality, expresses an idea or sentiment, and engages or 'moves' people.

Underlying all these points is a feeling that organization designers, and probably managers in general, spend too much time trying to be scientists or engineers, and not enough time trying to be artists – processing the world into a factual mode when they should also be processing it into a fictional mode. I have developed this view elsewhere (Bate, 1993 forthcoming) with regard to one particular kind of artist: the prose fiction writer.

These ideas will be elaborated as this book proceeds, but I hope sufficient has been said here to demonstrate that the culture perspective breathes new life into traditional conceptions of structure and structural change. In essence, the cultural 'position' is that, like the iceberg, most of an organization's form or structure lies submerged and invisible to the naked eye (the semantic layer); that organization designers tend to be working only at the tip of this iceberg (chipping away at only a very small part of it – a surface artifact), and need to go much lower; and that any structure – even one as solid as an iceberg – is a symbolic as well as physical entity, which requires the services of artists, and not just craftsmen, to shape and change it.

Box 2.1: Managers as fiction writers

Managers, surprising though it may seem, have a good deal in common with artists, and it may not be stretching credibility too far to suggest that poets, troubadours, and prose fiction writers are their main comparators. What they have in common is that they are all professional language-users; language is their stock-in-trade; it is basically all that they have to rely on to get them through their working day. For them language therefore has to be something precious, not a thing to be wasted in idle conversation or held in reserve for purely factual discourse, but cultivated as a precision instrument with a very special dramatic purpose: to create the illusion of something, a virtual experience. Their sole aim, one that they nourish and allow themselves to be constantly seduced by, is to fabricate a successful illusion of life, one that is ultimately convincing and 'real' for their audience. Theirs is the art of contriving appearances, appearance being the only true measure of a successful fiction – or as Trollope said 'the air of reality is its supreme virtue, the merit upon which all its other merits submissively depend.'

'Good managers', like good poets, troubadours and fiction writers, are therefore people who possess this virtue of being able to create a particular illusion of life for those whom they are seeking to influence: 'If you can get people to take your fiction as fact, it seems the air of reality must have been achieved' (Langer, 1953: 291). In short, good managers are people who can make the potentially unacceptable acceptable. Like artists, they are the manipulators of meaning.

While the culture perspective is very much about structure and structural matters, it does, however, oblige us to question the traditional conception of structure currently found in academic and practitioner circles. As Gagliardi has pointed out, 'A designer sensitive to the cultural dimension of organizational phenomena will have to question the concept of structure devised by the classic theory of organization still widely and implicitly used in practice', a questioning that 'should then lead us to enrich the traditional concept of organizational structure, sharpening our eyes to the complex weave of instrumental and expressive, material and symbolic, programmable and non programmable elements that are created in the situation' (1991: 5)

Changing culture to change strategy

Just as structure is implicit in culture, so too is strategy. As I observed before, cultures do not 'have' strategies, they 'are' strategies; they are the ways and means an organization or society has developed in order to cope with the basic 'life problems' relating to its survival and growth. 'Directional orientations' is what the anthropologist Florence Kluckhohn (1963: 221) calls them – a definition of culture with a suitably strategic ring to it. The enormous cultural variation that exists between organizations – what makes IBM unique and different from HP, or McKinsey's different from McVitie's – is a tribute to human ingenuity in conceiving of an apparently infinite number of strategies for coping with these life problems (Bate, 1984: 61). On closer scrutiny, however (but being careful never to lose sight of the richness and diversity that exists), we find that the strategies in question are all derivatives of just two basic, prototypic or generic forms. Each of these offers a very different (but equally valid) 'class' of answer to the question, 'Why change culture?'. The two varieties, which will be examined in some detail in the next two chapters, are:

1 *Strategies for order and continuity ('conforming strategies')*
   - Purpose: maintenance and development of culture
     The strategic intention may be stated as 'changing in order to stay the same' – a change *in* culture. Cultural *development* rather than change.

     In these processes there is 'motion' but not 'movement' (in a translational sense). Energies are expended in efforts to keep the culture intact and in the same place, while at the same time strengthening it. Like a boat on a moving tide, it needs to move forward through the water in order to remain over the same spot on the sea bed. Although it may sound paradoxical, cultural continuity actually requires a continuing process of change.

2 *Strategies for change and discontinuity ('transforming strategies')*
   - Purpose: change of culture
     The strategic intention may be stated as 'changing in order to change' – a change *of* culture. Cultural *change* as opposed to cultural development.

In these processes there is 'movement' as well as 'motion'. Our metaphorical boat leaves one 'spot' and moves to another. This is the way we normally think of change.

My view is that organizations develop distinct preferences for one prototype rather than the other during different periods in their history, turning their backs, at least for a time, on the alternative possibility, and frequently getting 'locked' or 'frozen' into their chosen option for longer than is good for them. The two are not separate, however, but connected by the somewhat perverse fact that continued adherence to one class of strategy actually creates a growing need for the other, and ultimately triggers a 'switch' to the other; in other words any strategic cultural type has built into it the conditions for its own termination and transformation. This relationship of mutual dependence between opposites (order and change) and the conditions that lead to the switch from one class of strategy to another will be examined later, but now we shall look closely at each type of strategy.

3 Strategies for cultural development

Get used to thinking that there is nothing Nature loves so well as to change existing forms and make new ones like them.

(Marcus Aurelius, *Meditations*)

In this chapter 'development' is interpreted as evolution towards greater order and continuity in an organization's cultural life. This is the first of the two types of strategy introduced in the last chapter. Its central idea is trying to do what you do best, better – and more often: variations on a cultural theme.

The people who pursue these strategies are committed *culture conservationists*: they wish to preserve and protect the cultural environment (The Order) that their predecessors or present-day 'elders' have created. This has tended to make them imitators rather than innovators, copiers rather than creators, improvisers rather than inventors, refiners rather than reformers, purifiers rather than perverters, balancers rather than boat rockers; people who see change as an adapting, correcting, conforming process – a process that is dedicated to making the culture last. Developers, yes, but changers, no.

Cultural continuity is their goal. Their strategies are mimetic and homeostatic, having much in common with the equilibria encountered in the natural sciences, which obey Le Chatelier's principle and adjust in whatever direction is appropriate to the opposition of external influences. They themselves are like people on the deck of a ship who lean one way, then the other, in order to counteract the movement of the waves. Their motives and actions may be inspired by loyalty to a person (e.g. Walt Disney, Thomas Watson of IBM, Richard Branson of Virgin) or an ideal (service, quality, relief of suffering), or driven by the desire to repeat a winning formula or cash in on a previous success – the latter being expressed by Edwin Land, the Chair of Polaroid, in his classic comment, 'If anything is worth doing, it's worth doing to excess'. This is the basis of the strategy: doing what you do best, better and more often.

Deal and Kennedy (1982: 5) claim that many companies have achieved success by pursuing a strategy of 'cultural continuity', this apparently enabling them to capitalize on the lessons and winning ways that their founders had fought long and hard to acquire:

> The lessons of these early leaders have been passed down in their own companies from generation to generation of managers; the cultures they were so careful to build and nourish have sustained their organizations through both fat and lean times. Today these corporations still have strong cultures and still are leaders in the marketplace.

Equally, there are those who claim that the opposite can happen, with organizations declining or failing precisely because they persist with strategies that shore up a pre-existing cultural order. For example, the BBC's chronic loss of direction during the 1940s and 1950s, immediately following a Golden Age in Broadcasting, was the consequence of respective administrations clinging on to the stern, snobbish, elitist, safe, grey, middle class, establishment, 'Auntie Beeb' high culture that its previous Director-General, Lord Reith, had created (originally in radio) many years before. This Victorian traditionalism was symbolized by Peter Black (1972) in his description of the BBC as the 'Biggest Aspidistra in the World'. While the Reithian high culture had been well-suited to middle-class British tastes in the 1930s, it became an anachronism in the Britain of the 1950s, a hangover from the past that left the BBC hopelessly out of date and painfully out of touch. It became, in effect, a monument to Lord Reith. Viewing figures plummeted as people switched to the alternative channels that were becoming available. Hardly surprising when you hear the following:

> As late as 1967, the BBC News Guide was warning editors against using squalid crime stories as 'audience bait', explaining: 'This would be to pander to the public and offend against our tradition of responsibility.' And the guide still contained this relic of the Reithian Beeb, a warning against over-adulatory obituaries of celebrities: 'The fact that a person has attracted in his lifetime a large personal following does not necessarily mean that his achievement is worthy of uncritical acclaim. You may feel obliged to note the death of an entertainer of meagre talent whose gramophone records – thanks to the activities of financially interested parties – have sold in vast quantities and who has been the recipient of such doubtful accolades as a place in the so-called 'Top Twenty'. We do not have to speak of him in terms more appropriate to a Menuhin or a Klemperer or a Fischer-Dieskau.'
>
> (M.Leapman, 1986: 35)

Having recently switched from a 'strategy of order' to a 'strategy of change', today's BBC executives might well squirm as they are reminded of the high and mighty, holier-than-thou attitudes of their predecessors. Certainly, the 'new culture' they are now trying to create, one of listening to and interacting with viewers, would have been a complete anathema to Reith, who believed in the maxim: never give people what they say they want, give them something different and they will come to like it – which reminds us just how recent the notion of a customer-responsive culture actually is.

However, what they – and we – need to remember is that at the time there seemed to be good reason for people continuing to hold such attitudes. After all, it is perfectly natural for any company to want to preserve its glorious past and the 'excellence culture' that made it glorious in the first place. Indeed, Peters and Waterman (1982) might have said that the BBC had shown the mark of true excellence by 'sticking to the knitting', persisting with what it did best, like classical drama and serious documentary. The point is that if a company is doing reasonably well, there will be a strong incentive to avoid tampering with any element of a tried and true formula (Miller and Friesen, 1980: 603). There is also a momentum attached to success: past success breeds pervasive continuity and turns an orientation into an ideology or piece of dogma. This momentum is the reason why companies that have been on a winning streak do not stop even after they have begun to lose heavily. Finally, there is the issue of vested interests in preserving the status quo: vested interests and their power base become inextricably intertwined with a strategy, and the political obstacles to strategic reorientation grow (1980: 604). In short, there will nearly always be a rationale for not changing an organization.

The story of the BBC underlines a bigger point, often made by writers, that strategy-making is not just a question of what you do but when you do it; it is as much as anything a question of judgement, in this case judgement about whether cultural conservation is still the best strategic option, or whether it has become a liability and should be abandoned. Unfortunately, being part of the culture actually clouds that judgement (the problem of 'schematic myopia' or 'collective blindness' which is discussed later), and it is often not as clear to insiders as it is to outsiders when a strategy has overstayed its welcome.

Clearly, the two different viewpoints presented here show that 'success' is not simply a function of the strategy adopted, but also of the time and place, indeed of the whole context within which it occurs, and it would therefore be quite foolish to make or to accept anyone else's generalizations in this area. It is perhaps better to start from the assumption that a strategy for cultural order, as indeed any other kind of cultural strategy, is intrinsically 'polyvalent', in other words just as likely to produce an outcome in one direction as in any other! The question is knowing when to use which strategy, and when it is time to try to make the switch from one to the other. A contingency rather than a universalistic view on these matters is what seems to be called for here: one that sees the effectiveness of a cultural strategy as depending not so much on the strategy itself but on the prevailing conditions in the wider environment within which it is situated and embedded. There is also the 'subjective environment' to consider in the sense that the definition of what constitutes 'success' will itself vary enormously from individual to individual and group to group.

Apart from being conservationists, cultural order strategists are also *evolutionists*, pursuing a course of development that will produce not so much a change as a 'growth of order' (from a lower level to a higher level of evolution). Their strategies may therefore be described as custodial, dedicated to keeping the form or species of culture alive, and the 'line' intact. Their guiding rule is that a change is acceptable if it produces a mutation of the existing form, but not if it involves changing the form itself. In other words, first order quantitative growth ('more of the same') is permitted but second order qualitative growth ('something different') is not. The surface shape can be altered, but the underlying form or matrix from which it is constituted must remain invariant: Disney can branch out and do different things so long as it does not do away with its Duck (i.e. its 'cartoon culture'). The Duck itself can evolve and develop so long as it remains clearly recognizable as Donald.

The multiplying processes associated with the growth of order account for much of the recursiveness in organizational life. Their role is not one of creation or production, but re-creation, reproduction and repetition. The processes describe a circle – 'closed orbits' or 'stable limit cycles' as they are called in mathematics: 'orbits spiraling around and toward a fixed closed orbit, with its own stable equilibrium point' (Cooke, 1979: 58). From the viewpoint of this strategy, change is a disturbance to be corrected. Like a thermostat, the strategy cuts in automatically whenever anything moves outside the accepted range, and acts in a self-regulating way, that is homeostatically, to counteract the change.

This comparison is very apt because, as with the thermostat, the primary function of this strategy – indeed of any strategy – is one of *control*. As Child (1984) has urged, we have to see culture as part of a strategy for control in organizations, a consciously designed strategy for developing pragmatic acceptance into a much more enthusiastic support for management's purposes. It is thereby a means of fashioning employees' behaviour along desired lines. Although there is nothing remarkable about the ends or goal of a 'cultural maintenance' strategy (managers have always been preoccupied with the issue of control), it does differ from traditional 'bureaucratic' and 'humanistic' forms of control in the means whereby it seeks to achieve it. Diagrammatically (cf. Ray, 1986) the 'cultural theory' of control looks something like this:

Manipulation of ———> Love of the firm ——> Increased
culture   and its goals   productivity

Spelling it out in more detail, Ray has this to say:

> The latest strategy of control implies that the top management team aims to
> have individuals possess direct ties to the values and goals of the dominant
> elites in order to activate the emotion and sentiment which might lead to
> devotion, loyalty and commitment to the company. In this sense, the use of
> corporate culture is analogous to Rousseau's notion of the individual
> citizen's relation to the General Will. When viewed this way, we find that
> man is free inside the society (the corporation) but the legislator (the chief
> executive) is to lead him to the knowledge of the General Will (corporation
> policy) which will serve the entire collectivity.   (1986: 294)

The fundamental concept of the cultural control perspective seems to
be that implicit control systems, based upon internalized meanings and
values, are a more effective means of achieving coordination than
external control systems which rely on explicit rules and regulations
(Denison and Mishra, 1989: 168). At the very least, 'culture' plugs a gap
in the battery of managerial controls by providing an internal (and
internalized self-regulating) mode of control. As Inzerelli has pointed out,
'no organization can rely entirely on external controls because not all
human activities can be controlled in this way and because external
controls generate their own dysfunctions. Every organization must rely to
some degree on its members' voluntarism and identification as
motivation to perform, that is, on internal controls' (1980: 2).

We can define strategies for 'controlled cultural evolution' more closely
still if we refer to the work of Perrow (1972) and various political
scientists and philosophers (cf. Feenberg, 1986). Perrow identified three
levels of organizational control:

1 Control which is expressed in direct orders.
2 Control operating indirectly through programmes and procedures.
3 Control exerted by operating on the ideological premises of action.

Strategies for cultural order and control belong very much to category
3. Recalling Gramsci's classical theory of power, category 3 is the notion
of culture as 'hegemony': a form of ideational control that works by
controlling the way people think rather than their behaviour – in short,
mind control. Interpolating in Bates's definition (1975: 352), we can say
that cultural hegemony in organizations is 'political (corporate) leadership based on the consent of the led, a consent which is secured by the
diffusion and popularization of the world view (culture) of the ruling
class (senior management)'. Gramsci was writing about a situation in

which a dominant class (the equivalent of shareholders or a senior management group) has control over the basic economic and political institutions, and attempts to utilize its monopoly access to those institutions in order to propagate values and norms (e.g. 'IBM means Service'). These then serve to reinforce its own position of dominance.

This process of control has three basic facets, all of them found in cultural control strategies within organizations:

> Firstly, there is the dissemination of the values and norms favoured by the elite group; secondly there is the denial, refutation and ultimately censorship of beliefs, values and norms which threaten the position of the elite group; and thirdly there is the attempt to define and limit the parameters of permissible and normal discussion of beliefs, values and norms.
>
> (Kirkbride, 1983: 238)

A strategy for cultural order, which is invariably expressed in the call for a 'strong culture', therefore depends for its effectiveness on the control of ideas – ideational control – and it is only as a last resort, when this breaks down or is in imminent danger of doing so, that the ruling group falls back upon the coercive power of the political society or state machinery in order to reassert its domination (1983: 239). The culture strategy's aim is voluntary support for its ideas, and to achieve this it must deliver or promise something of value to the led. That it does not always succeed in doing this to the satisfaction of all concerned is evidenced by the fact that coercive power is resorted to quite frequently in 'cultural' change programmes.

Such occurrences are a reminder that ideational control is not the simple and straightforward affair that cultural engineers would like it to be. In fact, one fundamental objection to it is that it simply does not work! Employees may be prepared to put on Donald Duck suits and sing the company song at the tops of their voices, but this does not mean that they will go so far as to lie on their backs, waggle their (webbed) feet in the air and surrender unconditionally to the will of the 'dominant' culture. In an uncertain world they may yearn for meaning, but it does not follow that they will buy any meaning (Gabriel, 1991: 439).

In matters of personal interest people are rarely gullible or totally compliant, and they never take kindly to being hit over the head with someone else's idea of a 'good thing'. They are particularly sensitive to the presence or absence of reciprocity in the working relationship, and tend, despite strong pressures from strong culture organizations to join in the corporate groupthink, to make decisions about the nature and extent of their involvement in a fairly cool, detached and calculative manner. As Willmott observes,

Instead of the deep internalisation of corporate values encouraged by the Corporate Culture gurus, a more likely orientation is one of conditional identification or even calculative compliance. In which case, employees are willing to 'realise' the values of the corporation only insofar and so long as they calculate that material or symbolic advantage is being derived from it. This mode of engagement, which Berger and Luckmann (1966: 192) identify as an increasingly common orientation in advanced industrial societies, is characterised as 'cool' alternation wherein 'the individual internalizes the new reality, but instead of it being *his* reality, it is a reality to be used by him for specific purposes. In so far as this involves the performance of certain roles, he retains subjective detachment vis-à-vis them – he "puts them on" deliberately and purposefully'. (1991b: 14)

Very much in the same vein, Gabriel (1991, 1992) has written about the way personal subjectivity – the 'I' as distinct from the 'We' in organizations – is able to reassert itself even against the odds. People do not go under, do not succumb to thought controls, do not allow themselves to be absorbed into the greater whole (not in Western cultures, at least). They have a number of social and psychological defences which prevent this from happening:

The workers . . . may submit to the managers' cultural assaults but they also resist them by developing their own sub-cultures and counter-cultures. These challenge or poke fun at the managerial shibboleths, expressing cynicism and detachment at managerial attempts to whip up commitment and enthusiasm. (1992: 1)

Gabriel goes on to argue (and I very much agree with him) that writers have tended to generate an over-managed and over-policed image of the organization. He proposes that 'there is within every organization a large uncolonized terrain, a terrain which is not and cannot be managed, in which people, both individually and in groups, can engage in all kinds of unsupervised, spontaneous activity' (1992: 2). He refers to this as the 'unmanaged organization'.

The defiance and resistance to which Gabriel refers are particularly prevalent in 'total culture' regimes; one might even suggest that the strength of such resistance is in direct proportion to the amount of coercion being applied. A nice example of the way a sub-culture with its own 'private language' can resist the will of the dominant culture is provided by P. Burke (1987). Apparently the inhabitants of Polish prisons go to great lengths to ensure that new inmates learn the prison jargon ('*grypserka*') as soon as possible after their arrival. Through this process cultural identity is created, communicated and reinforced, and unwelcome members of the ruling group are kept safely at bay. This language is a defence against cultural colonization and the suppression of pluralism. Even in prisons, it seems, there is an unmanaged organization.

To summarize, no matter how much power resides in the ruling group, there will always be a part of the organization where control attempts can be subverted and robbed of their effectiveness by informal, grass roots processes. This is another way of saying that no change can be exclusively managed in a coercive manner from the top down. Even when the odds are stacked against it, the informal system will be able to repel most kinds of ideological invasion if it so desires. There must therefore be considerable doubts about the effectiveness of the 'strong cultures' approach as a strategy for control. This is a vitally important point for all those involved in managing culture, because it requires them to acknowledge that it would be extremely unwise to rely on this type of 'top-down' strategy to achieve their ambitions.

Perhaps the word 'control' therefore needs to be amended to read 'influence' or 'attempted control', since any strategy, not least a strategy for maintaining cultural order, will invariably fall some way short of its designers' ambitions. The main reason for this, explored later, is that cultural order strategists are often blind to the pluralism of organizations: they do not see (or prefer not to see) the hundreds of small interest groups, with incompletely overlapping memberships, widely differing power bases, and a multitude of techniques for exercising influence on decisions salient to them (Polsby, 1963: 118), and therefore do not allow for organization control attempts operating in the reverse direction – with them as the target of a 'defensive' informal system or sub-culture. Nor do they acknowledge that in such a pluralistic system management's power superiority is no longer sufficient to permit the luxury of imposed solutions or directives (Fox, 1973: 194). In consequence, they are often ill-prepared for the resistance that they encounter on the way, and for the bargaining process that will be necessary if they are to create some kind of order.

According to some writers (Gagliardi, 1991; Willmott, 1991a, 1991b), the cultural approach has also added a fourth level of control to the management armoury suggested by Perrow (see above):

4   Control exercised by operating on people's sensory, aesthetic and emotional responses – playing on their feelings as well as their thoughts.

Willmott, for example, writes, 'No longer is the preserve of management control restricted to authorising and enforcing rules and procedures. For the key task and responsibility of management is now control of how employees *imagine* and *feel* about what they produce – of "giving employees a mission as well as a sense of feeling great" ' (1991b: 6, original emphasis.)

The range of positive feelings that strong culture strategies seek to engender towards the company and its leaders is wide, taking in loyalty, commitment, dedication, devotion, enthusiasm and even love and passion. The theory is that employees will act responsibly (the idea of responsible autonomy) and follow their leader if they 'feel' something for their company and come to respect, even idolize and worship, what it stands for. This idea of corporate idol-worship, much beloved by strong culture writers, was anticipated some thirty years ago by the psycho-analyst Erich Fromm. As far as Fromm himself was concerned, it was not healthy for people to be worshipping inanimate objects, like an organization or its products, or a figurehead hero or saviour, because this led to a loss of personal control and individuality – Hitler and the Nazi Party (a strong culture if ever there was one) being one consequence of this idol-worship:

> Man spends his energy . . . on building an idol, and then he worships this idol, which is nothing but the result of his own human effort. His life forces have flowed into a 'thing', and this thing, having become an idol, is not experienced as a result of his own productive effort, but as something apart from himself, over and against himself, which he worships and to which he submits . . . Idolatrous man bows down to the work of his own hands. The idol represents his own life-forces in an alienated form.   (1963: 61)

Having read accounts of companies that have attempted such emotional control, I am inclined to agree with him. One unfortunate byproduct of this strategy is that the recipients of control attempts may become alienated from themselves and detached from their own personal emotions. Hochschild's book *The Managed Heart* (1983) painfully illustrates this point. Its subjects are the air stewardesses in Delta Airlines who were told that their 'company smile' was the number one asset as far as airline profits were concerned. (Readers may also have seen the recent two-page advertisement from American Airlines which markets 'the smile' as a commodity like champagne: 'Welcome aboard America's Business Class. A warm smile and chilled champagne await you.' Having shown several pictures, including one huge one, of 'the smile', the advertisement ends (just in case we have not got the message clearly): 'When you fly American Airlines to America *this smile* is always there. It's a warm and friendly American smile. And it's part of everything we do . . . '). They should smile regardless of what they felt inside. The book is about the commercialization of emotion, and how attempts were made to manipulate feelings in order to gain competitive advantage. At one level the company was only asking its employees to provide a friendly and courteous service, but on another level it 'estranged them from their smile' – and hence from themselves:

> The workers I talked to often spoke of their smiles as being *on* them but not *of* them. They were seen as an extension of the make-up, the uniform, the recorded music, the soothing pastel colours of the airplane decor and the daytime drinks, which taken together orchestrate the mood of the passengers.   (1983: 8)

The negative effects of this company policy appeared to be such that many stewardesses found it hard to release themselves from the 'artificially created elation' and at the same time felt a sense of 'emotional deadness' towards their jobs. It seemed to affect their capacity for having 'authentic' feelings as their emotions became more the property of the organization than of themselves. To paraphrase Fromm, their 'life forces' had flowed into a 'thing' called an airline, a situation that resulted in the creation of a false, objectified, self.

This is, of course, only one perspective on the strategy and there are others still to be considered. Nevertheless it does raise fundamental moral and ethical questions about a managerial ideology – the strong cultures ideology – which until now has attracted surprisingly little negative comment from writers and commentators.

What we can say with certainty is that managers of strong cultures not only 'make meaning' for employees – the intellectual view of leadership favoured by many organization writers (cf., Smircich and Morgan, 1982) during the 1980s – today they also seek to 'make feeling' for them, taking as their central interest the liberation of employees' emotional energies and the channelling of these in the direction of the corporate goal. The management writer Tom Peters expressed this view of organizations as emotion-releasing/fulfilling milieux at a conference lunch for business-men in London several years ago:

> Leadership is one hundred per cent about emotion [pause]. End of story. I don't mean screaming and shouting. I don't mean crying and hugging. I just mean emotion. Because organizations are people. Period. That's all they are – they're people. And people are emotional. That's the definition of people – you, me, and hourly workers with or without names.

Companies were not slow to take up Peters' invitation to place 'feelings' at the centre of their attention. For instance, during the 1980s and early 1990s Pizza Hut's employee induction programme made use of a booklet called simply *Feelings* (I believe the idea came originally from McDonalds). In it – and very much in line with the thinking in strong culture companies at the time – the company talked about 'investing' in feelings to ensure the continuation of Pizza Hut's commercial success story.

What an employee should and should not feel was set out in detail in the booklet: basically, employees were only allowed to display positive feelings – 'warm fuzzies' – during the work period. Negative ones – 'cold pricklies' – were not allowed. These sentiments were cleverly anthropomorphized into two cartoon characters: a malevolent, spiky-haired, spiky-bearded dwarf (Cold Prickly) and an appealing, round-eyed, cuddly powder-puff creature (Warm Fuzzy). Warm Fuzzies were shown helping old ladies and giving out 'positive strokes' to all and sundry. Cold Pricklies were seen getting wet and angry under black storm clouds and showing hostility towards the more unconventional customer – depicted in one cartoon as an Afro-Caribbean character with long braids of hair, a flat cap, hippie dress and a studded leather bracelet! The coldest of cold pricklies was the Big Fat Zero: keeping customers waiting, refusing to smile or simply ignoring people altogether.

The booklet was, in effect, an attempt by a company to formulate a policy on feelings for its employees (feeling rules), requiring them to feel a particular way – even when they didn't feel like it! As the booklet suggested:

> Even when life gets hectic a smile is a Warm Fuzzy, especially when you're having a bad day.

A typical picture showed a Warm Fuzzy booting a Cold Prickly out of the door while two employees looked on approvingly and the rest of the Warm Fuzzy gang gave a salute and a thumbs up to the camera. As far as Pizza Hut was concerned the only place for a Cold Prickly was outside – out in the cold.

Of course, as I said earlier, no self-respecting strong culture would be naive enough to rely on controlling employee effort by 'positive feelings' alone. In parallel with this, the company had strong back-up behavioural controls as well: ten 'service steps' had to be followed to the letter on every order. Routines were specific, leaving (theoretically at least) little scope for individual discretion in interpreting his or her role. Waiters and waitresses were 'programmed' to adopt 'suggestive selling' techniques at every possible opportunity. In short, their behaviour was tightly scripted.

Returning now to feelings, we need to ask what precisely are these feelings that 'culture-shapers' are seeking to engender towards the company and its products? Two of the main ones are dedication and love.

Dedication

Dedication means getting people to feel that they have to or want to put work before their families: 'I'm sorry I'm so late getting home, but the customer had a problem and we never leave a customer with a problem' (Deal and Kennedy, 1982: 33). Or, as the Honda worker cited in *In Search of Excellence* might well have said, 'I'm sorry I'm so late getting home this evening. I have been straightening the wiper blades on all the Hondas I have seen on the way home because I just can't stand to see a flaw in a Honda' (Peters and Waterman, 1982: 37). These examples show that working in a strong culture is not to be viewed as a 9 to 5 affair. It has to be a way of life, a consuming passion, a mission. The company has to be a place of worship.

Not surprisingly then, it is institutions like the Roman Catholic church that are hailed as the model for today's go-ahead, strong culture company (Deal and Kennedy, 1982: 194). The RC church has everything: stability, durability, a dominant market position, but above all, a grip on the consciences and feelings of its followers. In a word, it is the ultimate Hegemony, the perfect Order:

> And how has the Roman Catholic church maintained its sway for so many centuries? Not by strategic planning systems. Not by layers upon layers of middle managers. But through one of the strongest and most durable cultures ever created. . . . It is a culture that is rich with heroes, stories, and mythologies; martyrs; missionaries; saints; a Polish freedom-fighting pope; heroes for people to identify with day-to-day. And finally, whether you agree with it or not, it is a culture founded on the bedrock of a set of meaningful (to its followers) beliefs and values . . . The Catholic church is an important model for another reason: not only has it built a culture that unites people and parishes, provides faith and meaning across countries, and offers something of value in return for one's efforts. But beyond this, the Catholic church has something in common with IBM, Mary Kay, McDonald's, the Polaris project, the US Forest Service, and countless numbers of other successful organizations – *all of them capture some of the same religious tone.* (my italics)

Love

Strong hegemonic cultures not only want dedication, they also want love. 'Love' has acquired new meaning in the strong cultures literature. It no longer means loving your partner or your pet hamster, but 'cherishing' strangers (customers) and loving inanimate and sometimes unglamorous objects (the product) – a hamburger, for instance:

> you gotta love what you do, you gotta care. Ray Kroc was serious: 'You've gotta be able to see the beauty in a hamburger bun'; all his stories are hamburger stories – love stories about hamburgers, really.
>
> (Peters and Austin, 1985: 288)

Or even a piece of garbage:

> Take Sunset Scavengers. Yes, Sunset Scavengers is a garbage company –
> most say the best-run garbage company in America. Boss Len Stephanelli's
> secret: 'I love garbage'.   (1985: xxii)

The pay-off for those who succeed in 'cutting the mustard' (or should it
be the hamburger?) is simply that they get to feel good about themselves.
They can walk tall (Big Macs?); they can feel they are doing something
useful for mankind; they can run into Shea Stadium and be applauded by
thousands of their colleagues as their name comes up on the scoreboard
in large, illuminated letters. Ordinary mortals can be winners, even
heroes. And if the unthinkable happens and they fail? Here's the rub:

> employees not only derive a sense of meaning and belonging from complying
> with the culture. They simultaneously experience a sense of anxiety, shame
> and guilt when they judge themselves to fail.   (Willmott, 1991b: 13)

Unfortunately, unlike the church described earlier, there may be no
confessionals on hand to cope with this eventuality, and no kindly priests
to grant absolution to those who fail their Corporate God. The outlook
in some cases can be bleak.

Methods of enforcement

How is the Order nourished and maintained in strong cultures, and how
do the leaders ensure that any change that takes place does so in a
controlled evolutionary way? The methods range from the 'soft' –
creating a situation where employees discipline and control themselves, to
the 'hard' – meting out good, old-fashioned punishments to hapless
cultural deviants. The former is usually the preferred option, while the
latter tends to be a last resort, used either when matters get out of hand or
when the leaders are in a particularly zealous or messianic frame of mind.
These two represent the opposite ends of a continuum, shown in Figure
3.1. The six types of method are now illustrated.

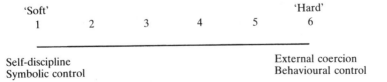

Figure 3.1   Methods used in the realization of a strategy for cultural order

1   Taking care of people

The boss allows humanness to pervade his organization.

(Peters and Austin, 1985)

'We think society today suffers from a pervasive uncertainty about values,' write Deal and Kennedy (1982), 'a relativism that undermines leadership and commitment alike. After all, in this fast-paced world, who really *does* know what's right? On the philosophical level, we find ourselves without convincing responses' (1982: 22). Organizations (say the authors) have the same problem: 'Unlike workers ten or twenty years ago, employees today are confused . . . their life values are uncertain; they are blameful and cynical; they confuse morality with ethics. Uncertainty is at the core of it all' (p. 16).

Enter Strong Culture, stage right: 'Yet strong culture companies remove a great degree of that uncertainty because they provide structure and standards and a value system in which to operate' (Deal and Kennedy, 1982). The strong culture, like a hospital or health farm, takes care of people, keeping them out of harm's way, while at the same time feeding and clothing them and helping them to grow well and strong. Of course, as with all total institutions, there are certain regimes to be observed; inmates must wear the same uniform, perform the same rituals, be prepared to put in superhuman effort, and submit to certain restrictions on their movement. And don't let them dare fail:

> [Leaders of strong cultures] are concerned with the set of beliefs and values they hold and in making sure these beliefs are inculcated in the people around them. On the one hand, this means protecting the people in one's organization – taking care of them in times of sickness, giving them full employment, and being otherwise responsible for the lives of those over whom you have stewardship. On the other hand, this means not permitting them to fail in any way.   (1982: 56)

The strong culture may be liberal but it is by no means *laissez-faire*.

In it, control resides in the ability of the leaders to resolve uncertainty and insecurity. Employees, like the patients in a hospital, tend to do what they're told because they value (and depend on) the care and attention they are receiving and do not wish to run the risk of being cast out into a hostile, uncertain and lonely world. They want to be good patients.

The lure of a strong culture is that it *feels* nice and secure. Happiness is . . . a warm sea:

> We are immersed in a sea. It is warm, comfortable, supportive and protecting. That sea is our culture . . . escape is by no means entirely desirable.   (Webber, 1977: 48)

The fact that it's 'sink or swim' means that they control themselves – internal rather than external control.

2   Giving people their heads

In strong cultures employees may be given a good deal of authority and responsibility for the things that happen on their 'patch'. The beauty of this kind of system is that people can be relied on to set their own standards and discipline themselves, while being aware of the 'deal': freedom is conditional upon the ability to 'deliver'. In this set-up, the leader's job is not so much to give detailed instructions as a broad mission, something for people to achieve in any way they think fit – just so long as they achieve it. The message is hard and simple: 'Here is the task; we're relying on you to go and do it; and don't come back until you've done it.' Employees make the corporate task their personal task, and derive a personal sense of purpose from the corporate purpose. Achieving the corporate goal is thus transformed into a personal crusade, indeed an act of personal redemption, which if successful deepens their commitment to the organization, and makes them ready to make bigger sacrifices next time around.

Peters and Waterman (1982: 318) describe this kind of control system as 'simultaneous loose–tight': 'the co-existence of firm central direction and maximum individual autonomy – what we have called "having one's cake and eating it too".' It is a system which, on the face of it, seems to have pulled off the impossible by merging the two apparent opposites of freedom and constraint. On the one hand, every man and woman can be a pioneer, an experimenter, an innovator, and a leader, while on the other hand the system exercises 'tight control' over them and ensures 'nothing gets very far out of line' (p. 320). A set of rigidly shared corporate values holds the key. And, of course, there is 'faith' (p. 318): people must be encouraged to have faith in these values. And if words like 'values' and 'faith' sound a bit 'soft', don't forget that it was these two authors who originally informed us that 'soft is hard'. For instance, we find when we read them that freedom can mean the freedom to earn a million bucks, or it can mean the freedom to hang yourself. Great American business leaders like Marriott, Hewlett and Packard

> were stern disciplinarians, every one. They gave plenty of rope, but they accepted the chance that some of their minions would hang themselves. Loose–tight is about rope. (p. 319)

In strong culture organizations, things may be soft but they are certainly never cushy.

3   Having fun

Control in any organization depends to a large extent on the leaders' skill in neutralizing criticism and disarming resistance to established values and practices. While traditional societies and bureaucracies tend to approach the task of managing differences with utmost 'seriousness', modern, enlightened, strong culture companies tend to approach it with a sense of 'fun'.

The strong culture company is a 'fun' place to be: its employees laugh a lot (and loudly), they play practical jokes on each other, they indulge in horseplay, they put on fancy dress and poke fun at themselves, they have regular beer-busts, and they are always giving each other 'jokey' presents and awards. These pranks and japes would seem to be more at home in the traditional English public school or the West End than a modern, commercial organization. However, there is a serious side to this fun that makes it quite good business sense as well, and apart from giving pleasure, it can also act as a powerful mechanism of control.

As Willmott (1991a) has observed, strong culture companies have used fun and playfulness strategically as a means of endearing employees to core values and objectives, and gaining compliance to dominant sentiments and truths. They achieve their desired effect by getting everyone to join in (shy gooseberries beware!). A bond of loyalty and affection and a strong sense of community are created (Judas's beware!), people learn to laugh at themselves and have a good time (killjoys and spoilsports beware!), and the asking of 'process' questions – like why are we doing this? what's the point? why this way? – is discouraged (critics and sceptics beware!). All serious dissension that might have existed is swept away on a wave of fun. As Willmott puts it,

> the gurus of Corporate Culture prescribe 'large doses of hoopla and celebration'. The value of these rituals, Peters and Waterman observe, resides in their power simultaneously to convey a positive valuation of employees and demonstrate the homely, caring quality of the organization. Of particular interest and concern is their capacity to inhibit critical reflection by ironicising the activity in a way that neutralises its serious examination. Referring to the award of 'Attaboy' plaques given 'for exemplary service' in one large US company, Deal and Kennedy observe how, in giving these awards, 'the company laughs at itself in a gentle way.' As Peters and Waterman observe of these 'productivity programs': 'yes, it's hocum, and – like so many situations we see – it's fun'. Moreover – and this is how criticism is effectively neutralized – employees themselves acknowledge it to be hocum *and* value it for its playful quality. As a consequence, anyone who questions the value or ethics of such programs – on the grounds, for example, that they are demeaning or totalitarian – is deemed not only to be disloyal to the company but is perceived to lack a

sense of humour or to ascribe undue importance to something that is transparently trivial.   (1991a: 10)

4   Handing out 'personal' corporate jewellery and other symbolic rewards

On a December day in 1982, every one of SAS's 20,000 employees received a parcel in the mail. Upon opening it, each found a beautiful gold wristwatch with a second hand in the shape of a tiny airplane. In addition there was a memo outlining new, more liberal regulations governing free trips for employees . . . Also included was a second 'little red book,' entitled 'The Fight of the Century', and an invitation to a party. Finally, there was a letter from me, printed on quality parchment paper, thanking them for the great job they had done during that year in which SAS has vaulted from its worst loss ever to the biggest profit in its history.

(Jan Carlzon, president and CEO of Scandinavian Airlines (SAS), 1987: 113)

Strong culture companies, like SAS, make a habit of showering gifts on their employees. Some chief executives, like Carlzon, have a penchant for personal jewellery and all-night parties in airplane hangars (could this be the origin of the word hangover?), whereas others like John Harvey-Jones of ICI prefer cases of vintage wine for 'particularly meritorious' individuals (1989: 91). CEOs' shopping lists of gifts, perks and various other tokens of appreciation seem endless.

But why do they do it? Obviously, it is one way of saying 'thanks': 'We had asked 20,000 people to go an extra mile for a year to help pull SAS out of a crisis. Now they deserved our thanks in equal measure' (Carlzon, 1987: 114). And a 'classy' gold watch says it that much better than a fat bonus in the pay packet at the end of the month. (That line about 'Say it with flowers' just wouldn't be the same if it were changed to 'Say it with money'. Anyway money smacks too much of the capital-labour divide – something the modern business leaders are all trying to get away from.) On the other hand, it is not all unbridled affection and generosity. The giver expects a return on his tasteful investments. That return is an enhancement and extension of his or her control. Such control takes two forms, both involving the leaders' manipulation of the 'symbolism' contained in material rewards of various kinds.

(a) *cognitive control* (see Perrow's category 3 above): This is derived from the 'framing' action inherent in symbol (Van Buskirk, 1989: 255). Gifts and trinkets are used to symbolize, encapsulate and communicate the notion of what the senior executive wants his or her organization to be or to become. To put it another way, people's ideas and perceptions are symbolically 'framed' by what the senior executive considers to be an 'appropriate' definition of organization reality: 'The watch was a particularly appropriate gift. Not only was it an expression of our gratitude but it tied in with our successful effort to become the world's most punctual airline' (Carlzon, 1987: 114). Acceptance of the watch (and who could possibly refuse such a generous gift from such an important person?) is tantamount to an acceptance of the leader's vision and objectives for the company.

Similarly, attendance at a party also symbolizes one's acceptance of the leader's vision of the organization, this being in Carlzon's case a vision of SAS as a large 'family' of 'equals':

> The second phase was the party. We intended this joint symbol of recognition to underscore the fact that SAS is actually a *group*, albeit a very large one. We held parties all over the world to do it. Four thousand people attended the one in Stockholm alone, including mechanics, pilots, loaders, pursers, air hostesses, secretaries, salesmen, computer technicians, and everyone else, all of whom recognized that we had achieved something collectively – not just individually.   (1987: 114)

Symbolic events such as this are highly compelling: after all who could refuse a 'personal' invitation from the president to attend his party, and who would be so antisocial as to turn one's back on one's own family?

(b) *emotional control* (see category 4 above): Symbols not only communicate meanings and ideas, they are just as capable of communicating emotions. As Van Buskirk (1989: 255) observes, 'it is the emotion that resides within a symbol that often accounts for its efficacy'. Gift wristwatches not only communicate a message about punctuality, they also make people feel happy, grateful, loved, wanted and recognized; and they make them feel good about their company and its leaders. Take the response of SAS's employees to that December parcel mentioned above:

> The contents of the package may not seem so extraordinary, but the recipients were delighted. Scores of them sent me thank-you letters with messages like: 'There I stood, a grown-up, at the post office with my package, and I was so happy that I was ready to cry'.   (Carlzon, 1987: 113)

As Carlzon himself says, there is no doubt that symbols are important – for controlling people as well as motivating them. This control is exercised by using symbolic devices, such as those described, to 'trigger' positive emotions about the company and its leaders that make people feel submissive and compliant, willing to 'go there and back' for the people (and products) they love. Power, as the theorists tell us, resides in dependence. Employees in a strong culture are, to a greater or lesser extent, dependent – emotionally dependent – upon their organization (and therefore upon those who allow them to work in it). The organization satisfies feelings that previously only an institution like the family or the church could satisfy. Perhaps even more so: Carlzon describes the employee hysteria that accompanied the unveiling of a new 'Calvin Klein' designer clothes collection for his staff. As the fashion models danced to the strains of 'Love is in the Air', people cheered and cried with joy, barely able to contain themselves (1987: 116). One wonders whether they had shown the same enthusiasm when their wives had last brought home a new dress, or their husbands bought a new jacket!

5 Spelling it out

As we continue to move from left to right along the control continuum, the 'subtle cues' (Deal and Kennedy, 1982: 15) of symbolic management give way to grosser forms of behavioural control. The strong culture company is not just a free-floating entity of meaning and emotion, it is also anchored firmly to good old terra firma by a strong network of rules and norms. There is nothing vague or ethereal about these. As Deal and Kennedy say, strong cultures 'spell it out':

> A strong culture is a system of informal rules that spells out how people are to behave most of the time. By knowing exactly what is expected of them, employees will waste little time in deciding how to act in a given situation.
>
> (1982: 15)

Informal these rules may be, imprecise they are not. Put one foot wrong and you're in trouble:

> At Disneyland and Disneyworld, every person who comes onto the property (the 'set') is called a guest. Moreover, should you ever write the word at Disney, heaven help you if you don't capitalize the G.
>
> (Peters and Austin, 1985: 41)

Whereas 'shared values' at the higher level of a strong culture define the limits and boundaries of behaviour, the 'rules' on the ground level define the precise paths and walkways that must be followed. All 'successful' strong culture companies, say Deal and Kennedy, have these rules and all expect them to be observed: 'they didn't tolerate deviance from the company standards' (1982: 14). And if people don't rigidly conform? That's simple, say the authors. They don't survive (1982: 98).

6 Getting heavy

At the far end of the control continuum we have corporate fascism, a regime in which order is maintained by brutishness and inhumane treatment, even 'torture', of employees (the advantage of symbolic torture being that it does not leave marks!). All strong cultures need their bastards, say Deal and Kennedy – people who are willing to act as bullies and heavies:

> In contrast to the warm, humane managers promoted by business publications today, what businesses need are individuals concerned about building something of value and sensitive mostly to the needs of the organization they are trying to establish. Call it bastardly, but also call it heroic. The point is this: modern managers who try to be humane may at the same time undermine the values upon which the culture of the institution rests. Modern heroes may need to be hard and 'insensitive' to keep a company consistent with its goals and vision – the very elements that made it strong in the first place.   (1982: 56)

Their methods range from 'teaching somebody a lesson they'll never forget' in the 'school of hard knocks' . . . 'hazing', for example, which is the corporate equivalent of the roasting that Tom Brown received when he first went to Rugby School:

> Managers often transform new hotshots into sacrificial lambs by sending them to consult with the well-known bastard who can't stand young kids. The manager knows the bastard will knock the hotshots off their feet every time.   (1982: 65)

to outright persecution of someone, as both a lesson to him and an example to everyone else:

> NCR's John Patterson was unique in his tortures. One of his executives once returned from lunch to find his desk and chair parked outside on the curb in front of the factory. He emerged from the cab to watch his furniture get soaked in kerosene, then set afire. He got back in the cab, lest he too should be torched. This was not a humane way of being told you're through; but whatever the executive had done to deserve this, the deed was probably never repeated by others.   (1982: 56)

In summary, traversing the control continuum (Figure 3.1, p. 47) we have discovered that a strategy for cultural order has plenty of openings for both the Mutts and the Jeffs of this world, in other words, for methods of control and order enforcement that can be as soft and sublime as they can be savage and hard. Mundane examples of the strategy in use, like the one above, offer a salutory reminder that, as well as the practical dimension to strategy and strategic processes, there is always a moral and ethical dimension that needs to be considered too. What makes the strong cultures strategy so hard to assess in this regard is that it is such a hotch-potch of 'moral opposites': humanism and instrumentalism, expression and suppression, collectivism and individualism, totalitarianism and democracy, symbolism and materialism, submission and control, independence and dependence. If ever there were a challenge for both–and thinking, this would certainly be it.

As we conclude this section it is also worth noting how far the conception of 'culture' has strayed from its initial use in anthropology (see Figure 3.2 below). The culture concept began its life as a framework for thinking, not a framework for action or control. It was an academic paradigm and mode of analysis. The last thing anthropologists thought of doing was to take their data 'back' to assist in bringing about change or controlling the society's members. The first departure from this was the use of the culture concept in an OD setting as a concept for action. In recent years the use of the concept has strayed even further from its original source to its use as a form of managerial control and human engineering.

Let us move on and look at another dimension of the class of strategy we have been discussing. I have so far described the people who employ strategies for cultural development as conservationists and evolutionists. I should now like to add a third label and describe them as *integrationists*. They believe that the company is healthier, more innovative and generally more effective when the cultures of its parts have been fully integrated into a single, consistent and uniform whole – or, to put it another way, when the overall 'corporate' culture is 'strong' and its 'local' subcultures 'weak'. Order and development, to people of this persuasion, are a matter of striving to assimilate and integrate diverse orientations and interests into a single, common orientation towards the organization's affairs (Martin and Meyerson, 1988).

Recent reviews of the literature on organizational culture show that the majority of studies conceptualize the 'desirable' culture in this way (Meek, 1988; Young, 1989; Darmer, 1991). The core proposition is that an 'effective' organization is a unitary system bound together by a common task and common values. A key management task, therefore,

	ANTHROPOLOGISTS	OD PRACTITIONERS	MANAGERS
CULTURE AS:	A Framework for thinking	A Framework for acting	A Framework for control
UNDERLYING OBJECTIVE:	Discovery	Improvement	Control

Figure 3.2   Three conceptions of culture

is to enhance system integration. This requires that different sets of norms, values and beliefs be brought into alignment both with each other across the organization and with other parts of the system such that together they fit the demands made by the environment. Culture's specific role is to allow the organization to survive as an integrated, ordered community in its [various] environments.   (Green, 1988: 123)

The integrationists' ideal of a team-based, trouble-free cooperative environment – a kind of Commonwealth or European Community writ small – gives rise to development strategies whose intention is to move the organization from what Kanter (1983: 27) has termed a 'segmentalist culture' to an 'integrative culture' (see Figure 3.3). The general direction of the change effort is away from diversity and heterogeneity among staff and employees, towards greater uniformity and standardization. Integrationists do not just want to build an organization, they want to build a community. Culture holds the key to this: it is the 'glue' that sticks the different parts of the community together (Baker, 1980: 8). Community integration is achieved by homogenizing employee and work group values, and suppressing or synthesizing competing interests and claims. With such a strategy, plurality is squashed out.

The nightmare image of segmentalism (left hand side in Figure 3.3) – internecine strife, degeneracy, stagnation and anarchy – has been described in graphic detail in the strong cultures literature. However, as is so often the case, it has been left to the cartoonists to show it how it really is! For example, the cartoon on page 58 shows the various island territories of the segmentalist organization, each claiming its own identity (note the flag) and each doing its own 'disconnected' thing, oblivious of the others (note the short-sighted men with glasses), and blissfully unaware of the bigger corporate picture. Things may go reasonably well during nice weather, but wait until the storm breaks. It is doubtful whether anyone will see the approaching tidal wave until it is too late.

My own example of this island thinking comes from British Rail. So segmented had its five marketing organizations (Intercity, Provincial, Network Southeast, Freight and Parcels) become that, by the mid-1980s they were operating almost as independent businesses – a somewhat risky activity, given the fact that their trains continued to share the same track! Each sector was doing its own thing, carving out its own identity for itself: at one point, passengers walking on to the station platform at Didcot in Berkshire would be greeted with the sign 'Welcome to Network Southeast', and a bit further down with another sign saying 'Welcome to Inter-City', and a little bit further still, 'Welcome to Provincial'. Not surprisingly, they were more than a little confused as to where exactly they were (Didcot is not normally regarded as being in the Southeast), who actually 'owned' the platform on which they were standing, and

SEGMENTALIST CULTURE	INTEGRATIVE CULTURE
= 'bad' /dysfunctional/ low control Disorder	= 'good' /functional/ high control Order

Direction of desired change →

* Disparate values, interests, and beliefs	* Shared values, interests, and beliefs
* Breaking rank, going it alone	* Pulling together
* Tribalism and conflict	* Communitas and cooperation
* Compartmentalizing problems	* Seeing problems as wholes
* Ruled by standards of the past	* Ruled by visions of the future
* Meetings	* Teams
* Winners and losers/ them and us	* Confronting and transcending differences
* Anti-change/reactionary	* Change-orientated
* Weak coordinating mechanisms and lateral linkages	* Strong coordination mechanisms and lateral linkages
* Inward-looking	* Outward-looking
* Mechanistic, systems-dominated	* Creative, ideas-dominated
* Non-reflective	* Reflective
* Discordant	* Harmonious

Figure 3.3 The transition from a 'segmentalist' to an 'integrative culture'

what had happened to good old 'British Rail'. Had it been broken up and privatized without anyone knowing it? Had there been an internal coup? Segmentalism – sectorism, to be more precise – had led to a violation of the long-hallowed principle of the 'One Railway': the principle that BR should always present a single 'corporate' face to customers and never confuse them by revealing its inner organizational segments and divisions.

Another example, from the same organization, is the 'hot wheels' story. An Intercity train pulls into a commuter station at the height of the morning rush hour on a cold December day. A guard (on the 'production' side of the organization) notices smoke and steam pouring out from underneath one of the coaches. 'Hot wheels', he remarks – to no one in particular. It is obviously not a job for a guard, so he does not move. Nor does the train! Enter sub-sector manager, from the Intercity 'marketing' side of the organization, responsible for passenger services. (Puffing): 'Why isn't this ruddy train moving? There's a huge queue of trains building up behind.' The guard does not look at him directly – there is a good deal of antipathy between the production and marketing arms of the business; production people have been known to tell marketing people to get off 'their' platform; marketing people feel that production people are obstructive; their prickly interactions stem from deeply ingrained, mutually derogatory stereotypes of each other. 'Hot wheels', he says to the air.

At this point, an engineering manager passes by (no one has called him): 'What's up?', he asks. 'Hot wheels', the others reply in unison, studiously avoiding his eye (there is antipathy between the engineering and marketing sides of the organization: 'engineers' spend too much money; and 'marketeers' don't understand 'trains'). By this time passengers are hanging out of the windows and asking the same question – and, of, course, getting the same vague answer: 'hot wheels' (there is some antipathy between BR employees and their customers; in such circumstances the best way to avoid contact with anxious passengers is to play dumb; the less said the better). Five minutes later and still no one has climbed down to look, or gone in search of help. The train sits there and does not move. Three people stare into the void below the coach, a picture that symbolizes the three-way split that runs from the very top to the very bottom of this huge organization. A testament to the writer Frederic Raphael's description of life as 'inertia posing as pluralism'.

Finally, a maintenance engineer arrives uninvited onto the scene, and, ignoring the other three, climbs down to examine the problem. After a while, a greasy face appears: 'Hot wheels', he remarks (by now predictably). 'A brake was locked on because of the cold weather. I've freed it. You can take the train out now.' Ten minutes after the problem was first noticed, the train departs slowly in the direction of London Paddington. Ten minutes of segmentalism in action: no one communicating with each other, and no one either willing or able to organize an effective concerted response to the problem.

The second cartoon by Browne shows how efforts are wasted when people operate in an uncoordinated, segmented manner. The message is that an integrated approach to the task would have produced the necessary synergy to cut down the tree in half the time.

Reproduced by permission of Yaffa Character Licensing

The final cartoon (page 61) depicts four scenarios that are said to be extremely common in segmentalist organizations:

A   Deadlock and win–lose: people from different segments engage in an endless and futile tug-of-war, either making no progress at all, or making progress only at the expense of someone else.
B   Cut-and-run: realizing they cannot count on the cooperation of other groups in the organization, segments give up and go off and do their own thing, taking whatever resources they can grab with them.
C   Paper games: paralysis by paperwork; segments pass paper endlessly between themselves as a way of delaying or obstructing each other.
D   The organization reaches crisis point and collapses; in comes the CEO on a white charger and centralizes in order to restore order. Totalitarianism takes over from segmentalism. The organization goes from the frying pan into the fire.

These, as I have said, are some of the nightmares that integrationists (especially the more extreme 'communophiles') are known to have about segmentalism. Their dreams, on the other hand, are of a Joe Girard-type 'Uniculture' or monoculture, a place where everybody looks the same, feels the same, thinks the same, points in the same direction and believes in the same things – a stable state where individuality has become subordinated by and almost perfectly absorbed into a superordinate, cooperative whole. An organizational *ganzheiten*, which raises civilization to new heights. Well, if not civilization exactly, then certainly car sales:

> Companies are, after all, only collections of individuals. If they all believe and behave as Joe Girard does, they will undoubtedly succeed at what they set out to do. And that is the real challenge for management: to make thousands and thousands of people Joe Girard-like figures who have a strongly ingrained sense of the company's value.

> (Deal and Kennedy, 1982: 24)

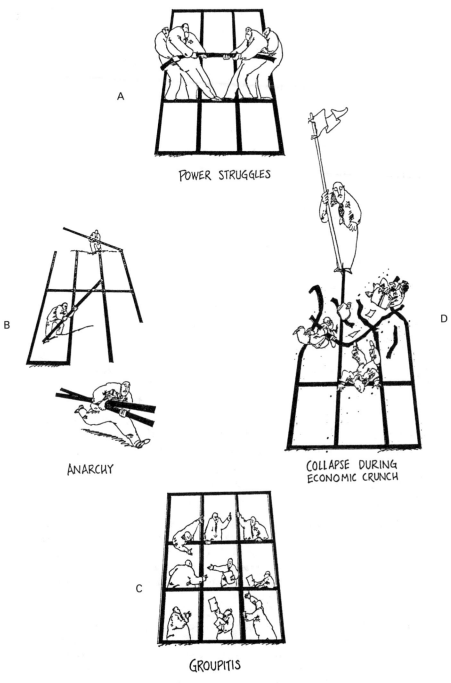

POWER STRUGGLES

ANARCHY

COLLAPSE DURING
ECONOMIC CRUNCH

GROUPITIS

If we were to switch language and express the integrationists ideal in scientific terms, we would say that their aim is to increase 'symbiosis' and reduce 'de-symbiosis' within the company:

> In symbiosis, parts sacrifice their individual autonomies so that the superordinate system (the whole) may have greater autonomy in its relationship with other systems in its ecosystem. In de-symbiosis, the parts of a system are relentlessly committed to their individual autonomy and not only avoid sacrificing for the superordinate, but are prepared to obliterate other parts as well as the whole even when this threatens its existence. Hence, the parts are not interested in the viability and autonomy of the system as a whole. In this sense, stalemate is a 'de-biolic' process antithetical to the health of a system, since it works to remove life from the system, which becomes stale and would eventually disintegrate and decompose, losing all integrity and identity. (Baburoglu, 1987: 5)

So what is one to make of the integrationists' ideal of organizational symbiosis and communitas? The first thing to say is that this talk of the 'integrative culture' will have a familiar ring to it for many readers, since they will have encountered it before in a somewhat different guise. The idea of an integrated culture is not new, but basically a re-working of an abandoned, and – interestingly – largely discredited, management ideology from the 1960s and 1970s: what industrial sociologists (cf. Fox, 1966; 1973), industrial relations theorists (cf. Clegg, 1975) and political scientists (Polsby, 1963; Kerr, 1964) used to refer to as the 'unitary' frame of reference or ideology. Take, for example, Fox's definition (1966: 3) of unitarism which, though written some twenty-five years ago, might easily have been describing the integrative/strong culture ideas of today. In fact, insert the word 'culture' in one or two strategic places and one can almost hear SAS's Jan Carlzon saying it!

> A unitary system has one source of authority and one focus of loyalty, which is why it suggests the team analogy. What pattern of behaviour do we expect from the members of a successful and healthily-functioning team? We expect them to strive jointly towards a common objective, each pulling his weight to the best of his ability. Each accepts his place and his function gladly, following the leadership of the one so appointed. There are no oppositionary groups or factions, and therefore no rival leaders within the team. Nor are there any outside it; the team stands alone, its members owing allegiance to their own leaders but to no others. If the members have an obligation of loyalty towards the leader, the obligation is certainly reciprocated, for it is the duty of the leader to act in such a way as to inspire the loyalty he demands. Morale and success are closely connected and rest heavily upon personal relationships.

So why was this viewpoint abandoned – by the academics at least? The main objection was that, while representing for many people a vision of what organization ought to be like, the unitary frame of reference did not adequately reflect what it was really like or could ever be like. Unitarism was a utopian ideal (at least for managers and any other dominant group), but pluralism was the inescapable reality. In industry there was no such thing as the Common Interest – only managers using the idea of a Common Interest to persuade others (not even successfully) to accept *their*, i.e. managerial, interest.

Restated in cultural terms there was no such thing as an organizational culture, only a 'federation' of sub-cultures each primarily concerned with protecting its 'turf' and each striving to become the dominant ideational force (Duenas, 1991: 3). Going back to Kanter, 'segmentalism' is not an organizational dysfunction but an inescapable feature of organizational reality itself.

To the sceptics, unitarist ideology – 'integration', in today's parlance – was a sentimental illusion, the kind of utopian outlook that hard-headed and practical people would be a lot better off forgetting. Real world people, they said, should know that the real world was not like that. Differences and conflicts of interest between individuals and groups – some of these intractable – were (literally) the order of the day, and no amount of wishful-thinking would ever change that basic fact. Nor could any single group ever hope to be able to impose its will unilaterally on the others or be able to count on undivided loyalty because power in the modern organization was too diffuse, and rarely coincided with formal authority structures – hence Fox's comment (1973: 194) about management's power superiority being no longer sufficient to permit the luxury of imposed solutions. Invariably, an informal system would spring up in response to attempts by the leadership to impose its will, and afford protection for other interest groups (i.e. sub-cultures) to continue to pursue their sectoral aspirations. Furthermore, not only was unitarist ideology naive, it was also dishonest. Leaders pretended to be interested in providing a better and brighter future for all, but were really only interested in the present, and the maintenance of a status quo that primarily served their own interests (witness in this regard the abuses of unitarism in the discredited communist regimes of Eastern Europe). In this context their ideology was not so much vision as deception.

For pluralists, on the other hand, the challenge in maintaining order or ensuring sensible and controlled development was not to ignore, suppress, gloss over or eliminate differences between people – actions that were likely at best to enjoy only a limited and temporary success – but to face up to these differences and find ways of jointly coming to terms with them. In short, *managing* the inherent 'pluralism' of the situation in respect of goals, values and aspirations, not squashing it out.

Progress was therefore marked by the creation of some kind of fragile order – a 'golden mean' arrived at by way of a process of multilateral negotiation between the parties concerned, or if not a golden mean exactly, a negotiated order that reflected the real locus and distribution of power within the organization. The terms of collaboration were settled by bargaining between recognized and legitimate interests; order was created and sustained through a network of contractual interdependencies between individuals and groups, a network of tensions held together in a state of dynamic equilibrium – 'antagonistic cooperation', as Simmel (1955) once called it. This order was not created unilaterally or consensually, but by a process of joint regulation, a negotiated rather than an imposed order.

One more flashback to the 1960s should be sufficient to sum up this alternative frame of reference for order and development. The following extract, which is worth quoting at length, begins with a rejection of the unitarism that is so beloved of today's strong culture writers, and then goes on to describe the preferred alternative.

> The whole view of industrial organization embodied in the unitary emphasis has long since been abandoned by most social scientists as incongruent with reality and useless for the purposes of analysis. If we are to have a model which explains the growing accumulation of evidence about how industry actually operates, we have to abandon ideal prescriptions which reflect wishful thinking rather than accurate observation. We have to see the organization as a 'plural society, containing many related but separate interests and objectives which must be maintained in some kind of equilibrium.' In place of a corporate unity reflected in a single focus of authority and loyalty, we have to accept the existence of rival sources of leadership and attachment. They need to be accepted, above all, by whoever is ruling the plural society in question. *The problem of government of a plural society is not to unify, integrate or liquidate sectional groups and their special interests in the name of some over-riding corporate existence, but to control and balance the activities of constituent groups so as to provide for the maximum degree of freedom of association and action for sectional and group purposes consistent with the general interest of the society as conceived, with the support of public opinion, by those responsible for its government.*
>
> (Fox, 1966: 4), my italics

Translating all this into the language of culture, a pluralistic organizational culture would be created interactively and participatively, relying upon processes of patient negotiation between the various parties involved.

By taking a backward look over time we have therefore discovered two strategic options for cultural order and development: the 'uniculture' option (see Box 3.1), the strategy currently in favour among strong

Box 3.1: Option 1 for cultural development: The Uniculture.

Type of strategy: Pre-planned; top-down; non-emergent.

Preferred by: Strong cultures writers and human relations writers; also many senior management practitioners because it is

a) a mechanism of defensive reassurance:

If you believe a basic harmony exists, any apparent demonstration to the contrary is due to faults among the governed – to stupidity, or short-sightedness, or out-dated class rancour, or an inability to grasp the basic principles of economics, or the activities of agitators who create mischief out of nothing.

b) an instrument of persuasion:

Managers seek to persuade their employees and the public at large that industry is a harmony of cooperation which only fools or knaves choose to disrupt. If they are successful in this, their jobs are made easier.

c) a method of legitimacy:

Propagating the idea that the interests of the rulers and the ruled are identical helps to confer legitimacy upon the regime. Their government is legitimate government; their sanctions are legitimate sanctions; they can be cruel to be kind yet remain free of guilt.

(Fox, 1966: 5)

Aims: Assimilation and integration of the workforce; elimination of conflicting interests and perspectives; creation of shared meanings and values.

Process: Order and equilibrium are achieved by unifying and homogenizing employee values, interests and beliefs; management uses its prerogatives to define a Common Aim for the organization as a whole.

Methods: Indoctrination and rallying cries, plus various other methods of ideational, emotional and behavioural control (see control continuum, p. 47).

Example: a recent initiative by a major British brewer to bring about 'cultural change' (in fact, to impose a managerially-defined cultural order) by way of a four-phase, five year programme of development. The aim of the first phase was, in the managers' words, to 'develop a cultural and organizational base for the pursuit of a common aim through increased, and more effective, communication, through training and through the introduction and funding of an assistant manager role in the house management structure to alleviate the increasing pressure on managers' time'. The 'common aim' was 'that every single member of the Division should contribute towards satisfying the needs of the customer more effectively' (Wood, 1991: 10). As a member of the Board put it: '[The programme] has really been driven by the belief that any organization has to have a common sense of purpose and it's only by everybody working to a common goal that the whole organization is going to move forward, otherwise there is just too much time spent in the organization internally in-fighting which results in a lot of energy and a lot of very inspired, dedicated and loyal effort being wasted' (1991: 12).

cultures writers and probably the majority of today's business leaders, and the 'pluriculture' option (see Box 3.2), the regular favourite of politically minded academics and (for reasons I will explain) many middle line practitioners: two very different strategies based upon two very different theories of organization development and effectiveness, both converging on the same goal (order) from totally different directions:

A third option: moving from either–or to both–and thinking

The test of a first-rate intelligence is the ability to hold two opposed ideas in mind at the same time and still retain the ability to function.
(F. Scott Fitzgerald, *The Crack-up*, 1936)

The person who can't ride two horses doesn't deserve to be in the bloody circus.   (Former trade union leader)

The dilemma, of course, in having two clear options such as these is deciding which one to choose – especially as they are so very different, and involve a host of considerations of a political, philosophical and ideological nature, as well as the normal pragmatic ones. Which path is one to follow? Should one, as the strong cultures writers suggest, recognize the anarchistic tendencies of corporate pluralism and seek to hold them in check with some kind of 'unifying' strategy, or instead, as the pluralists suggest, recognize the inherent political naivety of unitarism, and devise more realistic 'mediating' strategies for dealing with the perpetual conflicts that arise between different individuals and groups? The stark dualisms identified by writers from both sides seem to leave little scope for a third option or anything in between. They are set up in such a discreet way as to oblige us to choose between one state or another – segmentalism *or* integration, unitarism *or* pluralism, a strong *or* a weak culture.

Box 3.2: Option 2 for cultural development: The Pluriculture.

Type of strategy: Top-down, bottom-up and sideways-on; emergent.

Aims: Accommodation, interdependence, collaboration and peaceful co-existence between competing and participating interest groups.

Preferred by: Industrial relations writers and political scientists who believe that a unitary system is undesirable and unattainable. Also by non-managerial groups, like trade unions, who feel that they can exercise more influence in a pluralistic culture, where conflict and disputation (at a values and interests level) is expected, even welcomed. Possibly also by middle management groups who may want to pursue their 'local' bottom-line obligations – on which their performance is judged – without having to make sacrifices or concessions to the wider 'corporate' ideal (which they would argue is, after all, only their bosses' bottom-line obligations with a fancy label).

Process: Order and equilibrium are achieved by maintaining a viable collaborative structure within which all the stakeholders can pursue their aspirations, and participate in defining the terms of their interdependence; a process based on give-and-take (a struggle for meaning), and live-and-let-live (mutual adjustment of meaning).

Methods: Coalition-type bargaining, disputation, conflict and threat or use of sanctions.

I am inclined to criticize both models in equal measure, not so much for their content, which in each case is at least half-right, but for the kind of models that they are. Despite their substantive differences, we need to recognize that they are, in fact, identical in type, being the conventional – and in my view flawed – products of 'either–or' thinking. As the models demonstrate, this is a mode of conceptualization which loves to invent extreme polarities – simple dichotomies that carve up the world ('reality') into two parts: the one part 'good' – the bright, sunshine option, basically a statement about the nice things that will happen if you heed the authors' words; and the other part 'bad' – the dismal, shady, satanic option: what will befall you if you do not heed their warnings. Then it insults you by asking you to choose the 'obvious' option. My point is that life, not least organizational life, is simply not like that. The one-or-other models presented by the uniculturalists and the pluriculturalists are not representations of reality, as they should be, but idealizations of that reality, models that bear little resemblance to the 'real world' and the real world decisions that have to be taken within it.

As readers will have gathered, 'both–and' thinkers, myself included, entertain deep suspicions about dualistic models. We believe that bipolarities like unitarism/pluralism, integration/segmentalism offer too limited and limiting a view of life, and prescribe too narrow a range of possible alternatives for action. Young (1989: 190), for example, has accused both the unitary and the pluralistic conceptions of being 'irredeemably simplistic' because of the way they attribute single, one-dimensional meanings to organizational events.

Furthermore, this type of model invariably paints a picture that is larger than life, a sort of organizational Hollywood made up of 'goodies and baddies', 'black and white', 'right and wrong': dramatizations of life that have little time for the mundane, grey, paradoxical, conflictual, complex and in-between life that most of us experience on an everyday level. We also believe that these kinds of model are biased, subjective and manipulative: they guide the readers' choice by fabricating and then grotesquely caricaturing a fictional, extreme alternative, producing inflated claims about the merits and virtues of their own 'preferred' – and equally fictitious – option, and using hyperbole, stereotyping, bombast, stylistic animation, the 'method of extremes', and other tricks of expression to give their own pet ideas the desired amount of directive force. Models like those described are monistic and one-eyed, having in this case caused integrationists to overlook (and therefore underestimate) the differences between people, and pluralists to overlook their similarities. Finally, we say that the models in question are not descriptive but prescriptive, normative rather than factual, ideological rather than objective, reflecting how their creators would like things to be and how they should be, not how things actually are.

'Both–and' is a fundamentally different conceptual approach to a strategy for cultural order and development which begins with the question, what do organizations and cultures tend to be like in reality and practice (rather than how we would like them to be)? It does not say that the 'either–or' models are wrong, merely that they are only partly right. It has a central commitment to the view that societies and organizations are rarely, if ever, one or the other – unified or diversified, differentiated or integrated, cooperative or conflictual – but all of these things, in varying mixes and forms depending on the organization in question; not one model or the other, but both; both models rolled into one.

There is a growing support for this view (Quinn and McGrath, 1985; Young, 1989; Darmer, 1991; Duenas, 1991). Young, for example, has stated that in reality pluralism and unitarism are not opposites but *interdependent processes* through which values and issues are negotiated between organizational participants.

Consider your own family to get a feel of this 'both–andness' of life. In this social unit you will find differences and yet also transcendent similarities between the members. So it is in organizations. Furthermore, as with families, the possible permutations of pluralism and unitarism are infinite. To put it crudely, organizations or parts of them can be 'high' on one and 'low' on another, 'low' on both, or even 'high' on both. Consider, for example, traditional industrial sectors like mining and the railways, where there is 'high' pluralism within their unionized, adversarialist cultures, and 'high' unitarism in the form of shared and widespread dedication to the industry and the working community – a situation that either–or thinkers might have some difficulty explaining with their single concepts.

A slightly different angle on this is to say that organizations are made up of both unitarists and pluralists. Some are this way by nature, others by nature of their jobs. A shop steward, for example, would find it difficult to do his or her job if he or she were not a pluralist. An enquiry conducted among his colleagues by a British Petroleum manager for a management course, at which I was a trainer, revealed that frames of reference were hierarchically and occupationally differentiated within the organization (Figure 3.4). Senior managers (the higher grades on the chart), being the creators and custodians of all things 'corporate', were strongly unitarist and cosmopolitan in their outlook, as (for different reasons) were junior managers (lower grades), who were young and idealistic and who, as yet, had no territory to defend. Middle managers, on the other hand, were judged in terms of what they did locally on their 'patch' (i.e. segment) and whether or not they had achieved their 'bottom line' (segmental goal). To them, 'corporate' goals – whatever they were – were, as they say, for the birds: their own success was measured in terms of the achievement of local targets, and if this meant sacrificing the interests of other segments or the company overall, then so be it. As far as they were concerned, segmentalism was not so much an ideal as a rationale for personal survival and advancement.

What emerges here is the conclusion that strategies for managing culture need to deal with both sides of the equation, focusing in particular on the achievement of a synergistic relationship between the two and an adequate system of built-in checks and balances to prevent either of them from becoming dominant. 'Both–and' thinking is therefore an approach to cultural development which involves the simultaneous pursuit of unitarism and pluralism, integration and differentiation, with the

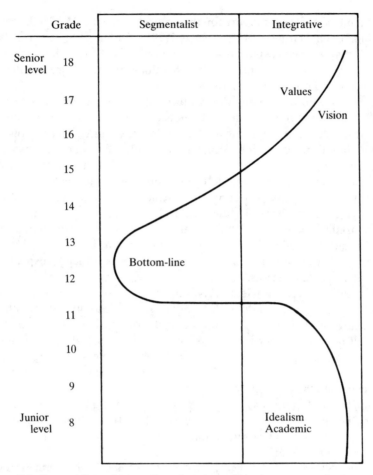

Figure 3.4 Segmentalist and integrative orientations within the same organization

intention of producing a hybrid 'culture' that is appropriate and optimal for the kind of situation in which it has to operate, and for the goals the system is trying to achieve.

What is interesting is that the 'original' culture perspective, as it first appeared in anthropology, was, indeed always has been, a 'both–and' perspective. It was the business 'gurus' and strong culture writers who abandoned this during the 1980s, having chosen to ignore the pluralistic aspects of cultures and focus only on the 'shared', unitary aspects – shared values, shared understandings, shared this, shared that. Anthropologists would criticize organization and management writers for disposing of the variability which they have always regarded as an important feature of culture. They might also wish to point out that cultures consist of similarities and differences, convergent elements and divergent elements, pluralism and integration, all of them rubbing shoulders and vying with each other in a loosely coupled system; and they would tell us that the culture perspective never presumed one or the other – that only came later when 'culture' had been transformed from an interpretive perspective to an ideology or strategy for managerial control. Their conception of any culture is as a 'multiplicity of human communities' – a phrase which incorporates the unitarism and pluralism inherent in culture. Sometimes, they would argue, organizations will be more 'pluri' than 'uni', and sometimes it will be the other way round.

Geertz offers a metaphor which captures the 'both–and' quality of culture perfectly:

> the elements of a culture are not like a pile of sand and not like a spider's web. It's more like an octopus, a rather badly integrated creature – what passes for a brain keeps it together, more or less, in one ungainly whole.
>
> (1984: 18-19)

We might usefully apply this metaphor to the two very different kinds of strategies that have been on offer for developing 'effective' organization cultures:

1 The integrative (strong cultures) strategy: this has concentrated on the development of an organizational octopus with small legs or, an even greater relish, an organism with no legs at all – more like a jelly fish than an octopus.

2 The pluralistic (weak cultures) strategy: here the preferred idea is of an organizational octopus with a small head and many legs; each leg moves independently with the 'centre' playing a coordinating rather than a controlling role.

The advantage of Geertz's metaphor is that it directs our attention towards the Darwinist argument that form or shape, by itself, is not the main issue in the survival of an organism or system. What is most important is the extent to which there is 'fit' between the form and its environment. There are no futile arguments in biology about the relative superiority of a jelly fish over an octopus. Similarly we should desist from arguments about the relative merits of unitary and pluralistic cultures. The central point is that 'effectiveness' (survival, growth and development) is not something that depends on the form itself but upon how well-suited that form is to the medium within which it has to function. Different situations and local conditions require different kinds of organization culture, ranging from an almost 'pure' uniculture at one end of the continuum – say, a hospital casualty department or a fighting regiment, to the almost 'pure' pluriculture at the other – say, a democratic parliament, debating society or liberal arts college.

The above gives an indication of the range of strategic choice available to culture developers. Their task is to construct a form that best suits their purposes. In this endeavour it is worth remembering that because different groups will have different views as to what this should be, the chosen option will always have to be negotiated.

Universal prescriptions and ideal-type scenarios are thus ruled out. In some situations and at certain times it will be appropriate for the organization to incline towards segmentalism and to be partitioned into separate cultural domains, whereas in others it will be more appropriate for them to incline towards unitarism and be closely drawn together in a jelly-like monoculture (as in a nation at war). As the contingency theorists say, 'it all depends'. Indeed, returning to Kanter and the strong culture writers, we can envisage a situation where it could actually be a retrograde step for a society or organization to follow the recommended path from segmentalism to integration. This, after all, is the same path that many societies have followed on their journey from democracy into fascism (although in certain situations even this might be defended by those involved). By the same token, it is not inconceivable that organizations taking this path may end up with their own brand of corporate fascism.

It is easy to be critical of the universal medicines offered by best-selling business authors. On the other hand it is equally wrong, not to say totally unhelpful, for contingency theorists to hide behind the argument that contextual diversity and local variations rule out the possibility of any kind of general guidelines being offered regarding the development of organization cultures. While it is true that individual organizations will have to discover the right 'mix' of unitarism and pluralism for themselves, and 'grow' situationally specific and relevant local strategies, it is still possible (indeed essential) for contingency and both–and thinkers to give a broad steer as to how they might go about this task. I propose to do this now, and will again use British Rail as an illustration. Before I begin, there are two main lines of thought that need to be drawn out.

First, because organization cultures consist of unitary and pluralistic elements, a strategy for managing and developing those cultures must address itself to both. In particular it will need to have a pluralistic commitment to providing mechanisms that will resolve, or at the very least contain, the disharmonies that exist between divergent systems of meaning within the culture. As Green has argued, you ignore the complexities of pluralism at your cost. The unitary approach alone will not work.

Organizations are multicultural, to such an extent that the imposition of a core-value complex on a plurality of sub-cultures requires 'a manipulative process based on propaganda and procedure'. Inevitably, this process breaks down when the complexity of social life defies managerial intentions.

(1988: 123)

Once this pluralistic orientation has been established, the possibility of simply turning one's back on differences is effectively ruled out. The aim should be to develop greater sensitivity towards multicultural differences, accepting – even welcoming – them, and continually looking for ways of expressing, accommodating and reconciling them.

Even the most committed 'strong culture' companies need to attend to pluralism. At present it seems they are only managing half of their culture – the unitary part. While they do need to do this, they also need a pluralistic strategy. In the case of Pizza Hut, for example, managers should accept that employees will frequently – and quite legitimately – be feeling 'cold pricklies' towards the company and its customers when they come in in the morning. The company should not be outlawing these feelings or trying to eradicate them by dictat (which will surely fail – who could ever hope to legislate successfully for feelings?), but should look for new ways to deal with them, for example by establishing a grievance machinery, granting negotiating rights to employees – or even paying them more. Managers need to be aware of local 'defensive' informal systems, and learn to work with them, not turn their back on them and hope that they will go away. It is difficult to envisage how a company can claim to have a caring culture unless it recognizes the fundamental human principle of pluralism.

At the same time a both–and strategy will also have a unitary commitment to creating and extending shared values and interests. People talk about the 'management of differences' in organizational discourse. Now the term 'management of similarities' must also be included in the strategist's phrase-book. The management of similarity involves a search for as much coherency as one can find in the cultural system, one that culminates in strategies that identify, enlarge and extend the common ground that exists between individuals and interest groups and 'exploits' the harmonies that exist between them. It is guided by neither utopian nor wishful thinking: we need to look for as much similarity as we can find, and where we cannot find any we must simply say 'we cannot find any', and then proceed as pluralists to manage the uncommon ground.

The second point is that one should not be aiming for a 'balance' between pluralism and unitarism. There is absolutely no virtue in the notion of a balanced culture. Quite the opposite, in fact: the thrust of my argument has been that different cultures need to give different 'weight' to pluralistic and unitaristic elements, and it may well be quite sensible and appropriate for them to be 'unbalanced' in one direction or another. In developing a strategy for cultural order and development, people should abandon all notions of balance. Instead their main concern, to my mind, should be studiously to avoid the natural temptation to drift toward the extremes.

Philosophies taken to the extreme are philosophies that have gone bad. This point is made very forcibly by Philip Toynbee (1976) in his book about the Spanish Civil War. Toynbee blames both sides equally for the carnage and suffering, the fascists for taking romanticism to the extreme, and the communists for taking classicism to the extreme. Like unitarism and pluralism, fascism and communism were harmless enough in moderation, but take them to these kinds of extreme, he says, and you end up with horrors like 1936:

> Romanticism gone bad becomes worship of darkness, death and suffering; contempt for common sense; the irrational urges of 'the blood' and 'the soil' elevated to first principles of action. Classicism gone bad becomes the equation of reason with the ruthless elimination of all 'unreasonable' elements . . . This has a very ugly ring in the light of what we know now, and should have known then about the fanaticism of all utopians.   (1976: 174)

Toynbee's story is a parable on extremism in general. It leads me to the view that it is the extremes of pluralism or unitarism that cause problems such as lack of innovation, resistance to change – 'isms' in the true sense of the word: philosophies that have become inflexible and obsessive dogmas; that have, in a manner of speaking, gone over the top, gone too far, or, in Toynbee's words, gone bad. Laurent (1989) makes the same point in relation to the 'strong culture'/'weak culture' debate:

> Although the cultural perspective on organizations may be promising, it does include a few traps. One of them stems from the popular idea of the 'weak' and 'strong' cultures. Organizations may die because of their strong cultures. The stronger is the culture, the more absolute the consensus on norms and behaviour, so the more we can expect rigidity, conformity, and sclerosis, and the less we are likely to see innovation. At the other extreme, organizations may die from weak cultures. If everything has a different meaning for each organizational member and if everybody has different ideas on what should be done, creativity may flourish for a while; but the whole edifice is likely to collapse from lack of consistency, co-ordination and direction.   (1989: 89)

If we recall the earlier stories about British Rail, it was not pluralism that caused the 'hot wheels' and 'Didcot Station' problems, but 'segmentalism' – pluralism gone bad. While I very much agree with Kanter that segmentalism is invariably harmful and dysfunctional, we have to be very clear about one thing: segmentalism is not pluralism. Segmentalism is the result of pluralism having *broken down* – not the presence but the absence of pluralism.

Such was the case in BR. For some years after the the Second World War, BR managed successfully to maintain order and achieve limited cultural development by pursuing a pluralistic strategy. There was a rough-and-ready order negotiated between a multitude of different interest groups, held together by the good faith that emanated from a unitary dedication and commitment to the railways, which allowed BR to make reasonable progress towards its goals. The order was tense, fragile and unstable, but generally 'held'. Pluralism, within a weak frame of unitarism, was, in a limited way, a useful coping strategy for the organization.

Subsequently, pluralism came under a good deal of strain as trade union power, Dr Beeching's axe, pressures for large-scale innovation, and competition began to grow. Things took a distinct turn for the worse as the Order based upon both pluralism and unitarism began to break down (this manifesting itself in strike increases, financial losses, resistance to essential innovation, and difficult relations with its Government paymaster). The story is a familiar one: segmentalism takes over when pluralism begins to decay, when the mechanisms for agreeing the terms of interdependence begin to crumble and break down, when corporate orientations begin to localize and fragment, and when muddling through with a purpose – a naive process relying on good faith and compromise – is replaced by cold war and deliberately constructed impasse among the various organizational groups or segments. This is basically what happened at BR, the 'Didcot Station' and 'hot wheels' stories being two very small examples of this. But, as I have already said, it happens not because of pluralism but because the pluralism of the situation is no longer being successfully managed.

BR's reaction to this cultural crisis was typical – and misguided. Instead of trying to correct the problem by reinstating a controlled pluralistic system, as it perhaps should have done, it overcorrected, swinging to the opposite extreme and adopting a unitary system of control. Almost overnight it went from the sublime to the ridiculous, changing from strategic option 1 (the pluriculture) – embodied in a 'messy' matrix form of organization – to strategic option 2 (the uniculture) – a one party state ruled over by the sector directors and publicly condoned by the Chair. The 'pluralism' of the matrix organization was systematically discredited. It was accused of being soggy, lacking in focus, wasteful of time and resources and divisive. Key interest groups were disenfranchised (for example, trade unions were ignored and the regional general managers, who had always been extremely powerful, were 'disinvited' from key meetings), and key figures were banished to distant parts and more lowly jobs, while in the meantime the one group of sector directors, hitherto their equals, was elevated to new heights of power and majesty.

This was classic either–or thinking on BR senior management's part, the result of a faulty logic which says that if one 'extreme' is not working the best remedy is to adopt the other: if one has a degenerate plant which is squandering its strength in excessive vegetative growth, the logical course of action is to prune the plant back to a single stem, and give it a good, strong dose of 'feed'. Unfortunately such action – predictably – was (to mix the metaphor) to take BR out of the frying pan and into the fire.

The rest of the organization had been told, in true military fashion, to fall in behind the sectors and embrace the new vision of a market-led, commercially sensitive organization. In the event, and not surprisingly given the political ramifications attached to this change of direction, this did not happen. When the sector directors turned around, they discovered – to their embarrassment – that no one was actually following them. In equally true military fashion, their 'colleagues' had decided to practice 'dumb insolence' in the face of a superior authority. Indeed, all of the groups, although their interests were diametrically opposed, had begun to think and behave in an identical ethnocentric manner, resisting one another and disobeying orders. The chosen 'change-makers' (the sectors), who had been expected to win new markets, generate more revenue, provide cost leadership, present a new railway to the travelling customer, and galvanize the fragmented organization into a united body, found defiance and desertion wherever they went (Bate, 1990: 92).

What had happened was that the attempted solution had become the problem, the paradox being that the imposed unitarism had led to more, not less, segmentalism. The uniculture strategy, having inflamed passions, was now found to be politically naive and incapable of quelling such passions. A summary of the story so far is provided in Table 3.1. It shows the features of the initial segmentalist culture (Variant 1) and the subsequent integrative strategy (Variant 2) used by BR's Chair in an attempt to get BR out of its difficulties – a strategy which, in the event, served only to compound and aggravate the difficulties.

Most of the table is self-explanatory, but I wish to draw attention to its overriding thrust and to several important details within it.

Variant/Extreme 1

Variant 1 is my distillation of the senior managers' own description of BR's 'initial' state. It summarizes the segmentalist situation described above, in which the organization had fractured into a congeries of quasi-independent, vertically structured interest groups, with widely differing

Table 3.1   Variants for cultural development

	Variant 1 Segmentalist	Variant 2 Integrative	Variant 3 Adaptive
Culture	Multicultural	Unicultural	Intercultural
	Many languages	One language	One language, many accents
Roles and	Contenders	Master/servant	Partners
relationships	Independence	Dependence	Interdependence
	Self-determination	Constraint	Responsible autonomy
Structure	Differentiation	Integration	Coordination
	Caucuses	Teams	Networks
	Strong vertical linkages, weak horizontal ones	Strong vertical linkages, weak horizontal ones	Strong vertical linkages, weak horizontal ones
Process	Subversion centred	Punishment centred	Penalty centred
	Confronting	Commanding	Persuading
	Accommodation	Assimilation	Adaptation
	Distributive	Integrative	Negotiative
	Conflictual	Cooperative	Collaborative
	X-led	Y-led	X–Y-led
	Informal	Formal	Informal
Primary	Interest centred	Authority centred	Issue centred
orientations	Clarity	Clarity	Ambiguity
	Simplicity	Simplicity	Complexity
	Closed	Closed	Open
	Loose	Tight	Simultaneous loose–tight
	First order change	First order change	Second order change
	Moving away from change	Moving away from change	Moving toward change
Outcomes	Deals	Pacts	Contracts
	Bilateral	Unilateral	Multilateral
	Concession	Compliance	Commitment

power bases and a multitude of techniques for exercising influence on decisions salient to them. Understanding across the 'sectarian divide' had broken down. Everyone was focused on pursuing local interests, frequently at the expense of others and the wider corporate interest. As Table 3.1 shows, BR had become multicultural. The problem was not so much that groups spoke different languages – this is nearly always the case in highly pluralistic cultures of large organizations – but that each of the different tribes insisted on using its own 'private language' and refused to communicate in a language that everyone else could understand. This attracted derogatory comments about other groups' languages (e.g. the so-called 'patois' of the marketing people and the 'jargon' of the planners), although few people showed any interest in becoming familiar with these professional languages. An often-cited story is that the CEO himself once marched noisily out of a marketing presentation, declaring that he had not understood a word that had been said. Not surprisingly, other people interpreted this as permission to behave similarly.

Different though the languages were, the one thing they had in common was that they were all languages of antagonism and division. Stereotypes, them-and-us attitudes, and betrayed trust are the hallmarks of such a segmentalist culture, all of which lead the organization to spiral downward into chaos and disruption.

Variant/Extreme 2

Variant 2 represents the 'natural' response to BR's problems, this being a switch of direction from extreme pluralism to extreme unitarism: give the sick patient a strong dose of direction and order, and that will produce a cure! This is the 'within-frame' solution of a machine bureaucracy, a commitment to purging the system of all its uncertainty and ambiguity and instituting a hierarchy of clearly defined roles. All discussions of matrix management concepts (considered 'messy') and notions of joint responsibility (considered 'fudging') and adhocracy (considered 'anarchy') are rubbished and then outlawed.

BR moved rapidly and efficiently from Variant 1 to Variant 2, leaving a stream of problems in its wake. For example, it became increasingly clear that in practice the sector directors were not going to be the new masters of the organization, despite official pronouncements to this effect. The language of 'business primacy' and 'sector-led', once so freely bandied around, was fast becoming mythology. The organization might be market-led but there was no way that it was going to be marketing personnel-led. The empire was striking back. As the pluralists would have foreseen, new oppositionary groups were forming in order to subvert sector strategies and safeguard their own interests. In short, Variant 2 was being proved politically naive and unachievable. Moreover – another point missed by the strong cultures writers – BR's employees had neither the skills nor the experience to achieve and maintain an 'integrative culture'. Teams rarely worked as teams, and people were much too proud of their individual or group identities to allow them to be dominated by corporate considerations.

At this time a team from Bath University, including two colleagues and myself, were hired as OD consultants. Our role, as we saw it, was to wean the senior management off this destructive form of 'either–or' thinking which was leading them to set unattainable objectives and to manage change by veering drunkenly from one extreme to the other. We suggested to them that the problems associated with the one extreme (segmentalism) had given way to problems associated with the other extreme (unitarism), and that neither in fact was an adequate basis for an organization development strategy. If the current extreme failed, as many were now predicting, what next? Would it be another case of 'all change' and more disruption as people struggled to cope with yet another reversal of direction? As we jointly explored this observation with them, we encouraged them to conceptualize their requirements in 'both–and' terms, abandoning this preoccupation with extremes and looking for a solution which would be more situationally contingent and more politically expedient as far as BR and its sub-cultures were concerned.

Variant 3

The notion of a third possibility – a hybrid of the other two but different from both of them – slowly began to emerge (Variant 3). This contained both pluralistic and unitary elements, a model whose aim was to manage conflict and cooperation simultaneously instead of hopping continually from one to the other. As Table 3.1 shows, this variant focuses less on the roles people play than on the type and quality of the bonds between them. The organization is conceived of as a network of relationships, mirroring the rail network itself. In cultural terms, this is a 'network,' 'contract,' or 'partnership' culture.

Philip Slater (1974) pointed out almost two decades ago that profound differences exist between a network and a community. Communities tend to be intimate and tightly knit, and their isolation gives people no choice but to interact with one another. As we have seen, Variant 2, the integrative culture, has all the features of the unitarist, community ideal: one culture, one language, strong hierarchy, restricted channels of interaction and communication, everyone knowing her or his place, clarity, and simplicity of purpose. Network cultures (Variant 3), however, are much more open, non-hierarchical, egalitarian, voluntary and permissive. They do not profess to have everything worked out before it happens (they are too pluralistic and multidirectional for this), and they learn to live with ambiguity and uncertainty. Complexity, contingency and informality are the norm. In networks, any attempt directly to control events becomes problematic to the point of futility.

If networks are pluralistic so, too, are they unitary. Whereas segmentalist cultures (Variant 1) abandon collectivity entirely, network cultures nourish it through reciprocal contracting arrangements. The parties, many of them potential adversaries, negotiate within a framework of jointly agreed rules and rights. Hence, while conflicts of interest (pluralism) continue, these are managed within a unitary framework of joint, agreed procedures. By following a philosophy of 'shared rights, different interests', the parties are able to merge pluralism and unitarism in the kind of network culture described.

For BR, the notion of a contractual culture – which previously had not been envisioned – offered strong appeal to the parties. This, they argued, would provide a way to avoid both integration and disintegration, yet clear the way to achieve coordination. As one might expect, the issue of control was the central preoccupation, and, fortunately, the contract solution proved acceptable in this regard. The idea of a partnership implied that nobody would be in overall control, but rather that control would continue to operate in a free market manner. Thus, the managers saw an opportunity for maximizing both independence and control – an appealing vision.

It must be emphasized that this was BR's chosen solution to the issue of order and development, one that involved putting the main 'strategic thrust' somewhere to the right of centre on the pluralism–unitarism continuum. The location might not suit others. This continuum represents the range of strategic choice available to culture developers. Their task, which involves a complicated mixture of diagnostic, judgemental and decision-making activities, is to find a place on the continuum which suits them – as did BR – and then manage it. Their overriding concern should be to avoid entering the danger zones of the extremes, and to concentrate on achieving the right blend of unitary and pluralistic processes for the situation in question.

Where this discussion leads us is to a rejection of the extreme conceptions of the 'strong culture' and the 'weak culture'. Both of these are traps for the unwary and both are likely to commit strategists to fatal courses of action.

The example from BR, while providing a valuable illustration of the problems associated with extremes of culture, is perhaps in some respects in the wrong chapter. The transition from one variant to another in fact represents a change *of* – as distinct from *in* – culture. The Chair's – and our – proposals were both transforming (as opposed to conforming) strategies, and it is to this group of 'second order' strategies that I would now like to turn.

4 Strategies for cultural transformation

symbols, like any other tools, wear out; they lose their usefulness. They become blunted and inapplicable, because the reality they were designed to deal with no longer exists.

(M. Peckham, *Beyond the Tragic Vision*, 1981)

all cultural forms are like exhausted soil, which has yielded all it can but which is still entirely covered with the products of its earlier fertility.

(G. Simmel, *Der Konflict der modernen Kultur*, 1921)

When the existing culture has begun to stagnate and lose its vitality and forward movement, then it is time for a different type of strategy for changing culture, one whose purpose is not to perpetuate and develop the culture but to transform it into something else. It emerges in response to a growing crisis, deficiency, malaise or disease of culture which can only be halted by changing the very cultural framework or pattern itself – the cultural structure. In such a situation a change 'in' culture is no longer enough; a change 'of' culture, both structurally and orientationally, is what is now required.

This calls for a 'transforming' rather than a 'reforming' strategy. Such a strategy deals with a radical, basic, second order change in an organization – a fundamental change of cultural identity – in contrast with the reforming strategies (type 1) which deal with cultural improvement and development. Type 2 strategies thus have higher ambitions. As Levy and Merry have put it, 'transformation' is the response to 'the condition in which an organization cannot continue functioning as before. In order to continue to exist, it needs a drastic reshuffling in every dimension of its existence' (1986: ix). In effect, what this means is a 'new' organization, a 'new' culture and a 'new' direction.

The strategist feels compelled to call a halt to development because he/she feels the culture no longer has the potential for delivering what it was originally set up to achieve. Its limits have been reached. It is seen as having lost its creative or reproductive capacity; the life has flowed out of it; it is withering and dying, in danger of being no more than an empty shell. Time and the natural ageing process have taken their toll. The organization is in decline, its strategies-in-use are no longer the right instruments for achieving its objectives. Simmel (quoted above) talks about the 'exhausted soil' of culture, while Heidegger talks about cultural symbols being 'all used up and worn out' and Peckham (quoted above) says its tools are 'blunted'.

Not only has the culture lost its creativity and vitality, and its ability to touch hearts and minds, it has also lost its direction: what was once a progressive linearity of development has become a regressive circularity of development; the 'virtuous' circle, with its infinite capacity for generating new combinations of the cultural material, has become a 'vicious' circle – a whirlpool or spiral of narrowing options and endless repetitions of constantly failing solutions; a framework of opportunities has become a framework of constraints. The strategy-in-use has become a strait-jacket; the solution has become the problem; and the 'vision' has become blind, short-sighted dogma, unable now to see the wood for the trees.

The above are just some of the different metaphors that writers have used to describe the core problem to which this second class of strategy is directed. What they all broadly refer to is a situation where an asset has become a liability, where culture is 'holding things back', acting as a brake on progress. The phrase that probably best sums it up is *cultural obsolescence:* the established ways of thinking have become *passé* and out-dated; they are stuck in a time bubble, remote from the problems and imperatives of present-day life. (Consider the ill-fated Communism of the Soviet Union, or even closer to home the rapidly receding Thatcherism of the 1980s, to get a feel for this notion of doctrinal or ideological obsolescence. More on 'isms' like these later.) What has happened is that the inertial forces within the structure of culture have weakened the organization by seriously impairing its capacity to adapt to the changing imperatives of its environment (Hassard and Sharifi, 1989). It is time to move on.

Further rearrangement of the contents of culture no longer offers a satisfactory answer or way forward. Indeed, most permutations of the old pattern have probably been tried already. Now it is the form or structure itself that must bend – there must be a fundamental change in the organization's pattern of life and direction of development. In Simmel's terms the organization needs to decamp and move to more fertile grounds, hence the broad concern of this second class of strategy being with 'movement' rather than just 'motion', cultural 'trans*form*ation' rather than cultural 'transition'. The aim of the strategy is to revitalize the organization by reframing culture, 'breaking the circle' and releasing the organization from the time warp within which it is being held hostage, allowing it to re-establish contact with the here-and-now, and to take up once more with the requirements of the modern world. The hope and expectation is that there will be cultural discontinuity, an occurrence that will disengage the organization from the now futile and counter-productive activity of repackaging and recycling useless recipes and formulas, and initiate a genuine process of renewal and replenishment, regeneration and innovation. In short, it will set in motion a process that will give the organization a new start.

In this section I shall be making a close examination of the problem of cultural stagnation and decline within organizations, in order to seek to establish its roots and origins, its manifestations, its implications for change strategies of a transformational kind and its connection with the first type of transitional strategy. I shall also be considering the steps needed to be taken by managers to develop relevant strategies for dealing with this problem. Following Simmel (1922: 17), who was one of the first people to write about cultural decline, my central argument will be that the struggle between the ongoing process of life and the inherent abstract rigidity of the cultural forms in which this process is structured is the fundamental motive force of cultural change. But first, a description of the *symptoms* and *side effects* of cultural degeneration within an organization.

'Normal' solutions no longer work: the 'resting on your laurels' syndrome

Success corrupts, absolute, success corrupts absolutely.   (Lord Acton)

The organization turns round one day and finds that its reliable recipes are no longer reliable, and its 'thinking-as-usual' routines (Schutz, 1967) no longer work as well as they usually do. Its common sense no longer seems to make good sense. The taken for granteds can no longer be taken-for-granted. While they are outwardly the same as they have always been, now for some inexplicable reason they seem to have lost their 'inner' power and attraction – emptied of meaning, like the 'shell' of the church in Philip Larkin's poem 'Church Going':

Grass, weedy pavement, brambles, buttress, sky,
A shape less recognizable each week,
A purpose more obscure.

The 'tragedy of culture', as Simmel put it, is that all cultural development leads in this direction. Decline is inevitable and inescapable, part and parcel of the development process itself. Even the most vibrant of cultural forms – including the grand and glorious civilizations of Greece and Rome – ultimately ossify and fragment, reducing those forms to incoherence and chaos.

What has happened to bring this about? To answer this we need to examine three interconnected issues: the pathologies associated with success, the mortality of culture and the inability of 'type 1' strategies by themselves to guarantee eternal life.

Writing about his organization's experience of this same problem in the mid-1980s, Jan Carlzon of the Swedish airline SAS wrote, 'when you reach your goal, you may become a prisoner of success' (1987: 121). He claimed that SAS's 'reversal' had occurred because people including himself had made the 'unforgivable mistake of assuming'. What did they assume? They assumed that the maintenance of the status quo, and the continuous pursuit of cultural conservation, development and integration was enough to ensure the continued success of the company. They assumed that the organization culture they had created in the early 1980s would go on for ever, continuing to pay handsome dividends. Unfortunately, in making this assumption they had unwittingly joined the long list of 'famous names of the past who clung to what they knew best without being prepared to adapt and change, and slowly but inexorably saw their business disappearing beneath them' (Harvey-Jones, 1989: 30) – for example, Singer, BSA and many of the forty-three companies that were originally in Peters and Waterman's list of 'excellent' companies (1982), and which since then sank dramatically in the ratings (*Business Week*, 1984). Lulled by their success into a false sense of security, companies like these turned their backs on their cultures, condemning themselves to the past and the realities of the time in which these cultures were first formed.

The point here is that culture is very much taken for granted, and the more successful you are the more you take it for granted – and neglect it. Success is the mother of failure: people in successful companies avoid major change; they settle for minimal 'tarting up' change and employ 'defensive' first order change strategies aimed at maintaining the cultural status quo. Unfortunately, as Harvey-Jones (1989: 23) has pointed out, for the modern company this is just not enough: 'Unless a company is progressing the whole time, it is, in fact, moving backwards. It is quite impossible to maintain a steady-state position in the marketplace.' This is precisely what happened at SAS. Despite (or, unbeknown to the parties, *because* of) the fact that the cultural status quo was maintained, 'a kind of reversal set in'; management 'started retreating', pursuing 'defensive strategies'. The result was that SAS lost its direction and forward momentum. Energy and motivation began to drain away, 'the atmosphere of togetherness' was being eroded, 'interests began to compete against one another', people were 'scattering in all directions' making different demands of the company. In short, the culture was disintegrating; the once-successful organization was failing.

The reason for this can be found in Peckham's opening quotation: cultures wear out, they lose their usefulness because the reality they were designed to deal with no longer exists (remember the Golden Age of Steam and the Golden Age of Broadcasting? Remember too those old sayings, 'pride comes before a fall', 'victims of success' and 'every dog has its day'). The message is clear: cultures cannot survive by endlessly recreating their past, no matter how glorious this may have been. There is never just cause for complacency. As the contemporary saying goes, even the winning team must be changed. At some point in an organization's development, the issue of second order cultural change has to be confronted. This will involve quantitative and qualitative change, the former in order to equalize the rate of change between the organization culture and its 'environment', and the latter in order to mirror and reflect major qualitative changes that have taken place in that environment.

It was this kind of second order change that Carlzon used to rescue his ailing organization, demonstrating in the process that, unlike human bodies, organizations can be revived and rejuvenated (though probably 'reincarnated in a new form' would be a better description). Carlzon put a stop to the internal squabbles by reminding people of the dramatic qualitative change that was about to hit them: the deregulation of the European airline business. When this had happened in America, he said, those airlines that were unprepared for this had found themselves caught up in a 'competitive hell'. Some of them failed to survive. SAS had a crisis to contend with (crisis being one of the preconditions for second order change – a crisis precipitated by the sole pursuit of type 1 change strategies and processes); it therefore had to pull itself together, cast off its old skin and grow a new one, one that was better suited to its commercial surroundings. For example, conventional assumptions about what constituted a fair day's work for a fair day's pay would have to go: people would have to do more with less and become 25% more efficient. Quantitatively, it was no longer enough to be among the leaders; SAS would have to become the most efficient airline in Europe, and the market leader in service, quality and safety. This second order change was appropriately called 'The Second Wave' – in cultural terms more like a Second Coming.

Disney was another failing company that enjoyed a Second Coming, thanks again to initiatives taken by its new CEO, the Carlzon-like Michael Eisner ('Mighty mouse of the movies', as *The Independent on Sunday* (23 February 1992) nicknamed him. More on the crucial role of leadership in cultural revivals in the last chapter of this book.) The story of Disney is that in the mid-1960s it woke up to find itself suffering from cultural obsolescence, the result of endlessly recycling previous 'hits' –

stories about cute, sentimental, patriotic, anthropomorphic cartoon characters, which though once well-suited to the simple and innocent tastes of the immediate post-war Western world, had come to jar with the experimental, rebellious children of the 1960s. The problem was that Disney had done nothing about this, believing that it was enough to carry on 'going through the motions' and producing yet more of the same. Success had made it complacent about its product, and blind to the growing problem of staleness. It had come to believe in its own magic. *The Independent on Sunday* summed up the prevailing situation well:

> Before [Eisner's] arrival, the company had been foundering since the death of Walt Disney, its founder, in 1966. Its assets were grossly under-exploited, and its image was rapidly becoming out of date. The geriatric Mickey Mouse and Goofy were struggling to keep abreast of a juvenile market that had tasted the pleasures of intergalactic war and thrilled to the adventures of Indiana Jones.

Eisner, like Carlzon, saw what was happening and set about the task of effecting a type 2 cultural shift. For example, on his very first day at Disney he approved the script of *Down and Out in Beverly Hills*, the studio's first 'R' (restricted) rated film – a sea change in Disney terms. This was followed by films like *Good Morning, Vietnam, Three Men and a Baby* and *Pretty Woman*. Disney's culture moved from animation to real-life (although the blend of the two in *Who Framed Roger Rabbit?* and the use of cartoons in video format demonstrated that you do not have to get rid of all the old culture when you bring in a new one). The transformation proved to be a remarkable success in financial terms. Disney's annual net profits rose from $98m to $637m in six years. Had Disney continued to stick with its type one 'maintenance' strategies, it is doubtful whether it would still be around today. Transformation, however, is a process not a single act, in which the old is phased out as the new is phased in – which means that even good 'ol Mickey may have to be put down at some point in the future. Faced with tasks as painful as this, it is little wonder that companies are so reluctant to change!

However, there is more to clinging on to the 'old' culture than simple sentimentality. In an article entitled 'The escalation of commitment to a failing course of action' (1992), Brockner considered the reasons why decision-makers, like the executives at Disney and SAS, frequently persisted with failing ventures (even to the point of suicide). Among the many theories reviewed by the author is one proposing that culture itself is to blame, that it has in-built devices that 'lock' it into irreversible courses of action. This is particularly true of certain kinds of culture, for example a culture that (a) makes people unwilling to admit failure or (b) values consistency in behaviour (1992: 57). I shall also be exploring this idea that culture brings about its own downfall, arguing that 'strong cultures' like Disney and SAS invariably get caught up in 'vicious circles' of thinking, leading to premature ageing and, in extreme cases, terminal decline.

Missed opportunities and unrealized ambitions: the 'I see no ships' syndrome

The organization is trying to do better and *could* do better, because better alternatives are available, but it does not do better simply because it fails to see these alternatives (Masuch, 1985: 15). It is suffering from cultural blind-spots: what Harris (1990: 25) calls 'schematic myopia', a cognitive or perceptual affliction that narrows the range of vision thereby preventing people from gaining a clear appreciation of the situation and of the actions that need to be taken to grasp existing opportunities. This is the paradox of culture: it provides a way of seeing but also a way of not seeing, or as Paul Ricoeur (1970) once observed of interpretive systems in general, it both reveals and conceals. Culture is a directional orientation: if we are looking in one direction we cannot be looking in another. Harvey-Jones came across this 'affliction' during his chairmanship of ICI. He called it 'collective blindness' (1989: 78), a failure by management to see either a crisis or an opportunity, even when it was staring them in the face. Bibeault (1982: 17) found it, too, in his study of crisis-afflicted, declining organizations, concluding that 'most ailing organizations have developed a functional blindness to their own defects. They are not suffering because they cannot solve their problems but because they cannot see their problems'.

IBM is a case in point. Its cultural myopia prevented it for a long time from seeing that the market opportunity had shifted from mainframes, where IBM had traditionally been strong and focused (70% of market share) to PCs, where it was relatively weak (30% market share). MIS departments were no longer attracted by the alluring sales and service contracts offered by the company; they now wanted personal products that would lead a corporate executive to say, 'This is good, it does everything I want done'. Its customers had changed as well, from the computer buffs of the 1970s – middle managers who were delegated by CEOs to deal with brainy machines, people who were impressed by IBM's computer wizardry – to CEOs themselves, people who were sceptical but also knew how important the choice of machine was to their success (Finney, 1989: 70). IBM persisted with its old ways, locked into a grid of assumptions about the market, the product and the customer that were no longer appropriate, and failing in the process to respond flexibly to or take advantage of the new opportunities that had opened up in the PC market.

Green (1988) has claimed that 'cultural blinkers' constrain the kind of strategic reformulation that organizations, like IBM, require. He writes:

> if we recognize that the whole strategic management process is rooted in people, then 'cultural blinkers' may also constrain strategy formulation. People bring their own intellectual baggage to bear on new problems, part of which has been conditioned not only by intrinsic cognitive limitations, but also by traditional or habitual ways of doing things . . . Because of the 'taken for granted' nature of assumptions underpinning traditional ways of doing things, people are frequently unaware of their cultural blinkers or regard it as heresy to challenge them.   (1988: 123)

A different but related problem is not so much that people are blind to what needs to be done but that they misread the situation and pick the wrong strategic alternative. For instance, we have the recent case of a well-known British High Street bank which decided to force early retirement on its older branch managers, in the hope of dispensing with its 'stuffy' image and attracting more custom. In the event it lost custom. Cultural blinkers had prevented it from appreciating that its older managers had in fact been an asset, their 'grey hairs' signifying the two most important customer requirements in the business: stability and security. The root assumptions and perceptions had been wrong. The bank now found itself with a group of people who, apart from not having these qualities, were associated with the 'yuppie' generation and high risk financial strategies.

The blind-spots we are talking about may be described as cultural dysfunctionalities. They place cognitive barriers on perception, self-reflection, learning, action and interaction (Hennestad, 1991: 55). The sum total of their effects is organizational underachievement. Nicoll puts it this way:

> These dysfunctionalities keep a system from reaching its full potential because in their cumulative effect, they lock organizations either into definitions of reality that have lost their timeliness or into unending, confusing conflicts.   (1984: 166)

Few organizations escape this affliction because, as I have already suggested, it is actually part of the cultural phenomenon itself, the residual product of growth and development. We must never forget that 'culture' (i.e. organization, strategy – see earlier discussion of these synonyms) is always a past solution to a past problem; it may be 'living history' (Malinowski, 1945), but it is history all the same. Any connections between present conditions and the conditions of its birth are purely coincidental. Culture, as Kluckhohn has pointed out, is inherently time-bound:

> [It is] the set of habitual and traditional ways of thinking, feeling, and reacting that are characteristic of the ways a particular society meets its problems *at a particular point in time.* (1963: 85, my italics)

As far as change is concerned, culture is a conserving not an innovating force; it can retain anything but create nothing. It has what Crozier (1964) calls a 'self-reinforcing equilibrium', comprising homeostatic rather than change-orientated processes. As Gagliardi (1986: 126) correctly observes, organization cultures usually change in order to remain as they have always been; the main reason why a firm changes is in order to preserve, not alter, its identity and purposes. Indeed, order-preserving cultural change of the kind described in the previous chapter is so natural that it is often quite wrong to regard it as a 'strategy'.

Because of its taken-for-granted nature, culture also lacks criticalness and reflection, and in this respect it provokes its own crisis. No wonder that new opportunities arising in the present are often missed: 'the culture' is not really interested in looking for them. Simmel puts this point in a slightly different way:

> But a peculiar quality of [cultural forms] is that from the first moment of their existence they have fixed forms of their own, set apart from the febrile rhythm of life itself, its waxing and waning, its constant renewal, its continual divisions and reunifications. They are vessels both for the creative life, which however immediately departs from them, and for the life which subsequently enters them, but which after a while they can no longer encompass. They have their own logic and laws . . . At the moment of their establishment they are, perhaps, well-matched to life, but as life continues its evolution, they tend to become inflexible and remote from life, indeed hostile to it. (Simmel, trans. Lawrence, 1976: 223)

Incorporating Simmel's point into our original metaphor of cultural myopia, we might say that cultural forms are blind from birth, or – if this sounds too extreme – always looking out of the back window.

Compulsive, repetitive behaviour: the 'round and round in circles' syndrome

Because it is locked in time, a culture tends to develop in a circular rather than linear fashion. Hence my reference elsewhere (Bate, 1990) to a 'circle of culture': a circle firstly in the sense of belonging to a social circle or community of people (with its own lingua franca and distinctive symbolic mode of communication), and secondly in the sense of being an immanent, enclosed and self-contained cognitive whole within which patterns of thinking and logic endlessly repeat themselves, producing 'more of the same' with respect to action and behaviour. Within a circle of culture there are a number of cognitive elements that make up a 'group' (Watzlawick et al., 1974). The interaction between the elements may be vigorous, even dynamic, but things still end up pretty much where they began. The system is invariant; it has plenty of motion but no movement:

> under these conditions one is always back at the starting point at the completion of a number of moves. One might, therefore, say that there is changeability in process, but invariance in outcome.   (1974: 5)

The natural development of culture therefore tends to be one of evolution from less order to more order (C1, C1.1, C1.2 etc.), stabilizing ('cooling' and 'crystallizing') and becoming more embellished and cluttered all the time – but always within the same fixed frame (C1). Figure 4.1 below represents this idea: it shows the increasing complexity within the cultural frame as the number of interactions between the same number of basic cognitive elements increases.

The striking feature about these development processes is their dynamic conservatism (Schon, 1973); they have a circularity to them which reproduces infinite permutations of the old, while producing little that is new. Dynamic they may be, innovative they are not; they are reforming not transforming processes. Individuals and groups continually re-enact what has gone before, condemned to the endless refinement of the inner elements of a static cultural form. Using contemporary scientific terms, we may describe cultures as 'autopoietic systems', closed, self-sufficient, and autonomous systems of thought that develop by making reference only to themselves.

Another feature of developing cultural forms is that, as they evolve, freedom of movement for the people within them (including the freedom to effect change) tends to diminish. What happens, in effect, is that

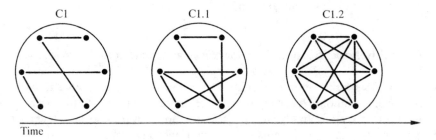

Time

Figure 4.1   The evolution of a cultural form

people become the prisoners of their own culture, hermetically sealed into a 'bubble' – a point visually symbolized by Escher in his lithograph, 'Development' (1937), which the artist himself has described as follows:

> Scarcely visible grey squares at the edges evolve in form and contrast towards the centre. Their growth is completed in the middle. An unsatisfactory feature of this kind of inward-directed unfolding is that there is so little space left for the freedom of movement of the most greatly developed figures: two white and two black reptiles.

The picture illustrates the point that the more a system – in our case a cultural system – evolves, the more restricted are the choices and the narrower the range of vision for those within it. It symbolizes the shrinking cultural space of the developing cognitive system as thinking processes become increasingly culture-bound.

© 1937 M. C. Escher, Cordon Art, Baarn, Holland

Given this important feature of developing cultural forms, it is not difficult to see why organizations have this tendency to go round and round in ever-decreasing circles. The reason is that the cultural process makes them inward-looking and egocentric, and isolates them from the external sources of new ideas. This applies even to those '*grandes idées*' which burst on to the management and organization scene from time to time – Total Quality Management, employee participation, even corporate culture itself. Unlike many others these have at least managed to get into the frame, but only to find themselves neutered as that frame closes in behind them, and begins to normalize them and make them respectable. The result is that an idea which may have been conceived as a 'palace' frequently ends up as a 'tent', blown away on the wind of culture.

What we are talking about here is not so much the failure to see a potentially frame-breaking idea (p. 87 above), as the failure to take full advantage of it. Total Quality Management (TQM) may be the latest to succumb. Whittle and others (1991) recently reported that widespread current experience of implementing TQM indicates that many companies encounter problems in sustaining it once the honeymoon period is over, resulting in disillusionment and loss of confidence in the strategy. The authors' conclusion was that this novel way of conceiving organization development is often 'spiked' by the existing culture of the firm: although TQM fundamentally implies cultural change, what usually happens is that TQM programmes end up adapting to fit the existing culture rather than the other way round. As this happens, they are effectively deprived of their impact and novelty.

The most extreme manifestation of the 'round and round' syndrome is the vicious circle, one whose own cultural logic turns in on itself, ultimately causing it to self-destruct. A most succinct account of vicious circles in organizations has been given by Masuch (1985). He claims, like Escher and many others, that humans produce forms which, though initially of their own making, end up, as the fictitious Doctor Frankenstein once discovered, controlling and tyrannizing them.

> They are somehow trapped in the web of their own actions. The hidden score is their own, but they don't like the music. Unable to stop, they play the unpleasant tune over and over again. The emerging picture begins to resemble a vicious circle. By trying to avoid undesired outcomes, human actors actually create these outcomes. And by continuing their activities, they continue to reproduce these outcomes.   (1985: 15)

They just cannot help themselves. They have lost control over their own destiny, powerless to alleviate their condition irrespective of their wish to do so. What is most ironic is that, like the person who struggles helplessly in the quicksand, their struggles for survival actually hasten their demise

– the attempted solution becomes part of the problem. As Masuch says, the key part of the theory surrounding vicious circles is that by trying to avoid undesired outcomes, human actors actually create these outcomes. And by continuing their activities, they continue to reproduce those same undesired outcomes.

Not even the experience of repeated failure or the threat of destruction are sufficient to push people into attempting a breakout from their cultural cell on death row. It is a simple case of not knowing what is on the 'other side': it just does not occur to them that there might actually be another side – an alternative, possibly more satisfactory, way of conducting their affairs. We need to refer back to the problem of schematic myopia described earlier for an explanation: simply, the limits of the 'circle' are the limits of their world. Their cognitive space does not stretch any further.

Gagliardi puts it this way:

> the experience of failure does not in itself lead an organization to explore routes which are different from those sanctioned by the group's basic values and point of view, just as the failure to catch fish in the Mediterranean would never in itself have induced the sailors of olden times to go beyond the Pillars of Hercules. For these reasons, many organizations will die rather than change, and in this sense we may say that organizations do not learn from negative experiences. (1986: 128–9)

This phenomenon (not unlike that observable in lemmings) has been described in the literature as the Einstellung effect: the tendency for people to persist with the same approach to a problem regardless of whether that approach is productive (Luchins, 1940). This effect has in the past been attributed to psychological causes, but what seems to be emerging now is a strong suggestion that it also has a link with cultural issues.

Masuch uses Cyert's case of a declining university to illustrate how a combination of vicious circles can bring about the decline (and, in extreme cases, the collapse) of an organization. His story goes something like this (with additions from me at the beginning and end): The organization, once a leading university in the country, has rested on its laurels for too long. Its early success has made it complacent. What is on offer in the 1990s is pretty much what was on offer in the 1950s. However, students' requirements have changed in the intervening years, and the university now finds itself beginning to lose students to other, apparently more enlightened and 'relevant', universities. The organization therefore finds itself facing decreasing growth rates. This reduces promotion opportunities within the organization and lessens its attractiveness even further (the first vicious circle).

Quality inside the organization declines, so that the organization has to look elsewhere to fill its top positions, thus decreasing promotion opportunities further (a second circle). The organization cannot maintain former standards of excellence and loses more students (a third circle). This creates an internal financial crisis, which is dealt with by raising tuition fees and freezing salaries. Two additional circles (four and five) are thus triggered: even more students stay away, while good staff members depart for better positions elsewhere. The university is now acquiring a poor reputation which it seeks to remedy by launching a vigorous publicity campaign. The morale of staff members declines further as they see funds being diverted from educational to marketing activities; in joining the rat-race, the university is also seen as selling its most precious asset – its distinctive identity in being something special, not just 'one of the rest'. Now there is nothing to differentiate it from the competition, and since it is now doing things the competition tends to do better, it loses even more staff and prospective students (circles six and seven).

The example shows clearly the self-terminating dynamic of a vicious circle, in which ill-conceived, though well-intentioned, remedial actions piled one on top of another can, if allowed to persist, eventually bring about the break-up of an organization. There is, says Masuch, a critical threshold – a point of no return – which if crossed causes the contracting circle to implode and the organization to collapse.

This notion of the vicious circle has also proved extremely popular in the wider field of the arts, the added attraction of such work being that it not only communicates what a vicious circle is but how it feels to be in one. Koestler, for example, did it with words, writing the following while under a sentence of death in jail during the Spanish Civil War (he was later pardoned and released):

> Life . . . is a constant repetition of the same situations, the same thoughts and schemes. One lives and thinks in a vicious circle. The mind is made giddy by it; there is no escape. There is no progress, even time does not move forward in a straight line; it reappears in the same form.
>
> (*Dialogue with Death*, 1983)

While Escher did it in pictures, such as 'Ascending and Descending' (1960), which, like Hesse's novel *The Glass Bead Game* (to be discussed later), offers a sober reflection on the 'strong cultures' ideal, raising serious doubts about the wisdom of blindly pursuing it, and challenging the conventional wisdom that has grown up in the popular management books around it. The top managers of the pictured organization are shown as the victims of a vicious circle, a closed structure of ineffectual and inconsequential behaviour that they themselves have created.

A rectangular inner courtyard is bounded by a building that is roofed in by a never-ending stairway. The inhabitants of these living-quarters would appear to be monks, adherents of some unknown sect. Perhaps it is their ritual duty to climb those stairs for a few hours each day. It would seem that when they get tired they are allowed to turn about and go downstairs instead of up. Yet both directions, though not without meaning, are equally useless.

But do all organizations ultimately succumb to VC (vicious circle disease!), and does it, once caught, normally turn out to be fatal? The answer, fortunately, is 'not necessarily' to both, that is so long as

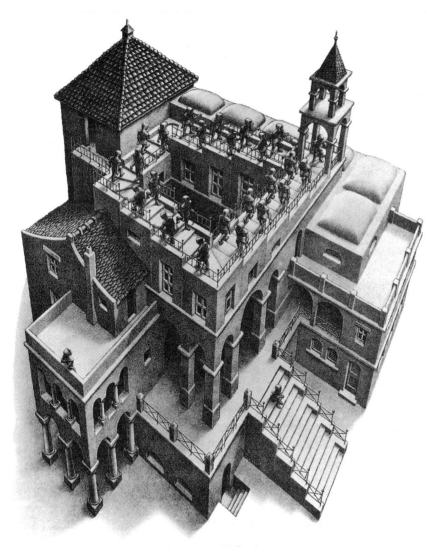

© 1960 M. C. Escher, Cordon Art, Baarn, Holland

managers are aware of the problem and are committed to devising appropriate preventative or remedial strategies for dealing with it. The former strategies can lead to a greater resistance against the disease, while the latter can lead to the revival and revitalization of ailing organizations that have succumbed. This is, of course, easier said than done because managers themselves – like the lizards in Escher's first picture – are trapped within the circle and often paralysed or blinded by it. They may very well be the last to see the problem and take action (hence the Chinese proverb: the fish is the last to see the water – though perhaps this should now be lizard).

As to the likelihood of an organization catching the disease, some types of organization are more prone to VC than others. As might be expected, some of the most vulnerable are the large-scale, Weberian-type machine bureaucracies – the British Rails of this world – whose dedication to order, routine and tradition positively encourages the formation of vicious circles: 'Such organizations look inward rather than outward. Customers, or suppliers, or competitors, or even what is going on in the outside world, seem of far less importance than the needless struggle to achieve and operate the perfect bureaucracy' (Harvey-Jones, 1989: 73).

During my research at BR I came across numerous examples of vicious circles of thinking within the management culture, where my research was mainly focused. (I am sure I would have found many of these plus some new ones in other parts of this diverse organization.) For simple identification purposes, and as a way of providing a rudimentary 'grammar' for managers to think and talk about their problems from a cultural viewpoint, I labelled the vicious circles in question with the suffix 'ism'. For a number of reasons, this label, which we tend to use unreflectively and rather loosely in everyday language, has a particular relevance to the cultural phenomena in question:

- In everyday usage 'isms' refer to doctrines, creeds, dogmas, orientations, ideologies and orthodoxies (e.g. atheism, cannibalism, communism, catholicism), all of them autonomous, self-referential, maladaptive and closed systems of thought – 'circles' of culture, in other words.
- These are owned and shared by a community of people – another indication that they are cultural phenomena.
- They frequently describe an abnormal or pathological state resulting from an excess of something. They are often compulsions which dominate one's life, and frequently lead one to go 'over the top' (fanaticism).
- 'isms' are intolerant (e.g. dogmatism): the language of Thatcherism was to dismiss anything that challenged or contradicted it as 'nonsense'.

- 'isms' can also imply decay or deterioration, a downward spiral as the grip of the habit or compulsion gets tighter and tighter – all of these being indicative of the vicious circles I have been describing.

'Isms' is therefore a term which, in the BR study, came to be used to identify and describe circles of culture which had the potential for becoming vicious circles, or which had in fact already done so. 'Bad habits of thinking' was what the managers themselves ended up calling them. My contention is that all organizations have such 'isms' – fixed, collective mind-sets that may have been functional in the past but have become dysfunctional in the present – though obviously not necessarily the same 'isms'. I say 'all' because organizations do not actually 'catch' or 'get caught up in' vicious circles; their very essence is that of the vicious circle. No matter what kind of organization we are talking about, there will always be maladaptive, misfitting and misaligned cultural orientations that will need to be identified and managed. They are an intrinsic part of the process of life which, from time to time, throws up forms, leaving them like flotsam on the beach before resuming its course. Such historical sedimentations, dead but by no means inconsequential, will always need to be located, used as a resource (see type 1 strategies for development) and at the appropriate time disposed of in some way (type 2 strategies for change). The task for the manager, as it became for managers within BR, is to become aware of and develop a familiarity with these circles, to explore their causes and consequences, and to devise strategies for breaking into them and controlling them – thereby avoiding the risk of them controlling the manager. This is the whole essence of the process of managing culture and bringing about cultural change.

A summary of a sample of BR's 'isms' is given in Box 4.1. More details about these and their relevance to the cultural change process have been given elsewhere (Bate, 1990) and need not be elaborated here.

I should, however, like to examine one aspect of cultural 'isms' that was not fully brought out in my original paper: namely their 'vicious', regressive nature. Segmentalism has already been described in some detail. Here therefore I shall focus on another 'ism' from the list.

Structuralism
This has been aptly described by the railway writer Michael Bonavia (1985: 21), as BR's 'Reorganization Fever'. Copious amounts of time and money were spent reorganizing or planning to reorganize structures (external consultants being the main beneficiaries). The overall aim was to achieve 'crystal clarity' in the definition of roles, responsibilities and reporting relationships, thereby making people personally accountable for their actions, and purging the system of all ambiguity and uncertainty.

Box 4.1   Cultural features/'bad habits of thinking'

1	**Segmentalism**	Pulling in different directions; lack of fusing mechanisms
2	**Conservatism**	The power of inertia; anchors and antibodies
3	**Isolationism**	The wall around BR; inward-looking
4	**Elitism**	Status-consciousness; weak vertical coordination
5	**Neologism**	Discontinuous change; fads and fashions; lack of consistent philosophy of change
6	**Structuralism**	Obsession with organization structure
7	**Pragmatism**	Strong on doing, weak on thinking; anti-conceptual; mechanistic; lack of vision

---

There was no doubt that BR did have a problem in this area. One story managers loved to tell was that if you went up to Edinburgh Waverley railway station and climbed out on to the platform and shouted loudly 'Who's in charge here?', eleven different people would step forward and say 'Me'. However, despite all their efforts to 'pin things down', BR had failed miserably in its endeavours. It was widely acknowledged that the structure had remained extremely 'muddy', and as far as personal accountability was concerned – as one manager put it – 'you can hide in this place for years without being found out. It's better than the Amazonian jungle'. Another story, verified by a number of different sources, was that for years a number of senior managers had been able to use their open rail passes to take days off during the week at their favourite seaside towns on the pretence of being out of the office on company business. Hardly an image of the level of accountability that BR was seeking.

My interpretation is that BR was caught in a classic vicious circle, in which the attempted solution had become the problem itself. Reorganization and the constant reshuffling of roles had left people unsure of what they were expected and authorized to achieve; just when they thought they had found out, it would be 'all change' again, and a whole new set of roles and relationships would have to be learned. No time was allowed for the structure (and 'clarity') to emerge, since the notion of 'development' had been completely suppressed by the all-important notion of 'design'. The constant upheaval of reorganization had also created the normal insecurity and low commitment and morale that one associates with the 'engineering of human souls'. People went into hiding, kept their heads down and generally avoided taking responsibility. A thriving 'defensive' informal system provided effective cover against attacks from above. Periodic reorganization also meant that people were usually moved on before any mistakes – and their sources – could be discovered. No wonder the structure was not coming clear. On top of all this, a change of Chair and CEO – and even higher, a change of Minister of Transport – every three to five years almost guaranteed that no reorganization initiative ever saw its way through to a proper conclusion.

The regressive processes arising from this structuralist mentality have been nicely captured by Bonavia. He writes:

> Most railway managers . . . would probably agree that the disruption caused by re-organization ('when you re-organize us, we bleed' as Gerry Fiennes, the BR manager turned writer, perceptively remarked) has gone far to cancel out the benefits. Once the decision to change has been taken, there is usually a freeze upon filling posts that fall vacant; this may last many months, meanwhile creating much difficulty in carrying on with routine duties. Then there is (usually) opposition from the Trade Unions to overcome, which may absorb a great deal of time and energy . . . Meanwhile most people are worrying about their personal future in ways that distract them . . . The grapevine becomes active and rumours circulate . . . Jockeying for position and lobbying takes place [*see how one 'ism' – structuralism – creates another – segmentalism*] . . . The physical removals can be disruptive . . . people will feel downgraded and embittered. Ascertaining the exact limits of authority and the new relationships takes time. (1985: 32)

The remarkable thing is that in all this time BR's senior management, as far as I am aware, had never stopped to ask why so much effort had produced so little in the way of progress towards its utopian ideal of a world purged of ambiguity. For me, this story illustrates the way cultural vicious circles produce a groupthink that numbs reflection and suspends critical judgement. Such circles effectively put thinking onto automatic pilot, while at the same time making it oblivious to its own limitations and unresponsive to the demands of the situation. BR is no exception in this regard: Gersick (1991: 25) has also described how strategists in organizations often get caught up in a kind of clockwork, fixed-term thinking, where they do things (like a strategic review or a restructuring exercise) at regular intervals for no other apparent reason than that it is time to do them.

Our solution, which consisted of turning the logic of structuralism on its head, was to suggest that BR fire the 'design and systems' consultants, bypass the technocrats, burn the burgeoning bulk of job descriptions, and let people get on with working things out for themselves ('take off the chains and handcuffs'). This was effectively replacing the notion of design with the notion of development, and central imposition with local negotiation. Such heretical, counter-cultural, upside-down thinking was hardly likely to be an unequivocal success but, as I have explained in the full account of the cultural change programme in BR (Bate, 1990), what it did was to prick the bubble, free them from the cultural 'spell' they had been under and reactivate their minds to explore new avenues – which they did. The effect of our intervention, in Louis and Sutton's (1989) terms, was to help organization members to disengage and then switch cognitive gears from 'automatic' to 'reflective' thinking.

Ashburner, Ferlie and Pettigrew (1991: 19), during their study of cultural change in the National Health Service, discovered that the rise of new cultures and ideologies seems always to be accompanied by a change in language systems. If this is the case, and I firmly believe it is, there is no doubt that BR did experience a switch of cultural direction at the senior management level at this point: the hard 'arrows and boxes' language of structure gave way to the softer 'bubbles' language of development. People began to talk about 'partnerships', 'networks' and 'negotiations'. Six months before they had almost jumped down our throats when we had suggested giving marketing and production managers joint responsibility for some parts of the business (structuralist logic says that someone has to be responsible and in charge – that equality and co-determination are fuzzy or soggy), but now they began to talk approvingly about mutual contracts and overlapping responsibilities.

And what about the original problem of lack of role clarity and accountability? In many ways what happened at local level was the equivalent of what happened when the Berlin Wall came down: people came out of hiding, stopped playing territorial games, and sat down and talked about roles and responsibilities with each other. Whatever ambiguity came with the switch from 'mine' to 'ours' was more than compensated by the increased flexibility that enabled people to move about more freely in order to deal with issues and problems as and when they arose. A growing solidarity between the parties made them increasingly accountable to each other, and in this way more accountable to the organization generally – the partnership became self-policing because it was now couched in social as well as task terms. People's social obligations to each other dovetailed with the realization of their task obligations.

It cannot be said that structuralism is a thing of the past, yet what is certain is that a new 'ism' has been born: developmentalism, a cultural form that has the potential for evolution and expansion for some time to come – before it, too, succumbs to old age and a loss of vitality, and needs replacing. It will now fall to evolutionary strategies to ensure that the full potential of this virtuous circle is exploited, while at the same time affording the vicious circle of structuralism a decent burial.

So much for 'isms' in isolation, but what is their effect in combination? In the case of BR seven 'isms' were identified (Box 4.1), and undoubtedly there were more that were not picked up at the time. For this reason it is worth speculating on their aggregate effect on organizational performance. My own findings leave me in no doubt that in certain areas the combined effect of these various mentalities could be quite devastating. Take innovation for example. I believe the story of BR's Advanced Passenger Train (APT) says it all. It is to this that the next chapter now turns.

5 Tales from the rails: the APT fiasco

It may be a cliché, but BR's Advanced Passenger Train – the APT – will probably go down in history as one of the most successful innovations ever to have failed. For some time to come transport industry analysts will be trying to unravel the mystery of how one of the most promising and far-sighted passenger train developments of all time turned into a huge failure, wasting nearly twenty years of research and development, and depriving Britain of the cornerstone of her intercity railway strategy for the remaining years of this century and beyond.

Had BR's plans reached fruition, APTs running at up to 250 km/hour would at this moment be whisking passengers along the country's rails in what the train's protagonists liked to call the 'squadron service' (Hughes, 1988: 50). And with the completion of the Channel Tunnel in the near future, the train would have provided the ideal mode of transportation for international rail travellers, well able to hold its own with the French high speed trains operating on the other side of the Channel.

Now this all needs to be couched in terms of what 'might have been'. The APT never made it into active service. The project was abandoned and today only one of the original trains survives – as a museum piece. The other prototypes went for scrap. A poignant symbol of the failure was a photograph which appeared in a national newspaper at the time, showing one of the APTs sitting forlornly in the breaker's yard, wheel-less and leaning over to one side. Burly men, sledgehammers in hand, were standing on the roof of one of the coaches, smashing out the windows below their feet. Hardly a fitting end for what had once been called the 'train of the future' (Nock, 1983: 7).

The story of the APT goes back some twenty-five years to 1967, when BR's Railway Technical Centre in Derby first launched its plans for a new generation of high speed trains. This was to be an 'all or nothing' approach (Potter, 1987: 195), offering both a challenge and a charter for radical innovation. The framework of objectives was ambitious and far-sighted, incorporating environmental concerns that have become fashionable only relatively recently. The broad objective was to build a high performance train to run on existing track. The list of specific objectives read as follows:

- Achieve a maximum speed 50% higher than existing trains.
- Negotiate curves at up to 40% faster.
- Run on existing track with existing signalling.
- Maintain standards of passenger comfort at higher speeds.
- Be efficient in energy consumption.
- Generate low community noise levels.
- Maintain existing levels of track maintenance.
- Achieve a similar cost per passenger-seat kilometre.

'These objectives determined the main innovations that the APT had to incorporate, which together represented the most radical jump in railway technology ever attempted' (Potter, 1987: 59).

The result, as one commentator (Hughes, 1988: 50) put it, was a train 'oozing with technological goodies'. Not content with making modifications and improvements to existing train technology, the scientists and engineers at the Derby Centre had set in motion a programme of fundamental research, its objective being to find solutions to hitherto intractable rail problems. One such example was the problem of 'hunting': ever since the 1840s railway engineers had been aware of the tendency of a train's cone-shaped wheels to vibrate uncontrollably as speed increased (rapid lateral oscillation) and to become unstable, thus effectively putting a ceiling on the maximum speed that any train could comfortably attain (approximately 100 mph or 160 km/h). The Centre members found a solution to this problem of 150 years' standing, an event as significant in the railway world as breaking the sound barrier in the aviation world.

Other innovations followed hard on the heels of this one: lightweight, aerodynamically designed body structures (weighing 40% less than conventional trains and giving a 30% fuel saving at comparable speeds); low unsprung mass technology (substantially reducing track damage, and therefore maintenance costs); and new non-friction hydrokinetic brakes that used the principle of a water turbine to bring the APT to a stop from its maximum speed of 250 km/h in the same distance as that taken by conventional loco hauled trains from their maximum speed of 160 km/h.

Most original of all, however, was the revolutionary concept of the 'tilting body' mechanism for the train. Railway lines in Britain were constructed in the second half of the nineteenth century when speed potential was not a major issue. It was more important to avoid offending the powerful landowners whose land had to be crossed than to concentrate simply on finding the shortest possible line between two points. The resulting railway network featured a good deal of imperfect, sharply curved track, resembling as one commentator put it, the 'proverbial dog's hind leg' (Nock, 1983: 84). Knowing that the high economic and environmental cost of the French solution (building new 'motorway-type' track) was politically unacceptable, the Centre concentrated on the cost-effective option of designing a vehicle that would run smoothly at high speed over existing track. In the end they did find a solution which, if the train had gone into service, would probably have equalled the French for only one-fifth of the cost (Hollingsworth, 1985: 215).

The method involved using a tilting body mechanism to counteract the powerful centrifugal forces exerted upon passengers as they hurtled round the tight bends. The tilting mechanism was designed to operate automatically whenever the train experienced these lateral accelerations. Sensing devices were installed which measured the effect of these forces on each separate vehicle of the train, and these would activate an electro-hydraulic servo mechanism which would smoothly and rapidly make the necessary adjustments. The amount of body tilt could be as much as nine degrees, which meant that at full tilt one side of the car could be as much as 400 mm (16 in) higher than the other. The theory was that passengers would experience nothing unduly strange or out of the ordinary as a result of travelling in this position (Nock, 1983). Because of the elimination of all centrifugal forces they should in fact enjoy an extremely comfortable ride. That at least was the theory.

The speed improvement on curves was expected to be anything up to 50 km/h, which translated into journey times meant that an average five hour journey would be reduced to less than four hours.

Other foreign railways, notably those of Canada, Italy and Japan, had begun to experiment with advanced concepts such as these, but none of them had approached the ambitiousness of the British scheme. Indeed, so far ahead of the field were the APT's innovations that licence deals to use them had been snapped up by more than thirty foreign countries.

By any standards BR seemed to have a winning package, and few would have predicted the débâcle that followed. First came the delays: it took two years for BR Research to persuade the British Railways Board and the Ministry of Transport to support and fund the APT project. Even after the go-ahead, there were frequently times when the project came perilously close to being axed. An industrial dispute over the proposed 'single driver operation' and the blacking of the APT caused a further fourteen-month delay to the test programme.

After some promising trials, in which British speed records were broken, various technical and manufacturing problems began to appear: the tilting mechanism was jamming or failing, brakes were overheating, failed bearings in the hydrokinetic brakes caused an axle to explode, and gearboxes were failing due to lubrication weaknesses and oil leakage through seals (Potter, 1987: 126-9). Some of these were just technical snags, while others were discovered to be fundamental design faults. In 1978 a combination of these led to the dramatic derailment of an APT prototype at over 160 km/h (100 mph). Miraculously no one was killed.

In 1981, a full three years behind schedule and under pressure to show results on £43 m worth of investment, the project managers decided the introduction of the train into public service could wait no longer. As later events were to confirm, this decision to 'go live' was to prove fatal for the train. The troubles began on the first day of the public launch. A group of newspaper reporters travelling on the train, who had consumed generous quantities of alcohol – courtesy of British Rail – began to complain of 'sea-sickness' every time the train went round a bend. The problems the waiters were having serving 'high speed' kippers were apparently nothing compared to the problems the passengers were having keeping them down!

Predictably, the following day's newspapers carried the story of the nauseous experience in full technicolour detail. From now on the trials and tribulations of the APT were to turn into a daily household spectacular. On another run shortly afterwards the train's tilting device failed, bringing passengers abruptly to their upright positions, and causing glass and crockery to be broken. Yet another trip was aborted because of ice-blocked air pipes and brake failure. Only one out of the first six trips actually reached its destination. All of this happened in a blaze of publicity during which time a spiteful and gloating press worked ceaselessly to turn the APT into a music hall joke. Fearing further public humiliation BR withdrew the train from service. Finally, in 1985, in a classic euphemism that only civil service-type bureaucracies can produce, it announced that the APT programme was to be 'deferred indefinitely.' In a word, scrapped. And so it was that the train was withdrawn from service, never having carried a single fare-paying passenger. It never ran again. From drawing board to scrapheap had taken nearly two decades.

The post-mortem: the anti-innovative culture within BR

Why did the APT fail? Why does any 'winning' innovation fail before it can be put to practical, commercial use? Clearly technical and manufacturing problems can never be underestimated, but are these alone an adequate explanation? I would argue that they are not. Joining with others who have also examined the APT fiasco (Potter, 1987; Hughes, 1988), I propose that the technical failures were symptoms of the much deeper problem of trying to manage a complex, innovative project within a largely unsympathetic bureaucratic culture. The stress is on the words 'manage', and 'culture': the APT failed not because it was a 'bad' train but because the project was badly managed and badly let down by the culture of BR:

> Some of the technical problems were certainly very difficult to tackle and there were some differences in engineering standards and approach between the APT project team and component manufacturers and train assemblers. But there was no reason why these should have produced a total barrier to innovation. It was in the management of the APT project that the true seeds of failure lay.   (Potter, 1987: 131)

To be more precise, it was within the management culture that the seeds of failure lay. It is my belief that this culture negatively influenced the APT programme in almost every dimension of its being, from beginning to end: strategy, concepts, attitudes, structures, systems, processes and responses. The 'isms' within this culture – its dysfunctionalities – dogged the APT programme throughout the duration of its life, and undoubtedly played a major part in its demise. To borrow a phrase coined by Harvey-Jones (1989), the 'isms' were the 'switch-offs' of innovation within BR, the negative mentalities that made it difficult, if not impossible, for radical, research-based innovations like the APT to succeed. What they added up to was a culture that paralysed the innovation process.

I should like to examine the ways in which the various 'culturisms' switched off the innovative process inside BR, and highlight their negative effects by contrasting them with their opposites – the 'switch-ons' of innovation. I have built up a picture of the latter from a literature survey, concentrating particularly on Kanter's work (1983, 1988) and *Business Week*'s (1989) special edition on innovation. Quotations included within the 'switch-ons' sections are from *Business Week* unless stated otherwise. For the inside story on the 'switch-offs' of the APT programme I have relied on my own interviews with BR's senior management and Stephen Potter's (1987) excellent account of the APT project. Quotations within these sections are from Potter unless otherwise stated.

Segmentalism

Switch-ons
Innovation depends on 'forgetting the organization structure' and 'putting together people who can get the job done, regardless of their function'. One has to tear down the organization walls and 'cross organization lines'. There has to be 'good cross-talk' going on, and a lot

of 'mingling', 'networking', 'swapping' and 'swarming' (Robert L. Calahan, president of Ingersoll Engineers). R&D must be changed from 'an individual to a team sport' (William Spence, Xerox), tying in more closely with business and marketing departments and production. There must also be inter-departmental, multidisciplinary teams where basic researchers mingle with applied engineers. 'The key is inter-departmental communications. Innovation is the product of endless in-house brainstorming' (Junichi Baba, adviser to Mitsubishi Electric Corporation).

All these fragments add up to a picture of Kanter's (1988) 'network culture', one that encourages flexibility, wide breadth of outreach, integration between those with pieces to contribute, boundary-spanning, intersecting territories and freedom for people to walk around and across the organization. Such an outgoing, cosmopolitan culture is intolerant of 'specialist boxes', inflexible, elitist hierarchies and local professional territories. It is a culture that supports coalitions and networks of interdependent, transacting members working together in multiple constituencies.

Switch-offs

At BR the picture could not have been more different. Its management culture, as I remarked before, was classically 'segmentalist'. In fact, Kanter's definition of segmentalism fits it perfectly:

> The contrasting style of thought . . . is anti-change oriented and prevents innovation. I call it 'segmentalism' because it is concerned with compartmentalizing actions, events, and problems and keeping each piece isolated from the others. Segmentalist approaches see problems as narrowly as possible, independently of their context, independently of their connections to any other problems.   (Kanter, 1983: 28)

As Potter has rightly pointed out, designing a high-performance train is one thing, but having the ability to win the support of a large number of departments and key individuals in order to smooth the development and testing process is quite another. The APT programme never did succeed in gaining support across the board from BR's management staff: 'It cannot be denied that there were serious technical and design problems, but the main problem was a divided attitude within the whole railway as to the credibility of the APT project' (1987: 133).

The roots of this 'divided attitude' are historical: there is a long record of segmental rivalry between various departments and professional groupings within the railway, this undoubtedly being encouraged by the strong emphasis that had always been placed on the bureaucratic principle of organizational differentiation. Unfortunately, the efficiencies arising from this type of structure have long been cancelled out by the ineffiencies of the segmentalist culture it created. Stand-up arguments became commonplace among heads of departments (1987: 56), and it seemed that the whole management system – as a system – was on the brink of collapse. Comments made to me by senior managers indicated just how far the politics had got out of control:

> To be frank there is an incipient power struggle going on all the time. There will always be winners and losers; the biggest loser is the railway.

> Cliques and alliances abound. The cliques become critical cliques rather than constructive ones. They gang up on ideas and they gang up against people.

> Someone tries to satisfy his bottom line but he's thwarted by somebody over here who has a word with somebody else and cuts his legs off.

There is much to be said for the argument that the APT was killed by politics. To put it more precisely, the 'power culture' starved the project of the good faith and the goodwill that it needed in order to succeed. It was also the cause of the interminable delays in getting the project underway: the fact that it took the BR Board member responsible for research, Dr Sydney Jones, two years to obtain the go-ahead for the APT was indicative of the sort of internal and organizational politics present in BR at that time (1987: 55).

The antagonisms between the research scientists and the railway engineers were probably the most destructive of all. Here were two sub-cultures that clashed on almost everything imaginable: values, attitudes (particularly regarding the best use of resources), and perceptions of role, status and function:

> In practice the APT project team found themselves in a very difficult position. The Chief Mechanical and Electrical Engineer was very supportive of the APT project, but within the Traction and Rolling Stock Design Department there was considerable antagonism. A number of key engineers viewed the whole approach of the APT as a threat to their professional reputation, their status and method of working. The APT was not only viewed as a frivolous high-tech irrelevance, but as something that was a distraction to valuable staff who could be better occupied in developing and building 'practical' trains. So while the senior management of CM & EE were sympathetic to the APT, at a day-to-day working level there was little support for the APT project. APT work got shunted down to the lowest level of priority. It would take days or weeks for even minor jobs to be done.
>
> (1987: 132)

Traditional engineers believed the APT was totally impractical and did not want to see resources wasted on the project, particularly in an area they felt was really theirs (1987: 55). Their concern was to build 'real' trains for today, not 'dream' trains for tomorrow. The scientists took the opposite view, accusing the engineers of anti-intellectualism, short-termism and plain stubborness. The APT ended up as the piggy-in-the-middle in this ideological struggle, caught in this cross-fire between the two warring subcultures. The 'fertile ground' (Kanter, 1988) upon which a thousand flowers might have bloomed had become a battleground, and the APT one of its casualties.

The segmentalist battle was also being fought on another front, between the 'innovators' and the 'book-keepers', the latter being the holders of the purse-strings for the APT. They were not at all impressed by the high-tech monster. To them the train was a high cost, high risk venture, one that hardly justified itself on financial grounds. The figures suggest that this attitude may have resulted in the low levels of funding that the project received during its lifetime: from its beginning in 1967 to 1982, investment amounted to only £43 m – which works out at under £3 m a year. To get a relative measure of the scale of this investment, expenditure on new motorways and other trunk roads over the same period was £5,300 m (averaging around £400 m per year), and the Concorde project alone cost £2,000 m to develop (£140 m per year) (1987: 58).

The root of the problem was that the finance people and the research engineers construed innovation in entirely different and incompatible ways. In rational terms, the book-keepers were right – the APT was not a sound investment, but then the engineers would argue that the whole point about innovation is that it is never a 'sound investment', that talking about it in these terms is to miss the whole point: innovation is a non-rational (risk-based) process that can only be evaluated in non-rational terms. If accounting logic were applied innovation would never occur. It was this difference in mental constructs that resulted in APT engineers accusing the financial planners of being short-sighted and narrow-minded, and the financial planners for their part accusing the engineers of irresponsibility and profligacy. Such professional grudges went back a very long way – were, one might say, part of the culture. The long view of history shows that the opinions being expressed by the financial planners about the APT were identical to those reputed to have been voiced by Baron Rothschild many years before, when he had pompously remarked to his railway colleagues:

> Gentlemen, there are three ways of ruining oneself. The first is through women; it is the most enjoyable. The second is with racehorses; it is the most exciting. The third is with engineers' ideas; it is the most certain.

Many would argue that the story of the APT in a nutshell is that the innovators fought the book-keepers – and lost. The APT fell victim to BR's inflexible, Soviet-style financial planning system. It failed, like so many innovation projects before it, because of the 'over-rigid application of cost accounting to policy decisions, which has dominated thinking for something like 30 years inside BR' (Bonavia, 1985: 9).

The story is still not complete: segmentalism also afflicted the relationships between R&D, manufacturing and marketing. The received wisdom is that the projects most likely to succeed are those that employ an 'in parallel' model of innovation, in which 'design', 'make' and 'market' activities happen at the same time with all three making constant reference to one another as they develop (simultaneous engineering). This is said to speed up the innovation cycle and lead to better decisions in all three areas. Although the APT project had a structure for achieving this (a multidisciplinary project team and a matrix management structure), the segmentalist mentalities found it so alien that it was never properly used. Segmentalist cultures, like BR, feel much more comfortable with an 'in series' model of innovation, one that allows departments to do their own thing with a minimum of contact and interaction. The problem with this 'design-build-test' model is that political expediency (turf issues) takes precedence over efficiency. Innovation cycle times usually end up taking much longer because people have to wait for others to complete and hand over their part of the job before they can begin their own, and because the blinkered way of working tends to produce a higher proportion of mistakes, wrong decisions and back referrals. This is the story of the APT: a segmentalist culture gave rise to an 'in series' innovation model which in turn resulted in numerous delays and mistakes.

One such mistake was assuming that the APT was a commercially viable proposition in the first place. What it all boiled down to was whether the time-saving between maxima of 125 mph and 140 mph or 155 mph was really worthwhile in commercial terms (Bonavia, 1985: 67): would it attract more passengers? The question was never seriously considered, indeed not even asked, at least not in the early stages of the project. The reason for this may be found in the 'in series' model of innovation that had been adopted: the first two groups in the chain, the designers and builders, were far too interested in the train itself to bother with questions about its potential uses and users. By the time the third group, the marketeers, had come into the chain and begun to discover from its surveys that customers were not greatly attracted by the marginally shorter travelling times offered by the APT, the project had assumed an unstoppable momentum and little could be done to halt it or change the line of its development. Perhaps it is fortunate that the project was finally stopped for technical and public relations reasons. If it had not been, it might well have been stopped – much later and at much greater cost – by commercial ones.

Conservatism

Switch-ons

Innovation needs a 'breakthroughs orientation', unconventional, con-troversial, heretical thinking, risk-taking, lots of asking 'Why?' about the status quo and a commitment to 'taking a gamble' and 'not steering the straight path'. Radicals and non-conformists, people who are prepared to 'go up the down escalator', are particularly welcome in this kind of culture.

Switch-offs

The APT's crime in the eyes of the BR culture was the very fact that it was innovative and symbolized change! It presaged a new generation of trains and a new form of management, and it signalled a switch from an evolutionary approach to rail innovation to a radical, research-based one. BR's conservative culture wanted none of these things. What it wanted was continuity not change, evolutionary rather than radical innovation, and it was prepared to fight the APT in order to preserve its normal way of life. This is one of the fundamental reasons why events unfolded in the way that they did: the conservative mentality moved against change and, being the bigger force, it won. As Hughes says, the conservatism in the railways was too much for the APT:

> Railways are a conservative business, and the innovative APT . . . was anathema to the traditionalist school in BR management. They believed it a waste of time, money and effort, resenting it as an intrusion in their domain. They fought it behind the scenes, undoubtedly contributing to its ultimate downfall.   (1988: 50)

To use the words of the managers themselves, what the project came up against were the 'anchors' and 'antibodies' within the BR culture:

> There are powerful, enormous anchors on the things you want to change. They are stuck in some pretty solid ground. Given BR's unbroken history of 150 years, it is not really surprising the chain is very long. It means you have got to work long and hard on your idea, but the trouble with that is that in the end it is easier to say 'blow it'.

> BR is an organism with some highly developed antibodies, so that if anything endeavours to permeate it the antibodies rush in, and they're incredibly strong, and they neuter whatever is happening.

The APT was not just a train, it was the counter-culture, an affront to conservative thinking in the railway – and was perceived as such. This is why it went down so badly. Potter (1987: 122) makes three observations in this regard: (1) the APT was a radical innovation in an industry which had long been organized with evolutionary developments in mind; (2) it was a project which, because it challenged established orthodoxy, inevitably became the focus of a lot of internal rivalry, particularly in departments where conventional trains were designed; and (3) because it was a radical development it required a different form of management (the project team), while the usual evolutionary design work continued in the functional departments. The imposition of one type of management on top of another caused overlaps and uncertainty in staff responsibilities. All three point to the fundamental mismatch between innovation and the prevailing culture.

Conservative cultures like BR can handle 'first order' innovation (updating, improving, evolving and amending existing technologies) but 'second order' innovations like the APT create very real problems for them. Not least, they upset the vested interests that have grown up around a particular technical development over a period of time (this is why people had been slow to abandon steam technology in favour of diesel and electrification in the 1950s, and why they were now reluctant to abandon work on conventional diesel trains in favour of the APT). However, the reasons probably go much deeper than this: the cultures of machine bureaucracies like BR were never designed with change or innovation in mind. Their *raison d'être* is order not change. Indeed one might plausibly argue that in rejecting change BR's culture was doing no more than what it was supposed to be doing – maintaining the organization in its steady state.

It is worth pointing out the overlap between this cultural mentality and the previous one. Much of the segmentalism in BR centred around competing conceptions of 'innovation', the one side represented by the conservative gradualists and the other side by the radical revisionists. Both sides lined up as follows:

The Grads	*v.*	**The Rads**
Engineers		Scientists
- evolutionary design		- radical, research-based design
- defensive, imitative		- offensive, novel and experimental
- following trends		- setting trends
- 'cut and try' (i.e. take existing designs as a starting-off point)		- 'frame breaking' (i.e. always begin with a clean sheet of paper)

The result of the match in the short term was a draw. The Grads won the right to continue to develop a conventional alternative to the APT (a low risk, low cost, rapid development cycle high speed diesel train – the HST), while the Rads were allowed to continue working on the APT. However, the long-term result was that the APT lost out because of resources going into the HST's coffers rather than its own. As might be expected the HST also made faster progress than the APT, causing many people to switch their support from the radical to the more conventional train. In many ways the fate of the glamorous APT was that it became less attractive the more the conventional HST began to blossom, and less likely to turn people's heads as time went on. Supporters of the APT might with some justification blame the BR Board for this development, for trying to square the circle with all the segments and in the process creating a situation in which the APT ultimately became the loser.

Isolationism

Switch-ons

Innovation processes need to be open to the skies if they are to flourish, not secreted away in the airless basement of some company research centre. 'Doing it all yourself' is now a discredited philosophy for innovation, having been replaced by the Japanese 'open door' approach in which boundaries between organizations disappear as competitors come together to Pool resources, form Alliances, and establish working Links (Kanter's PALS). Inter-company cooperation of this nature has been pivotal to the rise of Japanese industry. Particularly influential have been consortiums of competitors, like Hitachi, Fujitsu and Matsushita. One such consortium was the VLSI Project in the late 1970s which laid the groundwork for Japan's current domination of world-wide memory chip markets. This model has also been adopted in the United States, with scores of industrial consortiums being created so companies can conduct joint research on common problems. Here 'cooperation is one of the buzzwords for competitiveness'.

Pooling resources and sharing results has made for much faster innovation cycle times. Companies have also been able to recognize and respond much faster to changes in the environment, for example public alarm about pesticide use and the need to develop safer biological alternatives. This also raises another facet of the 'new approach' to innovation – the adoption of a stronger marketing focus throughout the whole process. Identification, qualification and quantification of the buyer's needs is now regarded as an integral part of product idea conception.

Switch-offs

News of the open skies approach to innovation had obviously not reached BR at the time of the APT project. Apart from one brief approach to Hawker Siddeley in the very early days, which came to nothing, the project proceeded entirely on a 'go it alone' basis. This meant that the burden of coming up with solutions fell on the shoulders of a mere thirty or so people in the core team – a very tall order indeed! The possibility of setting up a separate development company with wider contacts in the outside world was ruled out when the BR Board, the rail unions and the government decreed that the APT would have to be built using the accepted development and manufacturing structures of the rail industry (Potter, 1987: 122). Because of these self-imposed strictures there is no doubt that BR gave itself a very hard time in developing the APT and similar projects.

This closed shop attitude was symptomatic of the isolationist culture of the railways. In many ways it was the culture of the 'total institution', a sort of asylum where the inmates were safely locked away from the rest of society, condemned to live out the whole of their lives within it! As one manager remarked,

> The railway is an incredibly incestuous place. The traditional manager has very little contact with the outside reality. He knows nothing other than running railways. He knows nothing of the framework within which he has to perceive his own business.

Another likened BR to the Armed Services:

> You come in as a raw recruit and do your square bashing. The norms of the organization are knocked into you. And often norms are knocked out of you. And there are no more external influences after that. You are a member of the Body, you march through to retirement within that thing.

Other managers talked of the psychological 'wall' that separated them from the outside world:

> What reinforces narrowness is that we teach everything and do everything ourselves. All the railway expertise, by definition is inside the wall. How can you expect anybody outside the wall to know what he's talking about! If anything is to change we have to begin to breach the wall.

Given their perception of isolatedness, it is not really surprising that they naturally assumed that innovation involved doing it all themselves, with few links with relevant specialists outside the railway.

The consequences of isolationism for innovation were indeed serious. Because of it people had come to believe that railway problems were unique and that only railway people could possibly come up with the right solutions – which meant that a good deal of time was often wasted reinventing the wheel:

> The assumption is that the railways are different. This means we don't take advantage of knowledge and technical know-how elsewhere. Only now are we finding that, say, engines and gearboxes in lorries can be modified for use in trains.   (BR manager)

Another effect of this mentality was that it imposed a major constriction on perceptual possibility. Engineers saw themselves as railway engineers, rather than engineers in general or even transport engineers. They became isolated from professional colleagues and new developments:

> People become deep in terms of their particular specialization, but they're incredibly narrow. They do not know what is going on in the world around them. They end up knowing more about less and less.   (BR manager)

How different they were from the heroic boundary-spanning, kaleido-scopic thinking, comopolitan innovators that jump out of the pages of Kanter's (1988) writings!

BR's isolationist mentality also meant that often the last people to figure in its thoughts were its customers. As I said before, no-one thought of asking them whether they needed or wanted a train like the APT. Kanter (1988) would say that BR had broken one of the golden rules of innovation: stay close to need sources (i.e. customer requirements and tastes). There is no doubt that in the case of the APT the internal needs of the scientists were consistently given primacy over the external needs of the customer, with commercial considerations receiving far less attention than technical ones.

Certainly this cultural mentality had much to do with the project being 'technology-pushed' rather than 'market-pulled' (Potter, 1987: 78). This is not always a bad thing – after all, a purely market-pulled approach would probably mean that we would never have had the telephone, electric light, television or refrigerator, on the grounds that people cannot be expected to want something they do not know exists (or could exist) or have never thought of; we have to allow for the fact that innovation creates needs as well as responds to them. Nevertheless, a purely technology-pushed project, like the APT, can lead to a narrow and somewhat simplistic analysis of markets. For example, there is no doubt that the APT design team were obsessed by speed, did not give adequate consideration to other qualities like comfort, reliability and cost, and neglected to conduct a rigorous competitor analysis with regard to air and road transport. My point is that the APT may have been a better, more commercially viable train had the scientists and engineers not been making the commercial judgements in formulating the initial design specifications (1987: 78), had professional marketing people been involved at an earlier stage (rather than excluded by segmentalism), had contacts been made with designers in other industries (including competitors), and had there been a more open, interactive, dialogical relationship with customers and the market in general – in short had there been a better balance between market-pull and technology-push, and more openness to ideas from the outside world.

Elitism

Switch-ons
Innovation processes benefit from 'a flattening of the hierarchy', 'fewer single-stratum groups' and more multi-strata groupings and coalitions. Superior–subordinate relationships are replaced by partnerships, and a spirit of organizational socialism fills the air. To use an earlier metaphor, innovation requires taking away the ceilings as well as the walls! Conditions must exist for 'innovators to go across formal lines and levels in the organization to find what they need – vertically, horizontally, or diagonally – without feeling they are violating protocol. They can skip a level or two without penalty' (Kanter, 1988:190).

Switch-offs
Once again the situation in BR could not have been more different from what has been described here. As we have already seen, the horizontal 'walking across' was being prevented by segmentalism, but in addition to this the vertical 'walking up and down' was also greatly hindered by a culture of elitism which imposed a ceiling on vertical mobility. As a senior manager succinctly put it, 'Only directors talk to directors'. One critic (Heller, 1967: 67) has likened a top job in the railways to the position of a district commissioner in colonial East Africa, with perks like a pleasant office, minions at one's beck and call and an empire that is seldom interfered with by one's commanding officer. Servants – the 'unwashed multitude' as they were sometimes referred to in BR – were to be seen but not heard, and under no circumstance were they to consort with their superiors!

> The railways is a very hierarchical organization, everybody is status conscious and everybody knows where they fit in the pecking order.
> (Manager)

Everywhere in BR there were protocols to observe and hierarchical reporting procedures to follow – many of them incredibly complex and long-winded – before permission for a new project like the APT could be secured. Thus the APT had to go through endless review processes, gradually spiralling upwards to the BR Board level and culminating in the grand review of reviews. The process was mind-numbingly slow. There is little doubt that the APT became the victim of this class-ridden, hierarchical, status conscious culture. For example, it is a fact that the authority to construct prototypes took no less than seventeen months to come through – nearly as long as it took both to develop and build the prototype conventional HST (1987: 117).

If, as writers claim, innovation is also about nurturing human initiative then certainly the culture of elitism within BR did little to help in this direction. Because of it, nothing could happen without permission from the top. One had to get 'sponsorship' for a project, and only a very senior person or group could give this. Apart from the physical problem of having to wait a long time for a reply while the inevitable segmental battles between senior personnel were played out, there was also the psychological problem of feeling disempowered as a result of having to 'delegate' initiative upwards. Managers in the middle grades, rather than seeing themselves as the leaders of change, came to see themselves as the agents of the elite, their function being not to think for themselves but to carry out their leaders' will. Thus, in innovation matters, only the ideas of the elite were legitimate, and only its definition of the situation was allowed to prevail. The 'doers' felt a loss of ownership of the process, and wasted much effort struggling to retain whatever vestiges of control they still had available to them. Schedules, procedures, timetables, terms of reference – all of these things were decided at the top and communicated downwards. By no stretch of the imagination could this be seen as a satisfactory basis for pooling ideas, generating energy and stimulating the innovative process.

Another point about elite cultures is that they pay out on position rather than performance. Hence, the people at the top in BR took all the credit for the early success of the APT, while the superhuman efforts of those lower down often went unrewarded. Interestingly, the same rule did not seem to apply to failure.

Neologism

Switch-ons

Japanese companies are now looking to fund research into ideas that will not become a product for 10 to 15 years. Innovation needs longer term objectives like these – it requires 'being in for the long haul'. It also means persisting even when everything has been failing for months, or as the popular saying has it, 'when the going gets tough the tough get going'.

Switch-offs

Neologism can be defined as an obsession with the new and the newfangled. On the face of it this sensitivity to new ideas might be seen to favour innovation, but the BR research suggests a contrary interpretation. Innovation in practice requires a sustained process of change and development (see above; Quinn, (1985) also estimates that it can take anything from three to twenty-five years for an invention to reach commercial production). Ideas need to be worked up and worked on, coalitions have to be carefully constructed, resources have to be mobilized. All of this takes time and persistence which neologists simply do not have. They are attracted to the quick fix solution, and their curiosity is in newness for its own sake, not the content or even extrinsic value of that newness. The product of innovation and its application take second place to newness itself. When the newness wears off so too does the interest. In short, neologism is a distraction from innovation:

> The danger is that there is a peculiar sort of cycle on the railways where they have a continual stream of flavour-of-the-months. One trend can be completely reversed by another, not because a better way has been found but simply because it's the latest flavour.   (manager)

The APT may well have suffered at the hand of the neologistic culture inside BR. For example, one possible reason why the scientists did not fight tooth-and-nail against the decision to terminate the project was that the novelty of their 'new toy' had already worn off by the time the decision was being taken: they had solved some of the 'big' rail problems, like 'hunting'; the idea of a tilting train had been brought to fruition; they had proved that the train could reach its maximum design speed; so what else was there to be achieved? In a strictly scientific sense, the experiment had been a success. Perhaps it was now time to move on to another intellectual puzzle. If others wanted to do more with the commercial applications then frankly that was up to them.

As far as the other groups were concerned, it was a case of one 'flavour of the month' – the APT – being replaced by another, newer flavour – the HST. Thus it was that just when managers should have been steeling themselves against public mockery of the APT, and putting all their collective weight behind the project to get it through to the last stage, they were busily deserting the sinking ship – or should I say train! When push came to shove no-one, it seemed, had any stomach left for the fight.

The fate of all fashions is that they become unfashionable – and disappear. Perhaps the APT died simply because it went out of fashion.

Structuralism

Switch-ons

Innovation activities need a period of structural stability within which to get established, regularized and routinized (the 'incubation' phase). They need 'space' for relationships to settle down and work processes and patterns to develop. It is precisely because they are so unpredictable, uncertain, sloppy and chaotic that they need this discipline of a relatively secure, stable organizational environment within which to develop. As with plants, innovation processes do not like to be disturbed or moved. Kanter's (1988) maxim is that creating change needs stability. For example, high labour turnover is bad for innovation. You need a settled team (research suggests it takes at least two years for a team to begin to work together), one where members do not leave with valuable knowledge, where you do not have to re-educate new members, or have to fight an attempt to change direction.

Switch-offs

The structuralist mentality in BR was discussed earlier and does not require further explanation. What I wish to show here is how this particular cultural affliction paralysed innovation within BR and disabled the APT project. To refresh memories, the mentality in question was described by one observer as a 'fever' – reorganization fever – and by another as a 'pathology'.

> It has become a pathological thing; we tinker with the organization structure all the time. Change for the sake of change, that's all it is. When people see a problem, they perceive the answer to be 'change the organization' – the titles, the people, the jobs, etc. In fact, it's just shaking the bag around.
>
> (BR manager)

Nowhere was this 'tinkering' mentality more disastrous than in the APT project. The beginnings had looked promising: despite all of the obstacles and problems referred to already, the project did much better than most people expected, making remarkable progress on the development, construction and testing of the first APT prototypes during the first three years of its life. That was until structuralism struck. Potter takes up the story:

> just as the APT Project Group were beginning to win the enthusiasm of others within CM & EE [mechanical and electrical engineering] and to open trials with prototypes, a new managerial factor came into play that virtually brought any real progress on the APT to a halt. This was simply the total

> reorganization of the Mechanical and Electrical Engineering Department
> which, beginning in 1976, took four years to complete.   (1987: 134)

The ambition was admirable enough: to make the organization more customer-orientated and market-led by creating three new product groups (Freight, Intercity and Suburban). However, the act itself was ill-timed and totally misguided, indeed it broke every rule in the 'effective innovator's' handbook. Staff, including the APT Project Group, were reallocated within this new structure.

> The hundred and twenty APT posts were dispersed among nine different sections . . . The APT Project Group officially ceased to exist on 14 July 1980 and the APT Design Engineer was promoted to the new post of Inter-City Engineer, in charge not only of the APT but of all inter-city rolling-stock. The development work on the APT was to continue as a project sponsored by the Inter-City sector and conducted by staff allocated to work on it by the Inter-City Engineer.   (pp. 135-6)

The APT project had the rug pulled from under it. Because of the reorganization it did not just 'bleed', as Gerald Fiennes (1967) would have predicted, it positively haemorrhaged. Some indication of the disruption and upheaval the reorganization caused has been given by Potter (1987: 137). Members of the APT team woke up to find that they were working for bosses who had always despised the project. Understandably

> those who could left and obtained posts elsewhere which did not involve such uncomfortable conditions. This rapidly drained the project of its most capable and skilled people . . . Staff began to leave the APT Project Group from early 1977. Every single APT section head left in order to obtain an acceptable post either elsewhere in the railway or outside. Just as the APT was entering the crucial testing and debugging phase, key people were leaving prior to the whole team being broken up and dispersed. Just when the project required the strongest focus and greatest skill and resources, those resources were dissipated or lost.   (1987: 137)

The fact that the APT project never recovered from this blow must lead us to question why BR chose to reorganize when it did. The cultural explanation – granted, only one among many – is that the organization in question was governed by the immutable clockwork logic of its culture, one that periodically rang a bell to remind people that a structural change was due – not 'needed', I stress, but 'due'. The reason for a change of structure was simply that it was time for one. The mentality of structuralism assumes unquestioningly that it is more important to be on time than it is to be timely. Reorganizations, like trains, must arrive on time whatever the wind or weather.

History bears this out: reorganizations have occurred with remarkable regularity in the railway sector, every one of them justified on identical grounds: to make the organization more commercially and customer-conscious. The significance of this particular explanation is that the APT team was not reorganized because of anything that was happening or going amiss in the project itself – 'isms' like the one in question are so locked up in their inner logic that they have little time for here-and-now 'realities' – but simply because the alarm clock happened to go off at that time, making reorganization imperative. So ingrained was this mentality and so automatic were the thought and behavioural processes triggered by it that no one actually stopped to ask whether it was sensible or wise to be doing it.

Pragmatism

Switch-ons

The Japanese have shown that innovation requires a commitment to 'basic science' . Witness, for example, the big discoveries in fields like bioengineering and molecular biology, which have all used 'science-intensive' activities to break new theoretical ground. In recent years there has been a switch from the 'D' to the 'R' in R&D – the cult of the practical has given way to the cult of the theoretical. Projects also need to take on unreal, almost science-fictional qualities. Because the skies really are the limit these days, the last thing one wants is people who are boringly pragmatic and level-headed in their approach to innovation. Companies have to find ways of 'thinking the unpractical', supporting 'megaprojects' and 'tackling the longshot' – the superconducting supercollider, the space station, the space plane and so on.

Switch-offs

In many ways the futuristic, science-intensive APT was just too 'big' an idea for BR's pragmatic culture to cope with. The culture approved of 'doers' – practically minded people, pragmatists, sprinters and quick-fixers, but the APT required 'thinkers' – theorists, visionaries, marathon runners and long-shooters. Again there was a fundamental mismatch between the culture and the project.

Some of the flavour of this hostile culture is conveyed in the following comments from BR managers:

People tend to think short term about their bottom line next year and the year after, rather than think about the long term. That's dangerous in an industry with long-living assets, where you always have to keep your eyes looking forward.

People have lots of good ideas, but they are desperately afraid to talk about them.

The railways are naturally suspicious about ideas. Because of this, ideas will have to be rolled and rolled before they are allowed through. I don't know whether business generally outside operates like that or whether there is a little more of a relaxed, freer approach to ideas. We're far too slow in developing ideas. I can't put my finger on it but I suppose it's got something to do with us having been around for over a century.

There is a belief that action is the great thing to be valued. Standing back, thinking about problems is not considered to be a worthwhile way of spending your time. The action is all important.

Frequent bursts of well-intentioned pragmatism lay behind various drives to improve customer service or clean up the railway. Such events were known as 'Operations' (e.g. Operation Pride), being closely associated with the military-type culture of BR, one that preferred 'wind-up, instant action men' (Harvey-Jones, 1989: 102) to research boffins:

When you come to something fundamental, where there is a lot of concern, we will have a 'drive' or a 'campaign'. After a while we will all go back to our offices and think it's all over. We have got something off our chests but actually nothing has changed. We haven't tackled any fundamental problems.   (BR manager)

From these comments one can begin to get a sense of the kind of culture that the APT project was up against.

The dictionary defines pragmatism as 'a doctrine that estimates any assertion solely by its practical bearing upon human interests.' The whole point about the APT was that, like innovations in general, it was not the most practical thing to be doing and, as far as the multitude of vested interests was concerned, its pay-offs were of dubious value. Thus according to the logic of pragmatism, which was embodied in the highly influential 'empirical school' of engineering in BR, the APT was at best a distraction and at worst a complete waste of time. The general point emerging from this case description is that it was not so much that the train was 'objectively' wrong, just that it did not fit the subjective cultural schema of the management culture. The fundamental problem was that the culture had no way of appreciating, valuing or responding positively to the project.

If Kanter (1988) is right when she says that innovations need a fertile organizational ground in which to bloom and grow, it is clear from this story that the cultural terrain of BR offered little in the way of nourishment for the cultivation of the APT project. If each of the constituent microcultures – the 'isms' – represents a pocket of barren land, then laid alongside each other they create a desert. The APT did not stand a chance. It died trying to cross this cultural desert.

6 The Castalian Culture

There are a number of points and assertions arising from the APT case and the discussion preceding it that I would now like to put to readers for their consideration.

1   All organizations have 'isms' – vicious circles, maladaptive cultural processes, bad habits of thinking, call them what you will.

'Isms' are a universal phenomenon found in any and every kind of organizational configuration and one of the root causes of failure and underperformance. The task for management is to find them and do something about them. Together with their functional counterparts (positive-isms), they make up the DNA of organizational culture. The challenge, just as it was for Crick and Watson in the field of genetics, is to discover the implicit structures of these phenomena, make them explicit and reveal their rich, explanatory power. A strategy for dealing with 'isms' such as those found in BR is the basis of a strategy for cultural change. The intervention activities that arise from this strategy are directed towards interrupting and interrogating the established development cycle, switching off its self-destructing logic and delivering new symbolic modes into the organizational world.

   Claiming that 'isms' are a universal phenomenon is a lot less risky than it sounds. Once it is appreciated that regressive, circular thinking of the kind described is an intrinsic feature of a cultural development process that is itself circular in nature, the point makes itself. To put it another way, circularity is one of the 'developmental regularities' (Steward, 1955) of culture, one of its inherent properties, indeed an essential part of its character. Wherever there is culture there will be circular structures and processes of thought. Once we have accepted that cultures do not develop linearly but in a spiral fashion, we can then accept that 'isms' or whatever else we choose to call them will always be the residue or byproduct of such a development process. Not all of them will be 'vicious', of course, but my contention is that every 'virtuous' circle has the potential for becoming so, and left solely to the forces of natural development will always become so. This is because cultural forms have properties that allow for repetition, reproduction, adaptation and re-creation, but do not have the capability for changing or revitalizing themselves. They are:

- Multiplying processes: they naturally prefer 'more of the same' (quantitative change) to something different (qualitative change).
- Modifying processes: variation can occur but only within a fixed frame. Consequently they are unable to accept anything from outside the frame – the APT, for example.
- Amplifying processes: cultural circles are tragic circles of self-fulfilling prophecy whose features become more pronounced and ingrained with the passage of time. Consequently, they become more and more resistant to 'newness' and more and more likely to reproduce their ignorance and mistakes.
- Stabilizing processes: as I have said before, cultural processes are orbits spiralling around and toward a fixed, closed orbit with their own stable equilibrium point. They neutralize or counteract any thoughts and actions that come in from outside the range.
- Normalizing processes: circles of culture are deviation-correcting phenomena. Confronted with discontinuity and disorder they will always strive to restore or maintain normality.
- Habitualizing processes: cultural circles are taken for granted, commonsensical, automatic, preconscious mentalities. The longer they exist the more unaware we become of them, and the less likely we are to try to change them.
- Ossifying processes: circles of culture are petrifying, self-terminating processes. Their rate of change slows down as their creative resources are exhausted. Left to themselves they eventually wither and die.

We can see that these are all growth, reinforcement and development processes but none of them is a change process.

It is because of the above qualities that cultures ultimately lose their vitality and become emptied of meaning. The clear implication is that some kind of purposive human intervention and activity needs to take place if the natural ageing and shrinking process is to be halted and the cultural contents replenished. Culture cannot be left to grow with the superb aimlessness of the flowers of the field: it has to be tended – i.e. managed; in short, culture has to be 'cultivated'. The seasons bring a range of activities: old weeds have to be cleared and the soil turned over, new seeds have to be planted, the growing plants nourished and protected, and their ripe fruits harvested. All of these come under the heading of type 1 'development' strategies. However, as we know these cannot be pursued indefinitely or the garden ends up with exhausted plants and exhausted soil. All seasons come to an end, and the ground will at some point need to be cleared to make way for new plants. Disposing of the old and sowing the seeds of the new is the kind of activity that belongs to type 2 'change' strategies.

This metaphor is helpful because it reminds us that in the garden of culture timing is everything: knowing when the existing plants will yield no more, when the ground needs refreshing or resting, and when the environmental conditions necessitate a change of activity. The key decision is when to draw a veil over the old season and when to usher in a new one – that is, when to switch from a type 1 to a type 2 strategic orientation and when to switch back again. More on this later. Another point highlighted by the metaphor is that culture is a process – a never-ending process that embraces many different activities and constantly shifting focuses of concern. Getting everything correctly positioned and sequenced in this change process is another critical issue that will need to be considered later.

One objection to what I have been saying is likely to be that the maladaptive mentalities under consideration are not universal but merely a feature of large-scale operational bureaucracies like British Rail. While it is undoubtedly true that organizations like BR will always have an abundance of isms because of their unswerving commitment to order and stability, I do not believe they are exceptional. For example it is worth noting that the first place they were observed was not in a 'machine' bureaucracy but a 'professional' bureaucracy, the French civil service (Crozier, 1964), which is obviously a very different kind of organization from BR. Work with a colleague (Brooks and Bate, 1992) has uncovered similar circles in the British civil service, another professional bureaucracy. At the other extreme, Dyer (1986) found them in small, similarly stability-orientated 'family-owned' firms. Although the evidence is hardly conclusive, it does suggest that the phenomenon is ubiquitous and not associated with any one kind of structural configuration. This should not really be surprising, the point being that vicious circles are not an attribute of structure at all but the product of a certain kind of historical process – one that any organization, small or large, simple or complex, may have gone through.

2 Every organization will have its own unique set of 'isms' that it will need to identify and address in its own unique way.

It is the particular make-up and patterning of 'isms' that makes one organization culture different from another: Hewlett Packard (HP) is different from British Rail because it has 'isms' that BR does not have.

'Humanism', for example: embodied in the 'HP Way', this characteristic philosophy embraces human values of trust, respect, individual dignity, profit-sharing and employment security. There is no counterpart for this in BR, quite the opposite in fact: the culture depersonalizes and dehumanizes relationships and is not by any stretch of the imagination people-centred.

The task for the management is to find out what their particular organizational 'isms' are and set in motion a relevant and appropriate process for dealing with them. For this they will need a culture perspective. 'Isms' are invisible from any other perspective; unless people are 'thinking culturally' they will simply not see them. The various 'isms' need to be identified, labelled, described and explained, and consideration needs to be given to the manner in which they impact on organizational performance. Not all of them will be dysfunctional of course: some 'isms' will be a strength (virtuous) and others a weakness (vicious). The managers of change will first need to identify them and sort out which is which. Having done this, they will then need to devise relevant 'nurturing' strategies for the first and 'terminating' or 'transforming' strategies for the second.

The APT case examined in the preceding chapter showed that 'isms' reach into every nook and cranny of organizational life: innovation processes, problem-solving, relationships and many more. The message for practitioners must therefore be that you cannot simply turn a blind eye to them and hope they will go away. Cultural schema such as these hold the key to organizational survival and growth. This comment applies as much to successful firms as it does to the less successful ones, if not more so given the fact that today's virtuous circle will become tomorrow's vicious circle unless some kind of anticipatory remedial action is taken. There is always a need for preventive as well as curative medicine in the area of culture management.

Hewlett-Packard is a case in point. In the 1970s the 'HP Way' (humanism) was a classic virtuous circle, bringing the company profit and success. Nevertheless, by the 1980s the 'growing excesses' (Pascale, 1990: 230) of this philosophy had turned the virtuous circle into a vicious circle, and set the company on the road to decline. 'More of the same' had become 'too much of a good thing'. The phrase that HP itself used to describe the problem was 'terminal niceness': being nice had got rather out of hand; people were so busy being nice to each other that they were not facing up to their differences and were avoiding making necessary commercial decisions (such as reducing or relocating the workforce when business declined). These were just some of the many 'dysfunctional protocols' (1990: 232) that had grown up around the HP Way. Another problem was that the comforts offered by the HP Way had kept staff turnover extremely low (2% per year of employees with fifteen or more years' service), resulting in an ageing, less productive, workforce. Pascale is in no doubt about the harmful effects that this 'maladaptive ideology' is now having:

> The danger, then, is that the HP Way – for all its humanistic appeal – is becoming a maladaptive ideology of job security and autonomy. Employees at all levels tend to view employment security as more of a right than a privilege. When offered an opportunity to move (requiring an extra fifteen-mile commute to another facility), many refuse yet remain on the payroll. This has unquestionably led to some divisions becoming less competitive. The number of HP's product lines losing money has increased. (1990: 231)

Which brings me to my next point:

3 Some organizations are more likely to get trapped in vicious circles than others.

Least prone are the open, informal, continually reorganizing adhocratic or network kinds of organization. Most prone are the successful, hierarchic 'strong culture' organizations like HP. Their Achilles heel is that they have a strategy for developing culture but not one for changing it. They do not seem to have realized that the one strategy needs the other, indeed creates the need for the other: a strategy for cultural order and development without a strategy for cultural change has built-in obsolescence; a strategy for cultural change without a strategy for cultural development has no provision for reaping the benefits of a fruitful idea.

This brings us back to the recurrent theme of this book: the need for both–and thinking. Organizations need order and change, and hence development as well as change strategies – the first to exploit a virtuous circle to the full, and the second to cut in and terminate it when it threatens to become a vicious circle. Each offers something that the other cannot provide and each compensates for the weaknesses and side-effects of the other.

HP had the one but not the other – a development strategy but not a change strategy. It had the means for exploiting the benefits of the HP Way in the early days, but no way of terminating it when it had become a liability. The point is that cultural obsolescence, such as it was experiencing, cannot be 'evolved' away using a first order development strategy; in fact it was HP's tenacious pursuit of such a strategy (centred around the propagation of the HP Way) that caused it. This is a key point: it is precisely because pursuit of the one creates the need for the other that neither can afford to be excluded from the strategist's portfolio. What HP should have been doing was pursuing a strategy for order and then a strategy for change.

As all the cases mentioned have demonstrated, companies that depend entirely on type 1 cultural development strategies and never formulate type 2 cultural change strategies do so at their peril. Probably the most cogent illustration of this point comes not from a real example but a fictitious one: Hermann Hesse's novel *The Glass Bead Game* (1984 [1943]). For those not familiar with the book, it is an allegorical tale about a society that disintegrated and died because it was unable to let go of its glorious past and accept change, assuming right up to the very end that it could survive by pursuing strategies of order rather than strategies for change. (Günter Grass covered the same theme later in his novel *The Tin Drum* with little Oskar substituting for the Glass Bead Game.) The story is a modern tragedy (loosely based on the experiences of Nazi and pre-Nazi Germany) about an intellectually powerful, but naive and complacent, community that falsely believed it could 'develop' its way to even greater heights of civilization and sophistication without ever leaving the 'frame', and later when this failed continued to believe that it could 'develop' its way out of crisis and decline.

My main reason for drawing attention to this book is that its message is so different from what one finds in the best-selling business literature at the moment, and so damning of the so-called 'strong cultures' route to excellence (at least long-term excellence), that everyone should be aware of its provocative contents. The message is this: viewed from the normal perspective of maintaining order and control (see Chapter 3 above), the business gurus are absolutely right: the strong culture is ideal – but from the viewpoint of change it is a recipe for disaster. The following précis of the *Glass Bead Game* will hopefully whet people's appetites to explore this alternative viewpoint further. Its purpose is to offer a radical critique of the strong culture organization by drawing parallels between it and the society described in the book. The name of the society is Castalia, hence the title of this chapter.

The Castalian organization

The novel is written in the form of a biography of a master of the Glass Bead Game, Joseph Knecht, compiled by an anonymous scholar. The story centres on a land called Castalia, a tranquil and isolated province located in the mountainous region of a larger state. Castalia emerged out of the countermovement to an age of growing fragmentation within the larger state. This age was one of great chaos and confusion, the kind of situation described by one writer (Oakes, 1980: 43) as a 'culture of disorder that had lost its bearings'. Borrowing a phrase I used earlier, it was an age in which pluralism had broken down and anarchy had broken out.

Castalia is the antidote to this postmodernistic chaos, a society purged of all uncertainty and ambiguity, one in which anomie and triviality are eliminated, and meaning, purpose and an awareness of higher ideals are put back into people's lives. It is everyone's naive picture of the utopian society, the perfect order, the one reality, the ultimate in closed systems of thought, the furthest imaginable extreme of unitarist ideology. It is totally self-contained, totally integrated and totally static; a society frozen in time, apparently so perfect that it has no need of change. Castalia is Schubart's 'Harmonious Culture' (Sorokin, 1966), a culture animated by inner harmony and not requiring human direction or control. The idea of evolution or progress does not exist in such a 'cosmos' because Harmonious man sees the purpose of history as having been achieved, and lives peacefully in and with his world, as an inseparable part of it.

In modern parlance Castalia is the very last word in strong cultures. Against it even the Pizza Huts, HPs and IBMs of this world pale into insignificance. One might say that it is Disneyworld to the power ten. 'Organization Man' is but a shadow of 'Castalian Man'. People in Castalia have 'gone beyond all original and idiosyncratic qualities to achieve the greatest possible integration into the generality, the greatest possible service to the suprapersonal' (Hesse, 1984 [1943]: 16). One can almost see them mouthing together the words from that classic Monty Python film: 'We – are – all – individuals!' The irony is that the last thing Castalia allows a person to be is an individual. In order to be accepted one has to be prepared to let one's individuality be absorbed into the hierarchic function of the society: 'We find all the more worthy of our reverence the memory of those who tragically sacrificed themselves for the greater whole' (p.17). Castalian culture is the perfect synthesis of the individual will with the collective will, the ultimate in groupthink and personal disempowerment.

Castalia may be larger than life but does none the less contain all those features that modern strong culture organizations value and aspire to: order and tranquillity, ethnocentrism, historical continuity, strict adherence to routine, self-discipline, control, pride, stability, community, hierarchy, structure, a sense of tradition, loyalty and dedication, uniformity, ritual and ceremony – and, of course, excellence. The attraction of Castalia to such companies would be that it is a community of mind and soul – the pedagogical province ruled by Reason and Spirit.

The whole life of Castalia revolves around the highly venerated Glass Bead Game in which the nation's best minds compete to synthesize and rearrange the total contents and values of their culture in ever new, glorious and uplifting ways – a kind of cultural Lego for aesthetes and intellectuals in which surrealistic semantic cathedrals are constructed from the huge piles of the society's accumulated cultural material. A present constructed from the past and a past constantly recreated in the present. Hesse himself prefers the metaphor of the organ:

> On all this immense body of intellectual values the Glass Bead Game player plays like the organist on an organ. And this organ has attained an almost unimaginable perfection; its manuals and pedals range over the entire intellectual cosmos; its stops are almost beyond number.　　　(p. 18)

As might be expected, anything and everything is possible on an instrument as impressive as this. One school of players might favour synthesizing ancient Chinese temple plans with the harmonies of late Beethoven quartets; others might favour the technique of starting side by side, developing in counterpoint, and finally harmoniously combining two hostile themes or ideas, such as law and freedom, individual and community. In such a game the goal would be to develop both themes or theses with complete equality and impartiality, to evolve out of thesis and antithesis the purest possible synthesis. For virtuosi, like Knecht and the other Elders, the Game offers unlimited vistas, enabling the entire content of the symbolic universe to be grasped and manipulated at will:

> We draw upon the iconography
> Whose mystery is able to contain
> The boundlessness, the storm of all existence,
> Give chaos form, and hold our lives in rein.　　　(p. 415)

Readers will have gathered that Castalia is a metaphor for Culture (Schutz's definition of culture as a 'province of meaning' transposes nicely into Hesse's Province of Castalia), and the Game is a metaphor for the type 1 'development' strategies that are used to preserve and protect that culture. The HP Way is therefore a Glass Bead Game of sorts, as is the IBM Way or any other 'way of life' for that matter. All organizations have their Glass Bead Game, that is to say an established social, cognitive, affective, intellectual and linguistic process (note the parallels with Wittgenstein's concept of the language game) within which and through which the players (most notably the ruling elite) express and enact the meaning, purpose and direction in their lives. The Game is both a structure and a process – a fixed framework or structure of rules ('grammar') and a set of variations within it which make constant reference to it but never go outside it (again think of the rotating kaleidoscope, or, better still, forms in music, like the sonata form or fugue form, which allow for improvisation, variation and modulation, but always within the strict rules of their structure).

The particular genre of Game described by Hesse is typical of the strong culture firm. Its striking feature is its closed and immanent form. Hesse calls it the 'game of games' – a 'Royal Game' (p. 120) – which directly calls to mind Simmel's notion of the 'kingdom' or 'empire' of thought, a form of life that has established its own imperious, self-sufficient and autonomous existence. The self-absorbed monastic *ganzheiten* or high culture depicted by Hesse, and captured in Escher's pictures, epitomizes this type of cultural form. Cultures like this stand aloof and superior on their mountain perches. They have a strong inward focus, shying away from interaction with the outside world, which they regard as brutish, coarse, hedonistic, disorderly and unpredictable. In their most extreme form they are closed, isolationist, elitist, inward looking and unresponsive to the outside world (remember British Rail?). Inside them one 'ism' reigns supreme: dogmatism. This gains its strength from an absolute and authoritative belief in itself: 'Our way is the right way, other ways are false, wicked, godless' (Feyerabend, 1987: 84). Pity the godless – or should we say 'gameless' – try to inform them of the error of their ways, but failing that leave them well alone. In the immortal phrase, these are the cultures that stick tenaciously to the knitting.

The other feature of the Game which is so reminiscent of the strong culture organization is that it is an object of worship, with a spiritual as well as an intellectual focus. As Hesse states, 'We would scarcely be exaggerating if we ventured to say that for a small circle of genuine Glass Bead Game players the Game was virtually equivalent to worship, although it deliberately eschewed developing any theology of its own' (p. 40). Readers will recall similar references in Chapter 3 to 'idol worship' in the strong culture company and Deal and Kennedy's recommendation that the Roman Catholic Church should be the model for such a company. Hesse would have very much understood this metaphor, for he also based Castalia on that 'great organization', the Roman Church, in the eras of its greatest power, and Knecht on one of its 'greatest figures', St Thomas Aquinas. In the book the younger Knecht goes to Rome as an emissary from Castalia and returns with a concord between the two States.

In the Glass Bead Game people may only use type 1 cultural 'development' strategies, improvising on what is available but never being allowed to go outside the frame and create something new. The rules are fixed. Variations and alterations are subject to the strictest control. As Hesse himself says about the great 'organ' (i.e. structure) on which the Game is played, 'the manuals, pedals and stops of the metaphorical organ are now fixed. Changes in their number and order, and attempts at perfecting them, are actually no longer feasible except in theory. Any enrichment of the language of the Game by addition of new contents is subject to the strictest conceivable control by the directorate of the Game'

(p. 18). He tells us that at one time people with freakish memories played dazzling games and dismayed and confused the other participants. But now that is no longer allowed to happen. In the course of time such displays of virtuosity have fallen more and more under a strict ban and the Game has become narrower and more confined (remember Escher's Lizards?). The game describes a perfect circle, going nowhere, creating nothing: 'This meaningful and meaningless cycle . . . this endless oscillating game' (p. 272).

As one will appreciate, a 'first order', crossword-puzzle solving mentality is ideal equipment for becoming a master of the Game, a rule-following mind that derives stimulation from producing endless variations on the stated theme. The point of this vocation, if there is one, is reformulation not transformation: 'The most salient aspect of this new mentality was that serious men no longer produced new artifacts of objective culture' (Oakes, 1980: 43). The Game is a game of recall, a backward-looking game that requires nothing in the way of vision or deviation from the past.

The book traces Knecht's life from young novice to Grandmaster (Magister Ludi). At first he accepts the traditions of the Game as a lingua sacra or divine language. He is a willing and able pupil and rises rapidly through the hierarchy, finally receiving the 'last and highest' of calls, his appointment of Magister Ludi – the equivalent of CEO and at barely forty years of age! In time, though, Knecht begins to suspect the inevitability of the Game's disintegration, its inconsequentiality, its utter synthetic quality. He realizes that the Game is a matrix for dead culture, an aesthetic surrogate for real life (Burnham, 1971: 2). As Knecht himself puts it, 'the only creativity we have left lies in preserving [past culture]' (p. 261). He begins to wonder if it were not each intellectual's duty to free himself from the 'serfdom of time' and apply himself to living issues. Armed with the belief that no society can live beyond the realms of time and context and survive, he confronts the other Elders in a long letter of resignation. In it he accuses Castalians of selfishness and arrogance, of being stick-in-the-muds and noxious parasites on the outside world.

His main point is that Castalia is doomed because it has lost the capacity and the will to change itself. It has become a prisoner of its successful past. The strong culture that enabled it to reach its zenith has metamorphosed into a Model of Order, the be-all and end-all of existence. It has allowed itself to become detached from life itself. Flushed with success, trapped in their gilded cage, and believing in their own immortality, the denizens have even forgotten what the word 'change' means. This results in crisis:

To put it briefly: I have begun to doubt my ability to officiate satisfactorily because I consider the Glass Bead Game itself in a state of crisis. The purpose of this memorandum is to convince the Board that the crisis exists.

(p. 323)

It fails. The Board's response is to comment on the fascinating nature of his warnings, to thank him for his overanxious love, but to reaffirm that their position 'must be one of patient waiting to see what comes' (remember the 'I see no ships syndrome' in Chapter 4). In fact all his warning does is stir up resentment: 'One Board colleague raised his voice to ask whether it might not be described as dangerous, if not outrageous . . . for a Magister to alarm his Board by such images of allegedly imminent perils and tribulations'.

Knecht leaves Castalia a broken man, and dies shortly afterwards in a tragic drowning incident (trying unsuccessfully to recapture his youth). As might be expected his predictions come true. Castalia continues its decline and finally ceases to exist. Hesse describes the end of Castalia and its Glass Bead Game in a poignant poem, which is, in effect, an ode to the death of culture.

The Last Glass Bead Game Player

The coloured beads, his playthings, in his hand,
He sits head bent; around him lies a land
Laid waste by war and ravaged by disease.
Growing on rubble, ivy hums with bees;
A weary peace with muted psalmody
Sounds in a world of aged tranquility . . .
All, all are gone, and the temples, libraries,
And schools of Castalia are no more. At rest
Amid the ruins, the glass beads in his hand,
Those hieroglyphs once so significant
That now are only coloured bits of glass,
He lets them roll until their force is spent
And silently they vanish in the sand.

The parallels with Sorokin's description of the death of culture in the academic literature are unmistakable: 'Finally, weary, reluctant, cold, Culture loses its desire to be, and wishes itself out of the overlong daylight and back into the darkness of proto-mysticism, in the grave. It reverts in Danislevsky's terms to "mere ethnographic material" – historyless and formless' (1966: 189).

Castalia is a monument to the mortality of all forms of life. It shows that any attempt to maintain the existing collection of cultural forms as a timeless and permanent canon will result in failure (Oakes, 1980: 46). The fatal mistake its people made was to be seduced by their success into pursuing strategies of order when they should have been pursuing strategies of change. Castalian organizations take note!

7 Towards an integrated strategy for cultural change

Previous chapters have examined the different types of cultural change strategy in some depth. It is now time to begin our ascent back to the surface and take stock of where we have been. Along with this need for review there is also the issue of integration. I should therefore like to go just one step further before ending this part of the book and bring 'developmental' and 'transformational' strategies together into a single conceptual framework for cultural change. This will enable us to identify a number of key factors that need to be taken into account in the design of a comprehensive strategy for cultural change, and will provide guidelines on which type of strategy to use where, and when to switch from one to the other.

Overview

The important thing for anyone working in the area of cultural change is to follow the precepts of the 'both–and' philosophy and think in terms of order and change, development and transformation. Organizational life calls for a judicious mix of both. When this is missing it may lead to a Castalian tragedy – perhaps not organizational death, but certainly decline.

Organizations need both kinds of strategies because each fulfils an essentially different function at a different point in the cultural development cycle. *The skill is linking the strategy to the stage the cultural development cycle has reached.* In matters of cultural change, there is, as the saying goes, a time and a place for everything. Unfortunately, mistakes are extremely common, and people are frequently found pursuing strategies of order when they should be pursuing strategies of change – and vice versa. This is the kind of thing that the both–and strategy is seeking to avoid.

The 'both–and' idea can be applied in two senses:

In a cross-sectional way – across the organization

As I have insisted throughout, culture is not a homogeneous phenomenon. Indeed, one can go further than this and say that the notion of *an* organization culture, implying a single, unified entity, is pure myth. This myth, peddled for all its worth by many of the popular business books, has had the unfortunate effect of concealing the pluralism that is so characteristic of organization cultures. Perhaps it was Vico (1668–1744) who came closest to the real nature of culture when he described it as 'atomic entities of thought . . . each being logically an island, distinct or separate from other similar systems of interconnected atoms' (Berlin, 1980: 11). Not far behind comes Geertz with his 'octopus' metaphor for culture – the loosely coordinated creature described in an earlier chapter – and running neck and neck with him is Peckham, with his definition of culture as 'a loose package of diversities – an incoherence – not a structured system of compatible entities' (1976: 267).

My own contribution to this conception of culture as a plurality of heterogeneous mentalities is the notion of separate and overlapping 'isms' or habits of thought, circles or bubbles of culture floating alongside each other, sometimes colliding and bouncing off each other, and sometimes amalgamating into bigger bubbles; some of them virtuously taking the organization skywards, and some of them viciously dragging it down.

Whichever metaphor you prefer, it is always 'culture' in the plural, never in the singular. Thus, if at any time you were to stop the clock and examine organizational culture, you would find a whole range of mentalities, all of them different and all of them at different stages in their development. Some would be virtuous, while others would be vicious; some would be exploding, others imploding. This is where 'both–and' comes in: the managers of change need a portfolio of strategies to help them cope with this complex state of affairs. They must find ways of 'developing' some 'isms' while at the same time 'transforming' others, simultaneously employing both types of strategy in different areas of culture. This may sound difficult – and is – but is no more than the situation demands.

The idea of changing the 'whole' organization culture must be abandoned. Such an ambition is both silly and misguided – rather like turning in your car every time one of its parts develops a fault. In any case, as I said in the very first chapter, you cannot just 'turn in' your culture for a new one, even if you wanted to. Things are not as simple as that.

In a longitudinal way – over time

When we view culture 'over' time as opposed to 'across' time (as above), we see that it is not a static entity but an organic process. Each constituent mentality has a cycle of growth and decline which takes it through stages similar to those in the human life cycle – childhood, youth, maturity and old age (Spengler preferred the four 'seasons' of culture – spring, summer, autumn and winter, which is certainly in keeping with our earlier metaphor of 'cultivating' cultural change). Looking down the time tube we become aware of the need for a strategic process that uses both types of cultural strategy, the development one during the maturation period, while the form is still young and growing, and the transformational one later on when that form has begun to age and decline. Both–and in this sense therefore means that both types of strategy have a place next to each other in the cultural development cycle, where they can perform complementary functions.

One important difference between the life cycle of culture and that of the human body is that a culture's 'time-clock' is completely elastic. Apart from the fact that it has a beginning, a rise, a fall and an end, everything else about it is unpredictable – shape, trajectory and duration. These are subject to infinite variation, and any sub-state within the cycle may last from as little as a few months to an entire human lifetime. In some cases the cycle will be short, in others drawn out. Some cultures will make a come-and-go appearance and others will span years, even centuries. Some will burst on to the scene with a great clamour and others will creep in unnoticed.

This difference is crucial. Cultures are not physical entities. They are complex social phenomena produced interactively not biologically. They are a human product not a natural product. People create them, people sustain them and people change them. There is absolutely nothing about them that cannot be changed by human intervention. Indeed there is nothing more to them than human intervention.

The question 'can culture be changed?', endlessly debated in the literature, is therefore rather a futile one. Of course culture can be changed, in fact it is being changed all the time – continually at a first order level and periodically at a second order level. Cultural change is a natural by-product of human interaction and does not need to be planned in order to occur because it will occur anyway. Therefore the question we should be asking is not 'can culture be changed?' but 'is cultural change manageable?' This is the crux of the matter because it addresses the practical issue of whether it is possible for a person or persons to change a culture by intelligent will, by intervening deliberately and purposefully in the cultural cycle and changing its path of development and the nature and duration of its various phases. Obviously my answer to the question has to be of course it is possible, otherwise what would be the point in writing a book about strategies for cultural change? But it has to be said that on the whole this is not happening in organizations today – their cultures are changing, but not in a managed way. A major reason for the present state of affairs is that two vital elements have always been missing: an understanding of the cultural process that is to be managed and a model for intervening in that process. I shall now seek to rectify these omissions.

The specifics

A comprehensive strategy for cultural change needs to take account of the following:

1 The culture to be changed (the structural dimension)
2 Its origins and trajectory through time (the spatial and temporal dimension).
3 The life cycle of culture and the stage in the cycle the organization has reached (the processual dimension).
4 The environmental context within which the culture is situated and embedded (the contextual dimension).
5 The aims and ambitions of the parties involved (the subjective dimension).

Let us examine each of these factors in turn.

Gaining an appreciation of the culture to be changed

As Wilkins and Dyer (1988: 522) have pointed out, the flaw in cultural change programmes is frequently that they fail to take into account the nature of the culture to be changed. It is as though the process of cultural change is independent of the kind of culture that is changing. The simple rule for avoiding this is first get to know your culture and only then decide what it is you wish to change and how you are going to change it; in other words ensure that a proper cultural diagnosis is carried out before proceeding with the intervention. This is only practising what Organization Development (OD) has preached for years – that if you want to know where you want to be, begin by finding out where you are. The academic point is that any model of change needs a theory of order; only by finding how the present order is put together (i.e. structured), and why it persists, can we discover how to change it.

As we have asserted elsewhere (Brooks and Bate, 1992: 36), change attempts tend to be strong on prescription but lamentably weak on diagnosis, especially in cultural matters. Comments about the culture to be changed are often clichéd and superficial, revealing little actual research and little appreciation of its internal 'atomic' structure. To make matters worse it has not been thought necessary to understand the process of cultural change either. Here I very much agree with Hennestad (1991) who has claimed that most cultural change goes on 'behind the backs' of the actors, in a manner largely unrecognized by them, and often in spite of rather than because of a rhetoric and a formal programme that claims to be 'managing' cultural change.

It is essential to have a comprehensive understanding of the phenomena that need changing and the change process itself. In many ways this is standard OD. For example, W. W. Burke (1987: 73) defines OD as 'a process of bringing to the surface, that is, to the conscious awareness of the members of an organization, those implicit behavioural patterns that are helping and hindering development'. This nearly fits the requirements of a cultural change programme – but not quite. While the broad aim is the same (awareness), the focus of attention is different, cultural change being concerned not so much with visible 'behavioural patterns' as with invisible thinking patterns (Chapter 2).

The search for cultural understanding is not a one-off event, carried out at the beginning of the programme, but something that is ongoing and part of a continuous process of learning and discovery. In any kind of search it is essential to know what you are searching for. A recap might therefore be in order: the phenomena in which we are interested go by a variety of names – frames, cognitive maps, schema, tacit premises, cultural themes, forms and formats, *Weltanschauung* (world views), doctrines, dogmas, ethos, creeds, conventions, orientations, semantic systems, orthodoxies, *Gestalts*, mental domains, paradigms, protocols, and – of course – 'isms'! People must choose the labels they feel most comfortable with and which have most meaning for them. BR chose the phrase 'bad habits of thinking'. Other organizations where I have worked have chosen 'ologies', 'drivers', and 'corporate mind sets'.

Because these exist at both the organizational and sub-organizational level (occupation, profession, work group etc.), what one finds depends very much upon where one is looking, and the size of territory within which the search is taking place (the unit of analysis). Another point is that although this book has tended to concentrate on dysfunctional 'isms', a proper diagnosis would include functional ones as well – strengths as well as weaknesses. For example, when BR began to face up to the bad news it found there was good news, too: positive 'isms' like 'railway patriotism' (loyalty, dedication), intellectualism (pride in knowing and finding out, and using abstract reasoning), and liberalism (open-mindedness), all of them major sources of corporate strength. Cultural strategies cannot afford to be only problem-centred. They must be opportunity-centred as well, and this means dealing with the positives as well as the negatives.

As we can see, this first aspect of the strategic model is diagnostic. But it is not just this. It is also conceptual. One is not merely collecting data about 'the culture' but also learning to 'think culturally' and to use the language of culture (see Chapters 1 and 2). Culture is not an object but a perspective. The challenge is to see the organization from a cultural viewpoint, to reconstruct it culturally.

In order for this to happen one needs a language and some basic labels. Take the case of BR again: with the help of the 'isms' we were able to get the process of thinking culturally underway. Labelling is an indispensable part of perception and interpretation. It is the first principle of language (people may remember that in Chapter 1 I was likening the development of strategy to the acquisition of a new language), and is essential to all forms of discourse and communication (Miller and Johnson-Laird, 1976: 222). Before people can change a culture, they must first be able to think about it within their own minds and then be able to talk about it with others. They need a set of labelling routines for cultural phenomena. Labelling is a skill: finding a word that serves as a catalyst for some kind of inner cultural form or semantic unity is by no means a straightforward business. The label of the 'ism' proved highly effective, for it fostered the participants' awareness of the more problematic aspects of the organizational culture and enabled the managers to go on to construct a more sophisticated language for interpreting the reality culturally.

Labels not only capture reality, they also recreate it in a different form. For example, when the managers at BR began to take up these labels and incorporate them into their everyday discourse, something important happened. Reality itself began to change. No longer were the labels being 'fitted' to the reality of BR, now BR was being fitted to them – the organization was becoming its labels. Life was beginning to imitate art! The stress is very much on the word 'art': this first set of activities is more than just a 'scientific' fact-finding, descriptive exercise. It is also a creative artistic process which aims to produce a new representation of organizational reality for the members.

Establishing the origins and trajectory of organization culture (cultural archaeology and the architecture of culture)

Managers do not on the whole tend to be historically minded. Theirs is a language and outlook that prefers forward-looking concepts to backward-looking ones, hence the almost insatiable demand for words like 'vision', 'forecasts' and 'plans'. The culture perspective chooses to look the other way, putting the past back onto the agenda and giving it the weight that conventional strategic models lack. There is nothing nostalgic or sentimental about this, merely the conviction that present and future only become meaningful when they are set in the context of their past. Despite the separate labels we give to them, past, present and future are not discreet entities but interconnected phases of the same continuous temporal process. The task is to see that process as a complete and organic whole and to get a picture of the architecture of that whole.

The difference between this and the first cluster of activities is that the first was 'snapshot' diagnosis whereas this is longitudinal or 'telescopic' diagnosis – thinking culturally over or through time. Why do we need this? My belief is that any theory of change needs a theory of changing, by which I mean an understanding not only of how cultures are structured but also of how they change and develop – their process. Part of this understanding involves playing the role of cultural archivist and searching for the source of an organization's characteristic ways of thinking: there is much to be discovered about the child from an examination of its parents and relations!

Another task is to gain an appreciation of the 'architecture' of culture, and this too involves taking the long view. By doing this we become aware of the fact that the present culture is part of a much bigger historical pattern or architectonic unity, a *recurrence* rather than just an occurrence. It never stands alone but is part of a series – a series of displacements or mutations of earlier cultural forms (Foucault, 1972). Much of organizational life is repetition (though never exact repetition) of the past. What we may have believed to be a new or original idea turns out not to be new at all. For example, BR's 'business-led' culture of the 1980s was heralded as brand new thinking, but historical analysis revealed that many attempts had been made in the past to make the railways more 'business-led', and that this situation was repeating itself yet again. Even the rhetoric of change had been similar on these previous occasions. It was historical analysis that also revealed how regularly major reorganizations had occurred, and how obsessed people in BR had always been about structure and structural matters.

But so what? Is there really any advantage in knowing this? I believe that 'thinking historically' serves a variety of useful purposes: it provides an effective safeguard against corporate amnesia (and the associated problems of repeating the same mistakes or endlessly re-inventing the wheel) and provides invaluable learning from past experiences. It helps people to become aware of the vicious circles in which their thinking may be trapped (see Chapter 4). It also leads them to a different awareness of their present, which in turn leads them to ask different questions about their future: 'Why this, and why now?', 'How did we come to this?',

'Have we done anything like this before?', 'Why are we doing it again?', 'What became of it last time and will the same thing happen again?'.

Again traditional OD would have no difficulty assimilating this perspective, indeed it has always claimed that 'to diagnose is to identify the underlying forces and conditions which give rise to the present state of affairs' (French et al., 1983: 120) – and this must surely include historical forces. This needs to be made more explicit, however. For example, the popular 'present state/desired state' model would benefit from the inclusion of an historical element, so that a third question – Where have we been? – would precede the usual two: Where are we now, and Where do we want to be?

Thinking historically has a powerful existential element. It makes us aware of the ghosts of our past that are all around us, haunting us, meddling with the present and constantly threatening to control our thinking and action. As Henrik Ibsen once wrote:

> I'm coming to believe that all of us are ghosts . . .
> It's not just what we inherit from our mothers and
> fathers. It's also the shadows of dead ideas and opinions
> and convictions. They're no longer alive, but they grip
> us all the same, and hold on to us against our will. (*Ghosts*, Act 2)

This leads us to the realization that one of the important elements in managing change is freeing ourselves from these spirits and finding a way of respectfully laying them to rest.

Designing a strategy to fit the development cycle of culture

Cultures inevitably change in a routine, continuous manner. The question is therefore not whether they change but how they change. A sound understanding of the natural cultural change process is an essential part of any strategic framework; as far as this particular model is concerned, going in blind is not an option. This is easier said than done: we still have only a rudimentary knowledge of the cultural process and few writings that consider the topic with specific regard to organizations. The following comments are regrettably rather basic but should give some idea of what a 'process-sensitive' strategy for cultural change looks like.

The first thing to be said is that there is nothing especially unique about organizations so far as cultural change is concerned. Organization cultures develop in much the same way as cultures in every other area of social life – art, music, politics and so on. It is not that the organizational cultural process is *like* these processes: it is essentially the *same* process. What I am presenting here is a Theory of Culture as distinct from a theory of organization culture, a theory which postulates that cultural phenomena are cultural phenomena wherever they occur and in whatever form. From the vantage point of this wider theory it is more significant that organizational cultural processes are cultural than that they are organizational.

In every area of life, including organizations, cultures seem to have the same characteristic mode of development: the passage of time sees a succession of overlapping but discontinuous 'movements' – other words one might use are phases, orientations, ways of life, genres, schools of thought, epochs, generations, eras or periods. Call them what you will. In fact all of these terms have been used at one time or another in the social sciences. Each gathering movement is a separate cultural form with its own 'life career' (Sorokin, 1966) stretching from birth to death. Within each form there is immanent change: an unfolding of the potentialities of the system, the first order developmental change discussed earlier, what Kluckhohn (1963: 234) called pattern elaboration of same values or, more simply, intracultural variation. Though the main direction and the main phases of this unfolding process are predetermined by the inner forces of the system, there remains a considerable margin for variation and human intervention. At some point the 'power' of the system reaches its peak, and thereafter declines. The virtuous circle turns into a vicious circle.

Cultural life is perpetually in flux, constantly creating new energies and forces that cannot be contained within existing forms. Hence the evolutionary cycle is frequently interrupted by fundamental second order change, leading to the emergence of new movements or forms. For a while new and old run abreast of each other until finally one of them runs out of steam and drops out of the race. The new leaders become the front runners for a while before they, too, are challenged by younger, fresher contenders. And so the process goes on, a succession of first order and second order changes, a continuous transition punctuated by transformation, one form taking over from another. The new forms come and the old forms go but the process goes on for ever. No two races are ever the same. Change is never quite one or the other, first order or second order, Darwinian or Catastrophic, evolutionary or revolutionary, continuous or discontinuous, but a succession of all these things, a variety of orders and scales of change strung out along a zig-zagging, unbroken line.

The culture of art offers a good illustration of the process I am describing. In the chart shown in Figure 7.1, which summarizes the main art movements of the nineteenth and twentieth centuries, we can see most of the features of cultural change that have just been mentioned: the succession of separate but overlapping movements, the variable life spans of each (periods of continuous first order growth), and the breaks between them (discontinuous second order change). The chart also shows the variations in the degree of cultural pluralism in the system at any one time, ranging from periods when there were a number of movements (e.g. 1885–95) to periods when there was only one (1860–80). The labels below the chart are probably its most interesting feature. They reveal that the movements in question are none other than our old friends the 'isms'!

A chart showing the evolution of classical music would display similar features. The various movements would include classicism, romanticism, emotionalism, nationalism, modernism, symbolism and impressionism, chromaticism, serialism, dodecaphonism etc. Cultural charts for organizations must also look something like this, each showing different 'isms' and each 'ism' capable of being broken down into more 'isms' (circles within circles). An investigation across the whole spectrum of social life would reveal that cultural change always follows the same pattern: a progression of first order transitions ('development') punctuated by second order transformations ('change') of established forms – 'isms' if you prefer.

The problem with charts like the one opposite is that they are flat and two-dimensional and give no indication of the dynamism within cultural processes. To see this we need to picture cultural life in a different way, and depict change in terms of waves of culture. First there is the sea itself: the sea of life – reality – a vast, threatening and unfathomable entity. It represents all that is available, the raw material of life. The sea of life is a qualitatively as well as quantitatively infinite manifold of indistinguishable phenomena – as such it is unintelligible because it is a continuous, homogeneous and undifferentiated process. If this is the character of life, we need a sense-making instrument, a model or form for perceiving and organizing this watery world. Cultural forms are the waves thrown up from this sea, 'forms from the formless' Spengler called them. These social creations put features onto the flat and infinite expanse, giving it shape and the necessary contrasts to allow some sense of its meaning and significance to be grasped. Cultural forms are reconstitutions and synthesizations of the raw material of life, each one representing the human endeavour to express something about life and, in so doing, making that life more intelligible and meaningful.

The 'waves' analogy highlights some important features of the cultural process, all of which have important implications for strategic thinking:

- Its irregularity and unpredictability.
- Its energy and momentum.
- Its turbulence.

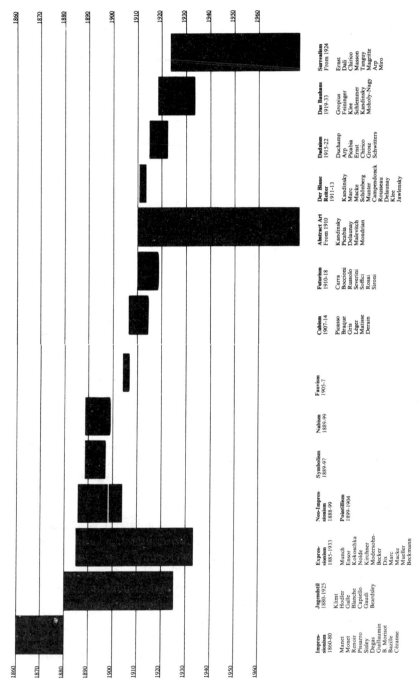

Figure 7.1 The principal pictorial movements. (Source: Schaeffner, C. (1969) *History of Art, Impressionism*. Editio-Service S.A., Switzerland)

Irregularity and unpredictability

In the ever-moving world of organizational culture we can never predict when and where a new wave will appear, whether it will be tall, small, long or short, what its effect will be, or how long it will last before returning to the sea. Some waves (e.g. fashions and fads) are very short-lived, barely rising before they sink back into the depths, while others, the 'rollers', possess all the power and energy to carry the organization along for considerable distances (e.g. some of BR's 'isms', and the 1980s 'total quality' and 'customer-driven' movements). Then there is the tidal wave, once a rare event but now occurring with increasing frequency in the stormy waters of mergers and acquisitions, a phenomenon that can cause considerable damage to anyone and anything in its path. No two waves are ever the same.

Given this type of environment, it is easy to see why planning-based models of strategy and change – the models that have guided our thinking for more than a century – have only limited use in the area of culture. The issue here is not whether planning (especially long-range planning) is a good or bad thing but that in a cultural environment as unpredictable and uncertain as this it simply does not have a role. This is an uncomfortable thought. In the search for an alternative we can, however, take some solace from the conceptual models traditionally used by the master mariners: they know where they are starting from and where they want to get to (and they usually succeed in getting there), but have little idea of the sea conditions they will encounter on their journey. Their logic is why have a plan for events you cannot plan for? Much better to wait and see, being prepared for all eventualities, while at the same time keeping open all the options for action and making use of every opportunity that arises. The strength of this approach is that it is actual rather than hypothetical, based on what 'is', not what 'might be'. It also incorporates the notion of incremental learning: finding out as much as you can as you go along and making corrections or adjustments in the light of this knowledge.

The main advantage of such a strategy is that it does not waste time trying to plan for the unplannable. It is truly interactive with its environment, being constantly 'on the spot' and 'of the moment'. If the weather is fair and you are making good headway it simply says keep going (the equivalent of first order strategies), but if an obstacle appears, the weather changes or you find you are going round in circles, you then need to change direction (second order).

In recent years there has been a growing awareness of the need to find alternatives to traditional planning models of strategic management, and this has resulted in a movement away from rational, linear or synoptic models of strategic decision-making (based on concepts of planning, procedures, systematic analyses and reason-based decisions) towards a conception of strategy as a relatively unstructured, highly iterative, socio-political process (Johnson, 1990: 184). This alternative conception is ideally suited to the world of culture and the high levels of unpredictability one finds within it. Indeed, one might even go so far as to suggest that a 'strategy for the unpredictable' is one of the most important, if not *the* most important, tasks in managing cultural change. It basically involves finding ways of working effectively in unpredictable environments rather than engaging in futile attempts to make them less unpredictable. Nicoll makes this point nicely:

> Our task, like that of the early sailor learning the rhythms of an ocean's winds and tides, is to discover enough to ride unpredictable forces respectfully toward a distant, yet desirable shore.   (Nicoll, 1984:169)

The Polynesian islanders are a perfect role model in this regard. Their particular methods of 'noninstrumental navigation' enable them to sail huge distances without the use of compass, sextant or charts. Their achievement has been to dispose of the encumbrances of scientific rationalism and still be capable of finding their way with pinpoint accuracy. While there is always the tendency among Western observers to regard such 'folk' methods as primitive and inferior to 'expert' techniques, research has shown that this is not necessarily the case. For example, from his study of the islanders Hutchins (1983: 223) concluded that their methods were highly advanced and in some ways superior to ours: 'The Micronesian technique is elegant and effective. It is organized in a way that allows the navigator to solve in his head problems that a Western navigator would not attempt without substantial technological supports.'

The Polynesian islanders discovered long ago how to ride the 'unpredictable forces towards the distant shore'. Modern strategy researchers are only now beginning to discover that this is one of the most important qualities of any model. Cultural change strategists in particular need to take note. Improbable though it may seem, their world and the world of the Polynesian sailor have a good deal in common.

The axiom for today's cultural change managers should be: Don't plan but be prepared. People who make rigid plans are all too often the ones who are the least adequately prepared!

Energy and momentum

Once created, waves are carried along by their own momentum. Organization cultures are the same. As they move they acquire an impetus which sustains the established organizational direction and resists any attempts to change that direction, even when the environment threatens that wave with extinction (Miller and Friesen, 1980: 591) –

Castalia being a case in point. The problem, however, is that if like poor Knecht (and Canute for that matter) you stand in the way of these waves and try to stop them, you are likely to end up getting knocked over and drowned.

Standing in the way of unstoppable cultural waves is not a sensible option. However, this does not mean that you are obliged to sit back and do nothing. Change strategists have a number of options open to them: it may well be that the current waves are in fact going in your direction (i.e. they have a 'virtuous' or 'functional' momentum), in which case the obvious thing to do is to surf or ride the waves, using the power within them to carry you to your destination (hangliders – and as far as I know surf-riders – call it 'following the energy'). Of course, this is only a feasible option if you want first order change.

If this is not the case, and the momentum is 'vicious' or 'dysfunctional', there are three further options to choose from: (a) try to deflect the waves, using their own momentum to do it (reframing strategies); (b) wait for the powerful waves to subside and then create your own waves ('new wave' strategies: since momentum is a variable – low to begin with, high in the middle and low at the end – the thing to do is wait until the third phase when it has begun to burn itself out); (c) wait for another wave that is going in your chosen direction and hitch a ride on that one (opportunistic strategies).

Whatever the chosen option, the issue of momentum, and the closely related issue of energy, must be central considerations in the formulation of strategies for cultural change. The main task will be to decide where the desired momentum for change is to come from (or how momentum in undesired directions is to be handled), and how the social process associated with this is to be managed. The stress is very much on 'social process': momentum is created and sustained by people acting collectively, not, despite the popular belief, by individuals acting on their own. Leaders must recognize that by themselves, no matter what their level of seniority, they cannot 'create', 'maintain' or 'change' the momentum of a culture.

Culture is a 'collective enterprise', socially created, socially owned, socially sustained and socially changed. The change manager's role is to formulate strategies for influencing and managing that social process, not to try to provide some kind of substitute for it. In matters of culture and cultural change, the strategic process is very much a social process, one in which debate, interaction, involvement and participation are not so much luxuries – or ideological imperatives for that matter – as basic necessities.

To summarize: one is intervening in an energy system, energy being a property of the system not the 'changer'. A strategy for cultural change does not create anything but rather exploits the latent or dormant potential within that system. The system in question is a social process.

The purpose of the strategy is to help in the cultivation and management of that process, and to provide it with the necessary momentum to produce the desired change.

Turbulence

This section focuses on another important strategic element: the politics of culture.

In any waters you must expect turbulence. The sea of culture is no exception. This sea is never at rest; Simmel, for one, has talked about the 'perpetual dynamism' within the cultural process:

> By the time one cultural form has fully developed, the next is already beginning to take shape beneath it.   (Quoted in Lawrence, 1976: 224)

The sea is a turmoil of competing systems of meaning. There are always strains and conflicts as different cultural forms – and the champions of those forms – fight for the same social space, always looking for the opportunity to undermine the others and achieve some kind of supremacy, no matter how precarious or temporary that may be (refer back to Chapter 3 for a fuller discussion of cultural pluralism). As Dyer says, conflict is an integral part of the process of cultural change. This is because of one very simple fact: cultural change processes are political processes, and as we know wherever there are politics there is conflict. Simple and obvious though it may be, this point is still frequently overlooked by the designers of a culture:

> the change process is fraught with conflict – managers are fired, employees quit, struggles for power are common. Such conflicts are largely neglected by those who suggest that culture change can be planned. Human beings are (wrongly) perceived as being fairly malleable in learning and adopting new perspectives, values and assumptions by those who see planned culture change as possible.   (Dyer, 1985: 224)

The struggle in question is essentially one between the proponents of the 'old' and the 'new', a scenario that is acted out daily – sometimes discreetly, sometimes very publicly – in just about every arena of cultural life. The former are the elders, those who claim timeless validity for their way of life and struggle to maintain this by pursuing defensive, stability-orientated strategies. The latter are the champions of change, the young turks, disrespectful of authority and indifferent about history, hell-bent on the pursuit of offensive strategies that will bring down the old regime and effect a second order change. Their goal is to be the new party of government in cultural matters – to put their 'idea' into power and to make it the dominant culture.

This struggle is the whole essence of cultural change. As Sorokin (1966: 324) put it, 'cultural change is the unfolding of a prototype of culture and its struggle against its predecessors'. Dyer also talks about the struggle between the proponents of old and new cultures, particularly where, as it often does, it follows a change of leadership. He tells what happens to the losers:

> After the introduction of new leadership, a period of conflict ensues between the proponents of the new culture and the old guard, who were either part of or supported the values and assumptions of the previous leadership. These conflicts may be short-lived . . . where the old leadership [is] deposed quickly by new management, or they may last for many years . . . The losers in such conflicts feel great resentment toward the new leaders and their values, and therefore they generally are not reeducated to the new beliefs. Most are quickly purged or leave voluntarily.   (1985: 217)

British Rail is a good example of this contested cultural terrain. During the 1980s culture and counter-culture fought it out as the old guard in 'Production' clashed head-on with the young turks in the 'Sectors', each parading before the other ideologies and styles of thought which they knew to be provocative and unacceptable. The one side valued service ('value for money'\the social railway), the other side profit ('money for value'\the commercial railway). These were life issues, issues on which no inch of ground could be conceded. As one participant put it – a sector manager in fact – 'there is a clash between those who seek professional management and those who see railways as a quasi-religion – something to which normal commercial disciplines shouldn't or couldn't apply.'

Dent (1990), who was also doing research in BR at this time, has provided an interesting analysis of the cultural struggle that was taking place. In the following extract, he talks about the 'symbolic contests' between the business directors (sectors) and those responsible for production. He also touches on the issue of momentum:

> Ideas evolved in stages. The Business Directors used the bureaucratic structure of the organization to secure changes in formal structures and systems. In parallel, they staged symbolic contests concerning the management of increasingly concrete aspects of railways affairs. As these events unfolded through time, the Business Directors created a momentum behind the 'business' culture. Through this sequence of symbolic contests, they redefined accepted criteria for action.   (1990: 20)

In British Rail the old guard were ultimately the losers. Within five years of the introduction of sector managers and the 'business-led' culture, every one of the old regional general managers in production had moved jobs (in most cases not by choice) or had left the railways, and the responsibility for production had been handed over to the business directors. This scenario is not untypical of what often happens: an ageing and flagging force is no match for a 'young' idea with optimism and surplus vitality on its side. However, as we shall see, things do not always happen in this way. Youth does not always win.

Rarely is it a simple two-way fight between the dominant culture and the counter-culture. Usually it is 'counter-cultures' in the plural: a multitude of rival factions fight amongst themselves for the right to 'get a crack' at the champion (the dominant culture) and knock him off his perch. Many eliminating rounds take place between up and coming ideologies before the actual final. In BR, for example, there were marketeers, financial planners, accountants, engineers and personnel specialists, all of them offering up visions of the future for others to try to knock down!

These contests and ideological power struggles hold the key to our understanding of the process of cultural change. To be more precise, we can say that the nature, magnitude and direction of cultural change is the product of the way the political-ideational forces resolve themselves – the 'resultant' of the 'vector' forces. By studying these forces and gaining a degree of familiarity with them the strategist can get a rough idea of the way the change process will unfold and where it is likely to end up. As already stated, the outcomes of such complex processes are impossible to predict with any degree of accuracy, but accuracy is not the issue here. The stress should be on scenario development rather than the specifics of what might or might not happen. All one is looking for is the ability to say that this particular scenario is more likely to occur than that one, and therefore that one should be thinking of doing this rather than that.

It may be helpful to conclude this part of the discussion with a brief description of some of the typical scenarios one is likely to encounter.

Absorption/Incorporation

The contest between the 'new' and the 'old' results in a win for the old. The revolution is put down and normality is restored once more. What may have begun as a radical, second order idea ends up having only first order impact – more an alteration than an alternative to the existing organization culture. This scenario is a reminder that the 'young' do not always win. In fact, according to Peters and Waterman (1982: 3), they rarely win:

> When we reorganize we usually stop at reorganizing the boxes on the chart. The odds are high that nothing much will change. We will have chaos, even useful chaos for a while, but eventually the old culture will prevail. Old habits persist.

One label for this scenario might be the 'Tianenmen Square' outcome.

Replacement/Succession

This was the ultimate outcome of the BR example described above: despite spirited resistance from the production side of the organization the business directors eventually gained the ascendancy for their culture. A label for this scenario might be the 'Eastern European' outcome: old regimes are overthrown and new regimes take their place. Symbols of the old regime are removed; statues are ignominiously torn down and the photographs and slogans of the old regime defaced and burned. Once powerful 'isms', like communism, are consigned to the cemetery of history. A genuine cultural transformation has occurred (Chapter 4), although true to the vision of Orwell's *Animal Farm* there is absolutely nothing to prevent the new culture reverting to the same practices as the old, and the pigs turning into humans!

Parallelism

The new culture comes in and establishes itself but the old culture refuses to lie down and die. The two cultures end up locked in a matrix of competing or contradictory outlooks, with neither side possessing sufficient critical mass decisively to dispose of the other. Situations like this are quite common and can last for considerable periods of time: for example, in music cultural movements like nationalism, modernism and impressionism managed to live together for many years; so too did various cultures in Yugoslavia until recently. However, matrix cultures, like matrix structures in organizations, are inherently unstable and tend eventually to collapse, leaving one culture dominant.

This scenario therefore usually resolves itself into one of the others described. This happened at BR: for five years the 'production' and 'business' cultures lived alongside each other before the latter finally won the day. This outcome would have been impossible to predict; for most of the time support for the competing ideologies was so evenly balanced that things could have gone either way. The BR example also illustrates how this matrix option can sometimes be used as a transitional phase, in which a new culture is eased in gently rather than forced in, thereby reducing the risk of rejection.

Collapse

In this scenario both cultures, the new and the old, end up the losers. The old has gone into terminal decline but the new has not been able to gain a secure enough foothold to claim rightful succession. The result is a cultural vacuum, in which organization mission, identity and purpose remain uncomfortably vague and indeterminate. Hennestad (1991: 177) and others have talked about this as the 'betwixt and between' period in an organization's cultural life, a period of great tension in which people know they cannot go back but do not know how to go forward. The organization may well end up collapsing because of this. Alternatively, the crisis might have the opposite effect, with the surge of activity so often born of desperation giving it a new lease of life.

The irregularity, momentum and turbulence associated with cultural processes are all important considerations in the framing of a strategy for changing those processes. All three features are present in the concept of a 'sea of culture'. Irregularity is represented by uneven wave shapes, the change of momentum by the rise and fall of the waves, and turbulence by the overlapping of the waves (Figure 7.2). Each wave outline represents the 'form' that a cultural movement acquires over time. Everything within that wave form is first order change, the implication being that a form can develop itself but not transform itself – 'evolution' of a form never leads directly to second order change; in fact spiralling evolutionary forces tend to take it further and further away from this. New forms – the result of second order change – are created outside of and separately from the old ones (though overlapping in time, and often precipitated by a limitation or crisis within the old) and develop according to their own immanent and self-sufficient logic. All waves or movements acquire their own distinctive shape, but their cycles always possess the same essential features of birth, growth, decline and death.

Let us now take a close-up look at a typical wave (Figure 7.3) and see where the two main types of strategy we have been discussing – the developmental and the transformational – fit into its contours.

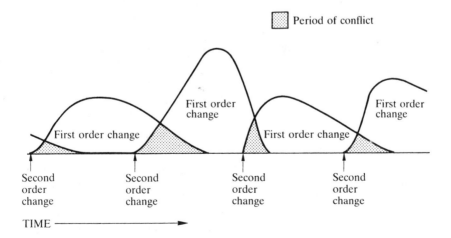

Figure 7.2   The moving waves of culture

First, it is necessary to say a brief word about the vertical axis: there were many possible labels to choose from, each slightly different from the others – momentum, weight, strength, vibrancy, impact, or significance. Any of these would do. However, the term I prefer is resilience, which I would define as the amount of 'life' or 'spring' in the cultural movement. Thus a high-resilience culture would be one that is still nimble and light of limb, whereas a low-resilience culture is a hardening, ossifying, rigidifying or stagnating culture, one that has little energy or spring left in its feet to drive it forward.

The figure is largely self-explanatory, but it might be helpful to point out some of its main features. The wave or cycle is divided by a vertical line passing through its apex. This line marks the point at which the resilience of the existing culture peaks and thereafter begins to decrease. Left of the line is the period of growth and right is the period of decline. Up until this point the cycle has been virtuous, functional and 'adaptive', but from now on it starts to become vicious, dysfunctional and 'maladaptive'.

The requisite type of strategy for the first period is a strategy for cultural development (Chapter 3), which is opportunity-centred and dedicated to the exploitation of the existing potential within the cultural

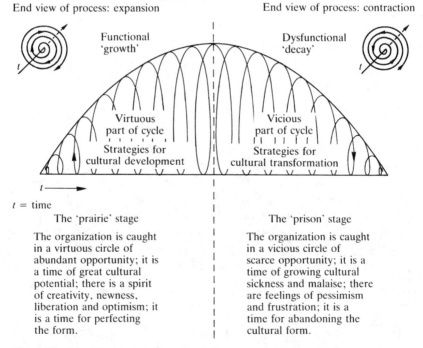

Figure 7.3 Selecting a strategy for cultural change

form. As the organization moves into the second period this type of strategy gradually becomes irrelevant and inappropriate. What becomes increasingly necessary is a strategy for cultural transformation (Chapter 4), one that will halt the decline by terminating the old directional orientation and giving it a new one.

Figure 7.4 provides additional details about the characteristics of the requisite type of strategy and the wide range of variants of each strategy that may be employed during the period in question.

Let us now consider how all this can be of help to culture strategists. There are three things that must be attended to when framing a strategy for cultural change:

First, find out where you are in the cycle (with regard to each of the organization's dominant cultural mentalities) and establish as best you can whether or not the appropriate\best\most 'process contingent' strategy is being applied. There is of course no suggestion here that you will ever have literally to draw the cycle as I have done! Nor should you expect to be able to pinpoint your position in the cycle with any accuracy. This is essentially a thinking exercise, not a test in trigonometry. Figures 7.2, 7.3 and 7.4 are heuristics; their purpose is to stimulate reflection, debate and discussion about the present 'culture in use', and help you to establish the scale, type and location of any cultural change that is required.

Secondly, identify how close each aspect of your organization culture is to the 'threshold' where a strategic shift from first order to second order change will become necessary. If you cannot plan a change (especially a second order change) you can at least anticipate it and take certain steps to prepare for it. Then you will not get caught trying to take remedial action when it is probably too late to do so. One purpose of this heuristic is to remind us that we constantly need to be looking ahead, identifying which cultural outlooks are coming near to the 'line' or have already crossed it, and making preparations for manoeuvring these out of the system and putting something in their place. As I have said, there is no such thing as forward planning in the world of culture, but there is still good reason for being forward-looking.

Thirdly, be prepared for the rivalrous politics that will be unleashed in the 'betwixt and between' period following a second order change (see the hatched area in Figure 7.2), and try to anticipate the direction they are likely to take and the manner in which the issues will be resolved.

Developmental strategies	Transformational strategies
* Frame-making	* Frame-breaking
* Change 'in' (form is fixed)	* Change 'of' (form changes)
* First order, stability-orientated	* Second order, change-orientated
* Continuous, incremental	* Discontinuous, step change
* Quantitative change/'more of the same'	* Qualitative change/something different
* Intracultural variation	* Intercultural variation
* Opportunity-centred	* Problem-centred

Intention

To take the organization further along the same track	To take the organization off on a new track

Examples of appropriate strategies

* Maintenance/restorative/suppressive strategies	* Renewal/revitalization strategies
* Protectionist/conservationist strategies	* 'new wave'/alternative strategies
* Consolidation/enhancement/retrenchment strategies	* Paradigm-shifting strategies
* Growth/expansionist/incubation/enrichment strategies	* Destabilizing/repositioning strategies
* Adaptive/alignment strategies	* Turnaround strategies
* Synthesizing/systematizing/integrating strategies	* Survival/'s——or bust' strategies
* Corrective/remedial strategies	* Decoupling/ break-up/'scorched earth'/dissolving strategies
* Imitative/'copycat' strategies	* Confronting/shake-up/deforming strategies

Figure 7.4   Characteristics of the requisite strategy

Assessing cultural lag: managing the interface between cultural change and changes in the wider environment

> But the deeper underlying process [of cultural change] is surely a perpetual struggle between life, with its fundamental restlessness, evolution and mobility, and its own creations, which become inflexible and lag behind its development. (Simmel, trans. Lawrence, 1976)

What has so far been missing from our model is a consideration of the wider world within which the culture is situated and embedded, and to which it must continually be able to respond and adapt. A focus on the culture alone is not sufficient: we must now begin to contextualize our model, which in essence means focusing on the issue of 'fit' or 'alignment' between the culture and its environment.

We may, for example, think we have a resilient culture but the question we also have to ask is, do we have a *relevant* culture? The two concepts are quite separate (though equally important). It is possible to have a resilient culture which is not relevant, and vice versa. What it is important to realize is that these two issues will often be in conflict: sometimes it may actually be necessary to pursue a strategy for phasing out a culture that is still vibrant and resilient (like Disney's traditional cartoon culture) on the grounds that it is losing or has already lost its relevance; or alternatively for reviving a low resilience culture on the grounds that its contents are still relevant and in demand. The problem of relevance can arise no matter where a culture happens to be in the development cycle - whether in the ascendant or descendant phases. There are no easy answers here: strategists will have to take each case on its merits and carefully weigh up relevance against potential. In some cases they may even wish patiently to pursue the 'Reithian' option (Chapter 3) of low resilience\low relevance, in the belief that given time the chosen culture will eventually catch on!

The central issue addressed by this part of the strategy is 'cultural lag' – the gap between a form of life (culture) and life itself (current circumstances). The term was first coined by the American sociologist William F. Ogburn in his book *Social Change* published in 1923. The term was new but what it was based on was a fairly obvious fact: that 'forms' (e.g. value structures) always change at a slower rate than 'life' (e.g. market, tastes, technology), and consequently always end up getting left behind. This is hardly surprising. Cultural forms are notoriously resistant to change. The reason for this can be found in their orientations and internal processes. As we saw in Chapter 4, they are naturally conservative in outlook and prefer to go round and round in circles, living in the past, than follow a straight line and keep up with the present. No wonder they are so often left behind by time.

The problem is that as the amount of lag increases so the contemporary relevance of the cultural form decreases. Life and form get increasingly out of joint – misaligned, dissonant, incongruent and maladjusted. The old ways and customs lose their meaning and significance. Yet ironically, long after they have lost their practical benefit, people continue to hang on to them, acting them out in their daily rituals and routines.

My colleague Adrian McLean has a lovely story to illustrate this point. The story is called 'Holding the horses':

> In the early days of the Second World War, a time-and-motion expert was called in to improve the rapidity of fire of some ex-Boer light artillery guns which, towed by trucks, were being used as mobile defence units. For some time he watched the five man crews practising firing. Some aspects of what he saw puzzled him, so he took some slow-motion pictures. He particularly noticed that a moment or two before firing, two members of the crew stopped all other activity and stood to attention, one hand held up, until the gun was discharged. He looked around for someone to explain this behaviour, initially in vain. Eventually he found an old colonel of artillery. At first he too was puzzled. Then, seeing the pictures again, he exclaimed 'I have it! They are holding the horses!'
>
> Old habits can become part of the organization culture. Long after they have disappeared, we can find ourselves carefully 'holding the horses'.
>
> (McLean: 1990)

'Cultural lag' is very similar to today's more fashionable notion of 'strategic drift' (Johnson, 1984: 9). This is clear from the various definitions that have been offered in respect of the latter. They refer, for example, to the gradually widening gap between an organization's actual environment and its enacted environment, and between the 'strategy in use' and the 'required strategy'. The second of these references can usefully be adapted to provide a working definition of cultural lag, as the gap between the 'culture in use' and the 'requisite culture'. The merit of such a definition is that it carries the clear implication that a strategy for cultural change comes into play to bring about a realignment between the required culture and the culture in use.

So much for the concept. Let us consider some concrete examples of cultural lag in practice:

● *BR's Advanced Passenger Train (APT)* was a victim of cultural lag (Chapter 5). The traditional management culture within BR was ill-equipped to give to the project the support that it needed. A more go-ahead, risk-taking (and less segmentalist) culture could have made all the difference. Unfortunately people often fail to appreciate that technological change needs cultural change, that is to say, an updating of the culture to bring it into line with advancements that have been made on the technical front.

- The culture of *Rank Xerox* had evolved to optimize the selling of 'copiers' as stand-alone boxes (Chapman, 1988). However, the 1970s and early 1980s saw major changes in office systems technology. Customers no longer wanted these stand-alone boxes. They had fallen for the 'total office' concept and were now looking for the complete works – multifunction workstations, the integration capabilities of networking technologies and the communication facilities of laser printers, electronic mail, fax, etc. Although Rank Xerox had actually been at the leading edge in the development of these technologies, it had been slow to exploit their potential in the marketplace. Cultural lag lay at the heart of the problem: the 'environment' wanted something that the traditional culture was incapable of appreciating.

  To produce integrated technologies of this kind a company needs an integrated culture, one in which people can bring their individual 'bits' together into a single whole. The problem at Rank Xerox was that its culture was more 'segmentalist' than 'integrative', reflected in a highly differentiated, chimney-type organizational structure. The existence of strong functional directors with clearly demarcated territories made intersegmental cooperation and communication almost impossible. The need for cultural change was recognized in 1986 by the new Managing Director, Mr David O'Brien, who set in motion a change programme aimed at reducing the gap between the culture in use (segmentalism) and the requisite culture ('an integrated team management philosophy'). That programme has continued to this day.

- *Company A* was a down-market men's outfitter founded in 1970, and relatively successful during the first ten years of its life (Johnson, 1984). However, from 1980 onwards the company suffered a severe downturn in both sales and profits. Cultural lag again seemed to be a major cause of its problems. Johnson's interpretation of what happened is that while managers had seen various changes occurring in the wider environment, the various 'recipes' or schema embedded in the company's traditional culture had prevented them from appreciating the significance of these changes.

For example a revolution in men's fashion was taking place in the late 1960s which, though observed by managers, was seen as of little relevance to the company for ten years, because the recipe emphasized the working man's market which was not seen to be much to do with fashion and a mode of operation which stressed cheap bulk buying. The changes were simply not

admitted to the arena of relevance to decision making that was defined by
the recipe.   (1984: 5)

The above examples demonstrate how the concept of cultural lag can
provide useful insights into the issues of organizational effectiveness and
survival. The notion of 'lag' implies that in order to have an 'adjusted'
organization all parts of the culture must eventually 'catch up' with the
most rapidly changing parts of the environment; and since an
organization must be fairly well 'adjusted' in order to keep going, the
size of the lag cannot grow continually larger (Davis, 1965: 627). This is
where the Castalia-type, strong culture organizations fall down (Chapters
4 and 6). As we know, they do not adjust at all well to environmental
changes and often display extremes of cultural lag (tensions, myopia,
exaggerated behaviour etc.). Certainly cultural lag helps to account for
the fact that often after a period of staggering success these organizations
take a sharp nose-dive in their fortunes. The good thing about the
cultural lag concept is that it puts the issue of *adaptability* right at the top
of the agenda in the debate about organizational health and effectiveness.
This is an issue to which we will be returning in a later chapter.

So we come to the strategy itself. To remind ourselves: the focal
problem is cultural maladjustment (a major source of organizational
ineffectiveness). The broad aim of any strategy should be to minimize
cultural lag and find a way of giving the organization a more adaptive
culture. This will involve making provision for the conduct of ongoing
audits or reviews of the culture in use (focusing on the issue of relevance),
stimulating dialogue about the requisite culture, and encouraging well-
founded judgements about the 'goodness of fit' between the two. The
strategist will need to scan both inwards and outwards, taking in both the
internal cultural environment and the external environment.

The strategy should be preventative as well as remedial. With review
processes like this there is much that can be done to prevent cultural drift
before it occurs, or at least bridge the gap before it becomes
unmanageably wide. At the same time we have to be realistic. Cultural
lag is a fact of life; it will never be possible – nor always desirable – to
equalize the rate of change between 'life' and 'form'. The idea of the
perfectly adaptive culture is a pipe-dream. A good deal of the strategy can
therefore be expected to be remedial. There will always be a long queue of
'isms' in the vicious area of our cultural cycle waiting for attention. Most
of these are the no-hopers, the cultural mentalities whose rate of change is
so slow that the chance of them ever 'catching up' with the present is
virtually nil. However, as we have already noted, down they may be, out
they most certainly are not. Long after they have lost their relevance such
anachronistic mentalities continue to exercise a powerful influence over
people's minds. It is for this reason that we cannot just leave them in the

cupboard and forget them. At regular intervals we need to locate them and dig them out, see whether they still fit or have a use, and decide whether or not they need to be sent to the next jumble sale!

This part of our strategy requires nothing out of the ordinary by way of methodology. For example, the 'present state–desired state' analysis used extensively in organization development (Beckhard and Harris, 1987) can easily be adapted to provide us with a picture of the 'culture in use' and the 'requisite culture', together with an assessment of the amount of lag between them. Companies are already doing this kind of thing, though they may not be fully aware that they are actually assessing cultural lag. For example, the data presented in the two columns of Figure 7.5 were generated during ICL's cultural change programme of the 1980s. All I have done is insert the labels we have been discussing.

Why this particular methodology can be commended to people following my approach is that much of the information on the one side of the equation – the culture in use – will already have been gathered in the previous phases, thus leaving them free to concentrate on the other side of the equation – the 'requisite culture'.

Another methodology which also dovetails nicely with our wider strategic framework is the one that we used in British Rail. As we planned

Culture in use		Requisite culture
Changing the outlook from being technology-led		→ to being marketing-led
Moving from tactical and short-term reaction		→ to strategic, long-term planning
Changing people's view from internal focus	C U L T U R A L	→ to external focus
Halting the urge to try to do everything		→ to concentrating on specialized target markets
Lifting people from parochial level		→ to company commitment
Getting away from being procedure-bound	L A G	→ to being innovative and open-minded
Moving away from being a UK exporter		→ to being a global competitor
Moving from a bureaucratic ER-dominated reward system		→ to paying for performance on an individual basis

Figure 7.5 Assessing cultural lag: a real-life example. (Adapted from Mayo, 1989, 'The ICL experience')

the next steps of our change programme with the parties concerned, following the 'isms' analysis and presentation (see earlier chapters), we began to reason that if the 'isms' we had identified were the characteristics of a maladaptive culture (i.e. the culture in use), then the next task should be to discover the features of its opposite number, the adaptive culture (i.e. the requisite culture). We pictured the maladaptive culture as a photographic negative, and then sought to reverse the image and find its 'positive' form. In the event, this process proved highly effective. People found they could fix both positive and negative images in their mind's eye, and see and feel how different they were in shape and texture. Having done this they felt they had reached a state of readiness where they could go out and begin the task of making the image into reality.

Assessing ambitions for cultural change against possible outcomes

For the last component of our strategy we need to go back inside the organization and take a look at what the actors themselves want – the 'subjective dimension' of the model; what is wanted as opposed to what is needed.

External fit between the culture and its environment is not the only issue in the design of a strategy. There must also be internal fit between the direction in which a cultural process is to develop and the ambitions and aspirations of the various groups involved: subjective as opposed to situational contingencies.

In a cultural change programme people need to be clear not only about what they want – and design a strategy that will satisfy this – but also about whether they are likely to get it, and whether there is anything that can be done to increase their chances of success. The issue of politics lies at the heart of these considerations (see the section on turbulence above). Politics and the processes of negotiation that accompany them are all about establishing targets and estimating what might realistically be achieved, what one is prepared to settle for, and where the support is likely to come from.

At the beginning of this book I promised in true Bush-like fashion ("read my lips") that there would be no simple models and no quick-fix solutions. I specifically mentioned that there would be none of the usual two-by-two matrix diagrams. Since I have succeeded in getting this far without such a matrix and am now coming to the end of the first part of this book, I hope the reader will allow me one small deviation from the rule.

The matrix diagram in Figure 7.6 is a heuristic, another aid for organizing our thinking. It advises that first of all we need to consider closely what kind of change we *want* (ambitions), and then we must assess what we can reasonably expect to achieve *in practice* (consequences). It is constructed around the two types of change that have provided the core structure of this book:

- First order change: one that occurs within a given form which itself remains unchanged,.
- Second order change: one whose occurrence changes the form itself (Watzlawick *et al.*, 1974).

The matrix diagram shows four scenarios for change. Scenarios II and IV – the first representing the more limited developmental type of cultural change and the second, full-blown transformational change – are the 'as intended' scenarios. People who select either of these are presumably satisfied that they will be able to achieve the kind of change they want. They may of course be right. However, they still need to consider very carefully whether this is what they actually want (people often misjudge the scale of change required), and also whether they might be deluding themselves in believing they can actually achieve it. There may in fact be no need for change at all – or certainly not second order change: it is all too easy for people to get carried away by 'big' ideas when it might be better if they stayed where they were (a case of 'better the devil you know . . .').

CONSEQUENCES

		First order	Second order
AMBITIONS	First order	II Anticipated developmental change	III Overachievement
	Second order	I Underachievement	IV Anticipated transformation

Figure 7.6   Different scenarios for a change programme

Scenarios I and III are the more problematical – and it must be said, the more likely – scenarios. The first relates to a common problem encountered by change programmes: underachievement, where outcomes fall short of ambitions. Change strategists must assess the likelihood of this happening to their own change programme. They need to ask whether they are being too ambitious, whether there is too much resistance or indifference to the desired change to allow it to occur, whether the timing is all wrong and whether there is sufficient political support and momentum to achieve the desired outcome.

The British Civil Service provides an example of underachievement – of a planned cultural revolution that never happened (scenario I). In this case the authors of the 'Next Steps' initiative (the chosen vehicle for second order change) were wrong to believe they could achieve their ambitions (scenario IV) using a top-down, 'invasionary' approach to change (Levy and Merry, 1986). Their big mistake was to ignore the pluralism within the situation (Chapter 3), and not foresee that local 'cultural infrastructures' – the outfield of the Civil Service – would resist, and finally succeed in repulsing, the invasion from above (Brooks and Bate, 1992). The clear lesson from this experience is don't overestimate your own power nor underestimate that of others. A strategy for cultural change needs to deal directly with the issue of the 'politics of acceptance', and find ways of building on existing areas of agreement, while at the same time managing differences.

At the same time, no one should overlook the possibility of scenario III, i.e. overachievement, occurring. A frequent irony of change is that the social or political dynamic for cultural transformation – the force that enables an organization to 'jump' from first order to second order change – comes not from the assumed or expected source, such as a 'formal' initiative like Next Steps, but from some entirely different and unexpected source, like a change of ownership, a public scandal, an environmental disaster, a technological breakthrough or a change in the legal framework.

I have nicknamed this the 'Gorby' scenario, in which a first order change process – something in the evolutionary cycle of a society or organization – triggers a revolution, unleashing uncontrollable forces and taking the change process in unforeseen directions (see the section above on momentum). It is unplanned and unwanted second order change, a reformation that becomes a transformation. When Gorbachev set out on his step-by-step approach to change in the Soviet Union, he could never have foreseen (and would hardly have approved of) the consequences: the death of the Communist Party, the democratization of Eastern Europe, an attempted coup, the break-up of the Soviet Union, and his own demise as President. Such are the limits of 'planned' change! As I remarked earlier, there is nothing so precarious and unpredictable as cultural change, not least second order cultural change.

This scenario is important because it offers to the strategist a reminder that unplanned transformation is always a possibility, at any time, and that what he or she must try to do is plan for the unplanned!

And so we come to the end of our description of the five major focuses of concern in a strategic framework for cultural change. If all of this sounds a bit of a tall order, especially for today's busy executives, it is perhaps worth reflecting for a moment on what we mean by 'strategy'. As I have defined it in this chapter and indeed throughout the whole of the first part of this book, strategy is more than just a set of tactics, methods or techniques that one uses from time to time in a military style campaign or operation; it is a constant, ongoing thinking process – a paradigm, a way of life, something one lives and breathes on an hour-by-hour basis, and not necessarily in the form that I have presented it. To put it as succinctly as I am able, thinking strategically is thinking culturally with a purpose, no more and no less. It is not something we 'make time' for, but something that is always with us.

One should not be too daunted by the prospect. The message of this book is optimistic. Corporate culture is manageable and it is changeable, but – and this is a big but – only if we are prepared to confront the complexities head on and learn the difficult skills of thinking culturally about strategy, and thinking strategically about culture.

Part Two Implementing Cultural Change

The focus of the book now shifts from strategy to implementation; from thinking frameworks to frameworks for action; from the 'why' of change to the 'what' and the 'how'. We begin by surveying current practice and examine the various, often strikingly different, ways in which people seek to effect cultural change in their organizations. The accounts that follow are based both on my own first-hand experiences of working with private and public sector companies on cultural change programmes, and on an extensive review of the available literature.

From a study of change methods currently in use I have identified four generic approaches to cultural change, which I have called the Aggressive, Conciliative, Corrosive, and Indoctrinative approaches. A character sketch of each (and its variants) is provided, together with an analysis of the reasons why people choose this method and an assessment of how well it appears to succeed in actually changing culture (Chapters 8 – 11). Readers may find their own organization's approach to change in these descriptions and in the light of what is said be able to evaluate its strengths and weaknesses, and decide whether an alternative method may be preferable.

A point that should be emphasized is that none of these approaches can be described as 'culture-specific'. The reality is that practitioners have tended not to discriminate between cultural change and any other type of change (nor indeed to see any need to do so). Certainly, the great majority of approaches to cultural change that I have encountered were not designed with cultural change in mind, but were simply borrowed and adapted from the current stock of change methods on offer. What we therefore find in practice is little, if any, difference between the ways people are trying to change culture and the ways they would typically go about changing structures, technology, operational systems, or any other aspect of their organization.

This clearly raises the important question of whether cultural change processes need their own indigenous, tailor-made modes of conceptualization, or whether they can safely continue to rely on 'ready-mades' and 'hand-me-downs' from other fields and paradigms. Up until now this question has been impossible to answer because of the lack of any explicit or relevant criteria against which the impact and effectiveness of attempts at *cultural* change could be assessed. This book seeks to rectify the problem by developing one such set of criteria and then using it to appraise the four approaches under discussion (Chapters 12 and 13). More importantly, these criteria may also serve as 'design parameters', affording organizations the opportunity to free themselves from convention and tradition and construct an approach to cultural change which is relevant and specific to their situation (Chapter 13). The resulting implications for leadership are also discussed (Chapter 14).

Since people may not be familiar with the labels I have given to the four approaches, the following outline descriptions using conventional OD terminology may be helpful:

Aggressive	Power-coercive; conflict-centred; non-collaborative; win–lose; imposed; the 'decree approach'; unilateral
Conciliative	Group problem-solving; win-win; collaborative; emergent; integrative; the 'joint approach'
Corrosive	Political; coalitional; unplanned; evolutionary; networking; the 'informal approach'
Indoctrinative	Normative–reeducative; the 'training approach'

(For a fuller discussion of these OD terms see Margulies and Raia, 1978: 29–54.)

8 The aggressive approach

Profile

This might be described as cultural vandalism, a wilful attack on the traditional values of the organization. Its purpose is to create disruption among the local population – to break a few windows – and to give clear notice of the intention of establishing a new cultural order. To quote one manager: 'The aim is to deliver a large shock to the system which leaves people shivering and shuddering, wondering what's going to happen next.' The Spanish, themselves no strangers to the effects of cultural vandalism, have a phrase to describe this condition: 'tiembla la tierra!' (the earth trembles). Brissy's neat phrase for this approach is 'leadership with a machine gun' (1989: 1).

The dominant discourse of the aggressive approach is physical and belligerent. For example, the world of boxing is often invoked in its indigenous language – 'getting the organization down to a fighting weight'; 'refusing to lie down'; 'outpunching opponents'. The language of the military is also drawn on – for example, 'running for cover'; 'being outflanked'; 'catching flack'; 'building bridgeheads' and 'avoiding blood-baths'.

Sensitivity is not exactly its strong point: 'What you need are some big-boots men to go out there and put things right. You don't want people who are capable of thinking for themselves. You want people who are capable of taking action.' Such comments are typical of what Deal and Kennedy (1982: 108) call 'tough-guy cultures', often found in the police force, construction and heavy industry, consulting, advertising, tele-vision, the movies, sport and entertainments. Relationships in these cultures tend to resemble arm-wrestling bouts: 'Every meeting can become a war game where the most junior person in the room has to best the most senior person in order to win respect. If the junior person doesn't fight, he or she will be dismissed out of hand as a lightweight. A comer is one who's aggressive whether right, wrong or indifferent' (1982: 110).

Time is of the essence in matters of change: there can be no delays or hold-ups. As one manager related: 'I can't afford the time debating all this through, arguing the toss with everybody, letting people challenge and delay my policies. I've got to have a quicker way of going in and getting what I want.' Tactics like these are most often employed when an organization is in crisis, e.g. because of declining profits or reduction in market share. The idea is to achieve rapid change by the suppression of alternative perspectives, this being justified by the scale and urgency of the task that lies ahead.

Like Faust, the aggressives unmake one world in order to make another (Czarniawska-Joerges, 1989). Work therefore begins in earnest on the invalidation and delegitimization of previous patterns and practices. This is tantamount to cultural arson. The past is debunked; history is re-written. Such events are common in human affairs, the case of Czechoslovakia illustrating this point nicely, if somewhat extremely (see Box 8.1).

Less extreme examples of cultural megashock and the re-writing of history involve the use of hyperbole to rubbish and bad-mouth a previous regime. In one organization studied it was recalled that managers had been 'too nice' and had let 'advantage' be taken of them. Work had become 'sloppy' and 'inefficient' and the organization had become 'a bloody great talking shop, all platitudes and promises but no delivery'. Corruption was widespread, with senior managers (i.e. 'senior villains') 'running their fiefdoms like it was the black market'. The system had broken down: 'No-one was in charge, and no-one was accountable."

It is by taking such liberties with history that the ground is prepared for the grand entrance of the liberating heroes, the incorruptible no-nonsense people who will sweep away the forces of anarchy and disorder, and restore peace once again to the organization. To quote from the election victory speech of Mrs Thatcher in 1979: 'Where there is discord, may we bring harmony.' This example brings out another point about the approach: that it is very much a one-man show, a case of 'I'll do what I bloody well like and don't you try to stop me'. Obviously one has not got to be too bothered about friends: 'The way this job works is that you have to be totally indifferent to your popularity within the organization' (manager).

The stress throughout is very much on the heroic, the concept Promethean:

The Heroic culture mentality and man view the world as a chaos that they must put in order by their organizational effort. The Heroic man does not live peacefully in the world but is set against it in its existing form. He is full of self-confidence and lust for power. He looks at the world as at a slave; he wants to master and mold it to his own plans. Nothing is static in the Heroic

---

Box 8.1   The President of Forgetting (*Source:* Milan Kundera (1980), *The Book of Laughter and Forgetting*)

Husak, the seventh president of my country, is known as the President of Forgetting.

The Russians brought him into power in 1969. Not since 1621 has the history of the Czech people experienced such a massacre of culture and thought. Everybody everywhere assumes that Husak simply tracked down his political opponents. In fact, however, the struggle with the political opposition was merely an excuse, a welcome opportunity the Russians took to use their intermediary for something much more substantial.

I find it highly significant in this connection that Husak dismissed some hundred and forty-five Czech historians from universities and research institutes . . . One of those historians, my all but blind friend Milan Hubl, came to visit me one day in 1971 in my tiny apartment on Bartolomejska Street. We looked out the window at the spires of the Castle and were sad.

'The first step in liquidating a people,' said Hubl, 'is to erase its memory. Destroy its books, its culture, its history. Then have somebody write new books, manufacture a new culture, invent a new history. Before long the nation will begin to forget what it is and what it was. The world around it will forget even faster.'

'What about language?'

'Why would anyone bother to take it from us? It will soon be a matter of folklore and die a natural death.'

Was that hyperbole dictated by utter despair?

Or is it true that a nation cannot cross a desert of organized forgetting?

---

universe. Like Prometheus, the Heroic man challenges any power and any god. He is active, tense, and maximally energetic. (Sorokin, 1966: 325–6)

Deauthenticating the authenticity of a previous way of life is seen as a necessary prelude to cultural change. Cultural coherency must be dissolved and ordinary reality allowed to come apart, so that habit and common sense are no longer reliable ways of coping with everyday reality. The ordinary language of the community must be continually checked for loose or stray values, and careful self-censored discourse encouraged among the population.

The temporary loss of cultural coherency creates massive ontological insecurity (Laing, 1971) among the natives. They lose the bedrock of protocols and conventions on which their way of life depended; their sacred grounds are trampled on; ordinary reality is fractured and normal mundane reasoning (Pollner, 1987) is suspended; there is what Mangham (1978) calls a *bouleversement* of the world taken for granted, a kind of psychological up-ending similar to having the rug pulled out from under your feet. People become helpless and disorientated.

This is all quite planned and deliberate on the part of the aggressor. A case in point is the Japanese brewery Asahi, whose market share had slowly declined from 36% to under 10% over a 35 year period. The revitalization of the company involved a cultural change process that was, by their own admission, not dissimilar to brainwashing. The account given by them of the way they 'unfroze' and 'refroze' the culture is quite chilling (see Box 8.2).

Box 8.2   Cultural brainwashing at Asahi. (*Source:* T. Nakajo and T. Kono (1989) *Success through culture change in a Japanese Brewery*)

The transformation of Asahi can be explained by using the following principle. Change in the corporate culture takes the form of the process of 'unfreeze', 'change', and 'refreeze'. Let us compare this process to the process of 'brainwashing' applied to the war prisoners held by the communist bloc during the Second World War.

First the prisoners' preconceptions were destroyed by pointing out the 'contradictions and errors' of capitalism (unfreeze). Next, they were taught the 'correctness' of communism. For those who did not change their minds, food rations were reduced, and for those who accepted this change of thinking, rations were increased (change). The change was then fixed and reinforced by the peer pressure exerted by fellow prisoners, etc. (refreeze).

To unfreeze is to destroy the conventional values. To achieve this, people are taught that their conventional values or ways of thinking are erroneous. In the case of the individual, each person is taught to reflect inwardly and confess the error of his ways. In the case of Asahi, the process of 'evoking a crisis mentality' corresponds to 'unfreezing'.

Fear also has a lot to do with it. To quote a senior manager in one of my own studies: 'If I leave people half-guessing about whether they'll have a job tomorrow they're much more likely to do what I tell them.' Others talked about 'management by panic' and 'motivation by fear': 'Things do tend to happen when there is worry about survival. I mean, the greatest motivator is fear. If you've got a bull chasing you across the field . . . ' Such bullying brings directly to mind Dunsing and Matejka's (1987) description of 'macho' managers' favourite intimidation tactics.

Methods employed may include witch-hunts, sackings and demotions: 'They "promoted" John from personnel manager to security man! They didn't get rid of him because they wanted people to see him still walking around so that they would say to each other "look what happened to him" '. This method is distinctly Skinnerian: 'The school of motivation here is mainly a large stick.'

As with all forms of rape, the significance of such acts of aggression is as much symbolic as it is physical:

> I call it symbolic because the vandalism is performed under circumstances from which the possibility of retaliation by others is absent. Empty houses are splendid targets for adolescent vandalism.   (Peckham, 1976: 23)

Having dissolved the coherency of the existing culture, denigrated history and created insecurity, the vandal next moves on to issuing his directions for performance. The two main features of these directions are that they are (a) cognitively simple – people who use this approach have little time for the overcomplicators of life and tend, as they like to tell you, to see issues in clear-cut terms (cf. Dunphy and Stace, 1988); (b) detailed – nothing is left to chance. The attention to detail exemplified by Harold Geneen during his seventeen years at the International Telephone and Telegraph Company (IT&T) can be quite staggering: 'They even tell you which handbill to put into which pigeon hole' (manager). Broad strategy is translated into detailed action by way of a rational top-down process involving the translation of directions into sub-directions, sub-directions into sub-sub-directions and so on, the intention being to eliminate all possibility of deviation. As one manager put it, 'everything is down to the hour'. Even language is subject to strict controls (see Box 8.3).

The style is thoroughly Procrustean: there is a scheme or pattern into which people are squeezed with little regard for their feelings or preferences.

> Management decides the firm must become market-driven so it sends out a memo to 6,000 employees saying 'starting tomorrow we are going to be market-driven'. And there it sits.   (Helms, 1988)

Having been produced, the cultural directions then have to be policed to ensure that they are being adequately reflected in performance. This may include a back-up 'informal' method using an extensive network of

---

**Box 8.3:   Memorandum to Directors/Managers
from Personnel Department**

BRIEFING GUIDELINE
Brief down to: ALL EMPLOYEES
URGENT - commence 09.00 hrs 20th October end Friday 21st
October
NOTE This text is issued as a guide to Directors and Managers
involved in briefing staff under their control.

It should not be read out to staff, but used as a quick guide (a) prior
to the briefing meeting, and (b) during the meeting as a discreet
check.

As far as possible brief the matter in your own words with normal
style and phraseology so that your discussion is natural, EXCEPT
that certain words and phrases in the written text are italicized; these
should be retained in your own version intact, since they are more
critical in retaining the correct emphasis or interpretation in the
matter . . .

---

spies and informers: 'They send people out into the system, often in the
dead of night, to check whether the carpets are being cleaned with a brush
or a mop!'

This sounds very much like the 'Design School' model for implementing strategic change described by Mintzberg (1990), which consists of
designing and disseminating a blueprint for the future through the
identification of clear objectives, the articulation of unambiguous
authority structures and the integration of specialist skills. The
overriding management problem is perceived to be that of controlling
against corruptions of the plan in its journey down through the
organization (Whittle et al., 1991: 2).

The ultimate ambition of such an approach is to establish a strong
integrated culture in which there exists a single source of authority and a
single focus of loyalty – a form of cultural hegemony through which
ideational control can be exercised by the ruling group (Chapter 3).

So much for the theory, but how do things actually work out? In
practice cultural change does take place but rarely in the direction
intended. With the sweeping away of cultural protocols, people feel the
need to re-group: some people join one camp, others join another. The
intended homogenization of the workforce does not therefore take place;
the culture becomes less unitary and more pluralistic; there are a

multitude of discordant voices, divided loyalties and rampant segment-alism. As the different factions struggle for advantage the organizational scene begins to resemble a battleground of adversarialism and coercion, sniping and backbiting. The paradox, one that we see repeating itself time and time again in oppressive totalitarian societies, is that 'it is not freedom but policing . . . which is the occasion for the occurrence of divergence and deviancy' (Peckham, 1976: 220).

What are the different factions? They will vary according to local circumstance, but as R. A. Rose (1988) points out there are broadly four types: the 'dominant' faction (those who support the ruling ideas); the 'enhancing' faction (those who have got 'carried away' becoming even more fervently attached to the values of the dominant culture than the dominant group itself); the 'orthogonal' faction (who believe in the dominant culture but also have their own separate values); and the counterculture (who repudiate the ruling values completely).

How this multicultural situation unfolds from now on will depend upon a whole range of factors, but what is certain is that at this point the aggressive tactics begin to lose their force. The threatened Armageddon has not materialized: 'It's like the Seventh Day Adventist predicting the end of the world. When it doesn't happen they just give us another date' (manager). It leads instead to the rapid politicization of the organization. Camps, cliques and alliances form to protect and advance personal interests and control the flow of information. 'Reality' is now shaped and presented in a carefully edited way to those above: duplicity and deception are commonplace. People find that effective resistance and self-protection are easier than they imagined. They become bold: 'I could hold the frontier against these guys with a single rifleman.' They opt out, testament to the idea that, despite the popular belief, you cannot actually cook a frog by dropping it in a pan of water: it will leap out.

The aggressors, on the other hand, begin to contemplate what went wrong. Their periodic reviews begin to take on the character of post mortems: 'we never had enough management information to show us what was really going on out there'; 'we/he/she/they should have taken an even stronger lead' etc. They are tired; their energy begins to drain because they are not getting the instant success on which they thrive; and like film stars whose latest movie has just flopped, their friends shun them.

To a large extent their own political naivety is to blame, as well as their elementary confusion of 'authority' with 'power'. Aggressive leaders often find themselves out-boxed by lesser opponents: 'I remember issuing a directive saying "no more cream teas for visitors" and several weeks later turning up as a visitor and getting the full 5-star cream tea treatment. They didn't bat an eyelid. It's part of the dumb insolence around here that you can't do anything about.'

They become embroiled in a change process that they do not understand and certainly cannot control. They may succeed, despite their dubious methods, in 'unfreezing' the old culture and unleashing new forces for cultural change, but what the situation now requires is a new form of coherency that will reconstitute these forces into some discernible form of order for those involved. Unfortunately, the aggressor possesses neither the skills nor the breadth of support to achieve this. The less belligerent people have left; even his friends have deserted him as the rats leave a sinking ship, and he is isolated.

He is trapped by the antagonistic culture he himself has created, and the energy he has put into it gives it an unstoppable momentum that carries it headlong into crisis and chaos (Chapter 6). The ultimate fate of this particular approach is therefore often tragic.

Recent evidence shows that, despite its questionable efficacy, the aggressive approach is being used with increasing frequency in organizations nowadays, and that its underlying militaristic imagery is gaining in popularity (Garsombke, 1988). Traditional behavioural science preferences for incrementalism and evolutionary change (Quinn, 1980, 1982) are showing signs of being rejected, along with the ideologies of humanism and gradualism that have dominated organization development theory for ten years and more. The gap between theorist and practitioner has widened. According to Dunphy and Stace (1988), for example, effecting change by 'coercive dictat' is a method that is now extremely popular with newly appointed chief executives and other senior appointees such as corporate strategists, financial experts and personnel directors. These people are showing a good deal of impatience with academic 'Quinnians', whom they believe have failed to come to terms with the fact that cautious incrementalist approaches to change are a time-consuming and unaffordable luxury and do not offer assistance to organizations operating in the much more turbulent environment of post-industrial economies. Cultural vandalism, it would seem, is back in fashion.

Rationales

The rationales informing the use of this aggressive approach might easily be missed or misinterpreted by theorists, partly as the result of the widening gap between theorist and practitioner, and partly because of the affront that the aggressive approach causes to the theorists' normative models. Orwellian images of sadistic, totalitarian regimes can easily flood the mind and become substitutes for constructive alternative interpretations. My own discussions with practitioners revealed that, from the native users' point of view, there was not only 'good reason' and adequate justification for the adoption of aggressive methods, but also the rudiments of a practical theory about the management of cultural change.

Survival

'Radical times demand radical remedies' (Dunphy and Stace, 1988: 321): the aggressive approach may be justified on the grounds that it is seen as a last-ditch effort to lift an organization out of crisis. Survival requires the declaration of a state of emergency in which normal codes of behaviour are suspended and deviant behaviour by the leaders must be tolerated. The social and heroic nature of the struggle makes a certain level of personal pain and sacrifice necessary and acceptable ('if it's not hurting it's not working'). It is simply a case of being cruel to be kind.

Redemption

The mentality is not only heroic but also messianic. The aggressive type frequently believes that he has a 'special mission' to perform, involving a legitimate struggle fought in the name of truth and goodness and sanctioned by the highest authority on the organizational earth. Aggressive change therefore enjoys some of the status of divine exemption. It is more than just 'change'; it is an act of redemption. Equally it is not so much a 'transition' or 'transformation', but a mode of organizational 'transfiguration': 'The Messianic man wants to change [the world] – not for his own self-will or self-satisfaction, but in order to fulfil the mission assigned to him by God' (Sorokin, 1966: 326).

In British Rail the language of the aggressors was often peppered with religious imagery and iconography, for example, one was chosen to 'fight the good fight' and 'preach the gospel' of the business-led approach. People recruited to the 'cause' were told to expect 'persecution', and 'crucifixion' could never be ruled out!

Initiative

Some aggressives claim justification for their approach on the grounds that they must seize the initiative in order to ensure a high probability of success. In this regard they are in fact following academically respectable principles – albeit not from the organization behaviour literature (of which they are frequently contemptuous). In industrial relations theory, for example, there is the 'power of the first bid' concept (where the person who takes the first 'shot' is thought most likely to be successful in defining the situation for others), and in the field of corporate strategy there is an almost identical concept of 'first mover' or 'attacker's advantage' (cf. Ohmae, 1983, ch. 5, 'Pursuing aggressive initiatives'; and Foster, 1986, ch. 7, 'The attacker's advantage').

Aggressors would argue that neither the humanistic nor the evolutionary traditions of organization development are appropriate when one is trying to effect radical and rapid second order cultural change. Humanistic practices of 'democracy' and 'participation' give a platform to the opposition and allow them to resist or 'doctor' the change, and the term evolution evoked strong responses from some managers:

Evolution is an ethos and a strategy for keeping things the same.

I've had it up to here with this word 'evolution'. Look. It's simple. It's the radical versus the rest; we're the radicals and they're the rest. The 'rest' will be holding on like mad to what they've got, and you can always count on them being in favour of 'evolution'. You know the jargon trips out. The number of times I've heard people say they're in favour of evolution not revolution, I could scream. And each time they say that they talk glowingly about something which a year ago they opposed bitterly. They resisted at every stage. 'Evolution' is the way they justify their resistance.

Innovation

While there may be a strong temptation to equate the 'culturally aggressive' approach described here with the 'revolutionary' approach so labelled in the literature (Pettigrew, 1985; Gagliardi, 1986), I believe it might be better described as 'rebellion' not 'revolution'. Rebellion is a cultural act whereas revolution is a political act. Unlike the revolutionary, the rebel's primary focus of concern is not power but cultural innovation: his theory is that to bring about a new form of organization and new patterns of thought and behaviour there has to be modal discontinuity (Peckham, 1970: 274) – a violation of traditional perceptual forms and expectancies. As Czarniawska-Joerges puts it (1989: 12), the rebel works against the existing social structure not by revolution but by behaving as if the structure did not exist.

At heart he is a hopeless romantic (Ebers, 1985), motivated by a self-centred desire to bring his imaginative conception into existence, and by the belief that in doing so he can transform the world. This idealism can be found in all forms of romantic behaviour. Unfortunately, such a naive concern for cultural substance over political process is what may ultimately bring about the romantic's downfall: immersed in his vision he often fails to notice the gathering clouds of opposition until it is too late.

In summary: on the face of it, the people who use this approach are just hangovers from the past – pre-civilization bullies and Theory X autocrats who did not study their management texts closely enough at business school. There is no doubt that they are vandals whose behaviour seems at times to be motivated solely by the desire to irritate and create trauma. But they are more than this: they are modern-day romantics, adventurers, rebels, buccaneers, people who spurn convention and flirt with the forces of cultural change, that rare breed that is only comfortable (and effective?) when it is playing the anti-role to the establishment truths. Regardless of whether or not we approve of their methods and goals, we have to concede that they belong to that small minority that is working at the level of second order change. If these people sound larger than life, the reason is that they probably are.

9 The conciliative approach

Profile

While aggressive change agents do not sit comfortably alongside ordinary academic and management mortals, practitioners operating in the conciliative mode have no such problem. They believe that they can achieve cultural change through non-dramatic, gradual and routine means. The special quality of their approach lies in its direct appeal to the common sense constructs of the organizational membership, its perfect dovetailing with the dominant paradigm, and its ability to provide epistemological certainty and security for those involved. The methods used have a 'distinctive grounding in nature and in reason' (Douglas, 1987: 112) – so much so that initially the change programme often goes on unnoticed by those involved.

The differences between this approach and the previous one are striking: change is a quiet exercise; gone are the thrills and spills, the frenetic activities, the bar room brawls and the naive and elemental idealism. As Harold Geneen might have said, there are no surprises. Change occurs by degrees, as the new culture is slowly grafted on to the old, without any of the fanfare and razzmatazz of the previous approach. Conciliatives reject the view that there has to be confrontation in order for change to occur: theirs is a Bing Crosby, conflict-free theory of change.

While aggressors tend to assume that the natives are hostile, conciliators prefer to regard them as reasonable people. This is not to say that clashes of interest are not expected to occur: it is simply that there is sufficient good faith in the relationships between the parties to enable them to work through their differences. For example:

> I have a lot of banter with my friends in engineering. One of them says that he and I have a love-hate relationship: he loves spending money and I hate him for it! I think it explains the way we work together.
>
> (marketing manager)

Contrast this with another view of the same engineering division expressed by an aggressive-type practitioner in the same organization:

> Engineers will always try to manipulate you into a situation where you pay much more than the situation requires. You just have to call their bluff and keep being very difficult and unpleasant, challenging them and refusing to believe what they are telling you.

In organizations I have studied the conciliative approach was characterized by a form of discourse that was flexible (people talked about 'elastic parameters'), accommodating ('room for all of us'), and egalitarian ('no interest is privileged'). The metaphors were peaceful ones – cricket, for example: 'My job is to roll the wicket, you know – keep things nice and friendly. My experience is that on a flat wicket people don't try to bowl bouncers.' Water was another: targets should be made to 'ripple down through the organization', ideas should be 'floated', and so on. Then there was gardening: one's role was to 'plant the seeds of change', 'cultivate the culture' and 'keep the paths clear of brambles'.

Whereas the aggressives are noted for their idealism, conciliatives pride themselves on their realism: 'I'm not a conceptual guy. I'm very much the pragmatist'; 'principles are the most dangerous things to fight for because they might not be worth a penny at the end of the day'; 'if you always have your eye on the horizon you miss the brick wall just in front of you'. Unlike the aggressives they do not believe they have any particularly historic mission to perform: 'they keep telling us we're in the vanguard of the cultural revolution, but I know that by 1994 there will be a new fad and we will have become the old guard'. As might be expected, this method of managing change tends to be highly eclectic. Sorokin's description fits it perfectly:

> [It] shows no unity of topic, style, and objective. It is an incoherent potpourri or hash of all sorts of topics, styles, and objectives.   (1966: 376)

However, significant for their absence are any kinds of directions for performance. Unlike the previous approach, there are no coercive dictats and no policemen or law enforcement agencies. By appealing to commonsense, which as Van Holthoon and Olson (1987) point out is a self-regulating body of natural law, external coercion is unnecessary.

Change thus becomes a routine, almost pedestrian activity, surrounded by a halo of mundaneity and of-courseness (Pollner, 1987): 'You just work away at the coal face, and ultimately you may get change'; 'Change is a backwards–forwards process – two steps forward one step back. Persistence and hard work, that's all it is. You just have to keep beavering away'.

So far I have largely been describing a style of managing, rather than a theory of cultural change. One might easily come away thinking that there is no coherent change theory of any kind, merely a rag-bag of old-fashioned calvinistic folk ideals pertaining to hard work, hope, sincerity and predestination. In my opinion this view would be incorrect. The conciliators possess a very practical theory for cultural change and a well-founded rationale for holding this in preference to any other. One of its most interesting aspects is that, contrary to much of the literature on the subject, it does not accept that there has to be a dialectical confrontation between different interests in order for change – even major change – to occur. Its belief is that the best way to achieve change is by processes of convergence rather than divergence, by conformity rather than deviance, by order rather than by rebellion. Mutuality is the key principle: 'You get your authority by not undermining other people's authority.'

It is claimed that all kinds of change, including second order change, can be achieved in this way. There is some evidence to support this view. For example, Pondy and Huff's longitudinal study of three school districts in America showed that it was possible to achieve far-reaching change without having to deviate from the normal everyday organizational routines:

> Fundamental shifts in organizational domain . . . result from the ordinary workings of day-to-day processes. Significant shifts, in fact, are not discovered to be fundamental until after they have taken place. Continuity with the past and adherence to routine are the expected state of affairs .
>
> (Pondy and Huff, 1985: 104)

The question now is, if the approach works, how does it work? Piercy and Peattie (1988) provide some clues. They have likened the implementation of strategy to fitting a parcel through a hole in a wall. In our case, the parcel corresponds to the new culture and the wall to the existing one. While I have already expressed reservations about equating cultures with things as solid as walls (Chapter 1), this analogy does have its uses in highlighting the contrast between aggressives and conciliatives in the kind of change tactics each might use.

As we have seen, the aggressive approach would be to blast a bigger hole in the wall, or even demolish it altogether if necessary in order to get the parcel through. The conciliative approach, on the other hand, uses every means at its disposal to avoid friction and make the passage of the parcel through the wall as smooth and trouble-free as possible. Piercy and Peattie give some examples of what its methods might be:

- Break the parcel into smaller pieces – then reassemble after they have gone through the hole. In other words introduce cultural change in incremental steps. This is classic Quinn, whose model of logical incrementalism (1980) lies at the heart of the conciliative approach. It is characterized by low profile, partial solutions to problems, a gradual unfolding of a strategic vision, and a use of language that de-emphasizes the novelty of what is being proposed (Pondy and Huff, 1985: 115). This last point leads directly into the next example.

- Use the right label – present the package in conventional terms so that it appears to fit with no difficulty. For example, use cachet words like 'excellence', 'quality', 'involvement', 'customer-service'.
- Thin end first – begin with the more acceptable elements and aim to get beyond the point where going back is more costly than going on.
- Grease the package – do various things to the package to make it politically more acceptable. For example, suggest it will 'increase security', 'enhance management control', 'give greater freedom/ accountability/competitiveness' etc.
- Grease the wall – soften up the opposition and gain their support. The key words are involvement, dialogue and participation. If all else fails be patient and . . .
- Wait for the wall to crumble – sooner or later the particularly obstructive members will die or move on or simply become less dominant, or the environment will become generally more receptive to the change being proposed. The whole basis of the gradualist paradigm is that systems can 'accept' any change given time and patience.

Rationales

Perceived lack of power

Unlike the aggressives, the conciliatives do not feel omniscient and do not believe they can compel anyone to do anything (see pluralist perspective, Chapter 3). For example, when the Chairman of ICL, Peter Bonfield, took over at a time of crisis he realized that 'total cultural change' was needed (Mayo, 1989: 18). However, he did not feel empowered to impose this unilaterally:

> I gradually realized that I lacked the levers to transfer my strategic insight into the hearts and minds of the organization so that they shared the imperative. They had to know why, not just what. An impressive programme of communication was not enough. I got immensely frustrated – thousands of bright people all working hard but not buying into the directions.

Conflict avoidance

This approach is rooted in the belief that people object at least as much to how things are done as to what is done, and therefore the best way to achieve substantive cultural change is to collude with, rather than collide with, the organization's normal way of getting things done. This gives a certain social legitimacy to the change programme and helps compensate for any disagreement over the substance of the proposed change.

Continuity

Discontinuity can of itself be a source of tension and resistance. People who are suffering from cultural anomie and trauma are unlikely to want to learn and experiment with new patterns of thinking and behaviour. Support for this view is offered by Feldman: 'some level of cultural continuity is essential for maintaining cooperative relations, effective leadership styles, and, above all, a sense of order . . .' (1986: 603). From the point of view of minimizing opposition, it is better to have gradual and continuous development of form rather than the sudden and discontinuous creation of new forms (Renfrew, 1979: 9).

Simultaneous construction/deconstruction (Gray et al., 1985)

Whereas the aggressives follow a 'scorched earth' policy of destroying, clearing and then re-building, the conciliatives believe that the old can be put to good use in the construction of the new: 'first you get the brickwork up, then you can take the scaffolding down' (manager).

Competence

The maxim is that you should 'stick to what you do best'. 'Competence' in this sense has three meanings: (a) institutional – continuing to use one's established competence in applying current rules and procedures to the achievement of goals; (b) interpersonal – persisting with tried-and-tested routines for dealing with others; and (c) linguistic – continuing to engage in the routine language games of the organization in which one already possesses a high level of linguistic competence, and through which one can participate in the management of meaning.

Obsolescence

The production of a new culture may be likened to the production of a new car: it evolves through a number of stages – initial idea, design, drawings, production, test, launch, further modifications and so on. The design will succeed if it can make existing models look out of date. One advantage claimed by the conciliatives is that their methods of change are sufficiently disarming to minimize opposition, and thus allow them to focus solely on achieving the 'grand design' that will render the present culture obsolete.

> The challenge is to come up with a design for this part of the organization – a philosophy, a mode of operation, some systems and policies – which will make the rest of the organization look downright old-fashioned. Our model will speak for itself. There can be no more tinkering about with the old designs – people making a modification here and another modification there. They will change because they know they have to change. They have no choice. They have been upstaged. We don't have to tell them that; they know their model's days are up. (manager)

'Cultural leadership' is therefore envisioned as being broadly similar to 'product leadership'. If the product is sufficiently innovative and original then it will sell itself and floor the opposition. This is the ultimate in leadership by example, its claim to superiority being that it is entirely voluntary. There is no invasionary force and no coercion. People simply discover for themselves that their own practices have become obsolete and empty, that there is a new imperative to which they feel compelled to respond.

This approach sounds very plausible, but does it work? The conciliatives may well be deceiving themselves: priding themselves on being in possession of a clever strategy for autocatalytic change, but actually being so paradigm-bound that they never progress much beyond the initial conforming stage. It is easy to be seduced by the cosiness of convention, to simply lose sight of any 'radical' conception one was once trying to achieve, and let oneself fall back into the ever-welcoming, but smothering, arms of Mother Culture.

One must remain sceptical about the possibility of achieving revolution by evolution. Certainly, the evidence from my own research leads me to suspect that the conciliative approach is more likely to be successful in bringing about first order 'developmental' change rather than second order 'transformational' change.

10 The corrosive approach

Profile

People using this approach see cultural change as an essentially political process, whose main purpose is to effect a major change in the locus and distribution of power and authority within the corporate hierarchy. Their view is that culture is the weft and woof of organizational politics, continuously shaped and coloured by volatile informal influence networks (Chapter 7).

This particular conception of reality tends to be reflected in a characteristically political discourse (Connolly, 1974). For example:

> The simplest way of regarding this culture change is as a power struggle between the radicals and the rest. The rest are always seeking to hold on to the authority and the status they have traditionally enjoyed. They have been successful in this over the years but our job now is to make them less successful. In any situation there will be winners and losers. My job is to see that we, the radicals, are the winners.   (senior manager)

At heart the corrosives are fundamentally pluralists – something which they have in common with the conciliatives. They do not see the organization in terms of formal authority but informal power: it is not the visible organization chart that is important but the invisible network of the power structure. In this network power is diffuse and multi-directional; it is shared and there is no dominant party, no single individual or group who enjoys the luxury of being able to impose a solution or course of action on the rest, no matter what the size of its police force (Chapter 3).

However, corrosives and conciliatives differ in the way they manage that pluralism. Whereas conciliatives are prepared to be open and accommodating in outlook, corrosives tend to be covert and devious, skilfully manipulating relationships in order to achieve their ends. Theirs is a zero-sum game conception of life in which gains are made only at other people's expense. Sorokin (1966) puts it well when he says that people who hold to this frame of reference see the changing world as booty to be grabbed, and everyone within that world as a potential enemy rather than a brother.

On the surface of this world there is peace and tranquillity, but beneath it there is a good deal of commotion and turbulence, an underground stock exchange where deals are struck and non-material goods and favours are bought and sold on a daily basis. This is all very different from the aggressives, whose simple response to pluralism is to ignore it or try to wipe it out! Corrosives work by erosion rather than by eradication, progressively undermining the power base of rival groups until a point is reached where they become either submissive or irrelevant.

Despite its covert operations, there is in fact nothing secret or exclusive about the informal system in which the corrosives participate. As Barnard (1938) pointed out in his classic treatise on this subject, membership of the informal system is not the privilege of the few, but a facility used by all. It is the natural consequence of human contact and interaction, hence anyone can engage in it and everyone does. The difference in the case of the corrosives is that they rely on it for the attainment of specific ends: the formal structure exists only to dot the 'i's and cross the 't's of decisions already taken by other people in other places. Their involvement in the informal network is neither accidental nor motivated by gregariousness.

This is not to say that business and pleasure are not sometimes combined, but social activities are usually regarded primarily as a way of cementing and strengthening the work relationship. The 'business angle' always imposes constraint upon the social side of things for, as Douglas (1987) has pointed out, in any political network no person can fully trust another. Relationships are contractual rather than social. A degree of collaboration is possible but full cooperation is not. Mistrust therefore to some extent deprives the relationships of their social value.

> No, they are not my friends so much as contacts. Although we have worked together for many years, I still don't know many of them well personally. Unlike a friend, you don't ask them for a favour unless you're giving them something back. When you are playing for high stakes it's very much dog eat dog, and it's really better that you don't complicate the relationship with too many personal ties and obligations. (manager)

This style of management will be familiar to industrial relations researchers and organization watchers, but what may be less familiar is the manner in which it impacts on processes of cultural change. The following rationales suggest that the pursuit of informal, non-legitimate and corrosive processes is indispensable to the process of cultural change and development.

Rationales

Performance-led culture change

Peckham (1976) defines culture as 'directions for performance'. He uses the term 'directions' in a very broad sense to refer to indications, signposts, codes of meaning, guidelines, instructions, orientations and definitions (which may be of a physical, linguistic, ergonomic, or visual type). By 'performance' he means both actions and institutions, the conventionally appropriate responses to cultural directions.

Peckham says that there is 'order' when there is symmetry in the relation between directions and performance. To bring about cultural change the balance between these must be disturbed. One approach is to change the directions, in the belief that this will lead to a change in performance (as for instance a 'no smoking' sign is intended to prevent people smoking). This approach of 'change by edict' is the preferred way of the aggressives. Hence,

DIRECTIONS ——————— govern —————————> PERFORMANCE
(culture)   (institutions)

The corrosives prefer to take the opposite approach, concentrating on the 'performance' side of the equation. Their management theory is simple – they just get on and do things, 'pulling' rather than 'pushing' for change.

> No memos, none of the rigmarole of putting something on next month's agenda (which I know will get thrown out) – we pick up the phone and fix things with each other. We just go ahead and make changes, and the formal system catches up sooner or later.

Their strategic map would look more like this:

PERFORMANCE ——————— governs —————————> DIRECTIONS

The paradox of this approach is that directions for change actually appear after the change has taken place! Or to put it more precisely, *de jure* status (legitimacy) is endowed upon a *de facto* development – the informal system leads the formal system, practice creates its own conventions. Culture endorses a course of action already taken and restores the symmetry of the relation – not the other way round. This is a reversal of Peckham's definition, and paradoxically implies that culture consists of 'performance for directions'.

The argument here is that the corrosive approach contains the three essential elements of cultural change:

- Tension: if there is no tension between directions and performance there is no dynamic for change. The corrosive approach produces such a tension by creating a gap between what the existing culture expects to be happening and what is actually happening. While cultural change may not take place, at least the potential for change is there.
- Action: the whole point about culture is that it is created by processes of enactment. It is more than an ideal, something that is real and actual. Cultural change can only be said to have occurred when people go out and do things differently. The trouble with the aggressive approach is that very often it does not lead to a change in actual behaviour – after the earthquake people basically pick up where they left off. The corrosive approach can at least claim to be putting the wheels of change in motion – letting actions speak louder than words, and setting a practical example for others to follow.
- Interaction: as I have insisted throughout, cultures are not changed *by* people but *between* people – in interaction. I have written elsewhere that

> Cultures are produced interactively and are therefore changed interactively. They are the product and the property of the interactants of a given organizational community . . . Cultural change must always have at its core some kind of participative communal activity.   (Bate, 1990: 40)

Thus the high-participation corrosive approach, with its multiple stakeholder interactions, contains one of the chief requirements for cultural change. In this regard it is much more likely to bring about change than the low-participation aggressive approach, with its simple and restricted interactions. This concept of interaction leads us into the next point.

Networks and culture change

The concept of the network is central to the theory of culture change. As corrosives would agree, the network is the basic unit of cultural production and modification: culture is produced on the loom of the network; change the shape of that network – by stretching it, extending it, or altering the thread or the weave – and the shape of culture changes with it.

Networks are not only channels of information and influence, but also channels of meaning – webs of signification (Geertz, 1973) – into which ideas are introduced and subsequently defined, developed, validated or corrected. From this perspective cultural change is a function of network complexity not hierarchical position: seniority alone does not confer the necessary power to effect cultural change.

The corrosives may be regarded as the people who choose to influence cultural change and development by varying the type, quality, shape and density of their relationships and interactions. They would argue that networks empower individuals (Brass, 1984), and individuals (in collaboration with other individuals) change cultures. In other words the network 'de-couples' them from the mother culture, while at the same time providing them with all the resources they need to develop new cultures (see the BR example in Chapter 3).

Networks have an impressive array of features for achieving this. They are (a) permissive (Mitroff and Kilmann, 1985), offering a 360 degree approach to any problem and an almost infinite capacity for deviant thought and behaviour; they are bureaucracy-jumpers and red-tape cutters (Mueller, 1987); (b) non-hierarchical (Kanter, 1988): within them people can take both the highways and the byways; they can go anywhere they like in the organization and avoid the trap of normal structural conventions; (c) self-reliant and self-helping (Mueller, 1987): networks take back some of the powers that have accrued at the centre, and offer a form of mutual help that pre-dates industrial society itself; (d) arenas for organizational learning, information-processing and meaning negotia-tion; (e) contextually sensitive processes (they respond to environmental shifts – see discussion of cultural lag in Chapter 7); and (f) flexible: they are polyvalent and multidirectional, and are highly tolerant of ambiguity, uncertainty and internal dissension. To put it briefly, networks have no respect for the boundaries and contents of the existing cultural paradigms within the organization.

One accusation that might be levelled at networks is that they only produce sub-cultures or minority counter-cultures rather than dominant cultures. There is in fact ample evidence to the contrary. As far as the scale of impact is concerned, one could argue that all of the large-scale cultural movements in history began from small-scale networks – socially transforming networks of people like environmentalists, feminists, civil rights activists, trade union activists (the Tolpuddle Martyrs, Solidarity workers in Gdansk), and many more (Mueller, 1987: 12) – rarely if ever from formal, top-down directives or initiatives from governments and establishment figures.

As with the first two approaches, however, we do need to be aware of the weaknesses and shortcomings of the corrosive approach to change. It could be argued that the above paints far too rosy a picture of networks, and overlooks their one serious drawback: the fact that, once established, they can so easily become order-directed rather than change-directed. The Old Boys Network is the classic example of a network that resists change and has as its main agenda the preservation of the status quo. There is nothing to prevent a network from practising only its defensive functions, dedicating itself to the neutralization of any new change initiatives and thus guaranteeing its own perpetuity. Informal networks can be as dedicated to order as they are to change. Therefore any approach that relies on the network as a vehicle of change must be regarded with suspicion. Things could so easily go the other way.

11 The indoctrinative approach

Profile

The last approach shifts the arena for cultural change from the rough and tumble of daily organizational life to the relative peace and quiet of the training centre, and focuses on the concept of cultural change as a *learning* process (Schein, 1985).

'Learning' is, of course, a very broad concept and incidental learning can be said to occur wherever there are people and whenever there is interaction. What makes the idea of establishing a new culture through training programmes so different, however, is that, as the term itself implies, the learning is planned and programmed, not incidental. There are designated roles of trainer or educator, a design for learning, a place of learning, a previously agreed body of knowledge to be imparted, and a professionally managed learning process. In none of the approaches so far mentioned can there be found an explicit framework for creating cultural change that is as strong and as organized as this one.

BT (British Telecommunications) is a typical example of a company that has approached cultural change from the training angle (see Box 11.1). ICL is another (Box 11.2).

Cultural training programmes obviously come in a wide variety of shapes and sizes. A small minority might be described as cultural 'exploratories', designed as an aid to personal consciousness-raising and development (cf. Marshall and McLean, 1985). The main purpose of these is existential: to give participants the opportunity of gaining a deeper appreciation of the corporate culture and the manner in which it impacts upon their daily lives. The experience is intended to be liberating: aware perhaps for the first time of the cognitive grounds that support habitual ways of doing things, people can work on freeing themselves from the tyranny of the cultural forms and attempt to regain some control over their psychological and social environment.

However, the great majority of education and training programmes have little or nothing to do with praxis or personal empowerment.

Box 11.1   'BT plugs into a cultural revolution' (*Source: Financial Times*, 27 March 1991)

In a small room several storeys above Glasgow's central station in Scotland a handful of aspiring revolutionaries gathers for a lesson in their new creed.

The ten people in the room are part of what BT hopes will be a sweeping cultural revolution. The new order created by the revolution will officially come into life on April 1.

The main message of the three-day course is simple: the new BT will not allow customer calls to get lost or to have them shunted endlessly from one department to another.

Thousands of training courses like this have been under way up and down the country to instil in BT staff a new sense of purpose – to serve their customers. Beneath the glitter of last week's launch of the group's redesigned corporate image, what really counts for BT's commercial future is whether the cultural revolution, dubbed Project Sovereign, is a success . . . Project Sovereign is one of the most ambitious attempts yet by a British company to overhaul its organization, management and culture.

Box 11.2   Achieving total cultural change (*Source*: Andrew Mayo, Director of Personnel, ICL International, 1989)

The second circle [in our model of culture change] is 'Education and Communication'. Everybody has to *understand* why we are doing what we are doing, to know why they have to shift their thinking. At a time therefore when many companies would have said 'Training is a postponable expenditure', major educational programmes were commissioned. Entitled 'Core Management Development Programmes', the objective was to communicate the strategic vision and the rationale behind it to all managers in ICL, and to reinforce the values of the ICL way.

Despite the variations between them, they all appear to be fundamentally very similar – and all raise the interesting ethical question as to when education is truly educative and when it has become just another word for controlling people (Chapter 3). The point here is that, although generally conducted in a cooperative and good-natured atmosphere, cultural education programmes are not egalitarian, self-directing or individual-centred. The language of training may seem so much more 'soft' and communal than that of the aggressives described earlier (for example, instead of 'directions' and 'rules' there are 'guiding commitments', 'persuasion' and 'conversion'), and this makes the training approach appear more legitimate and uncontroversial. Yet invariably what lies behind the democratic and pally facade is a learning situation as traditional and hierarchical as would be found in any family, school or apprenticeship scheme, one which 'imposes' itself more peacefully, but no less strongly, than the aggressive approach.

Culture programmes are, at the very least, socialization programmes: their aim is to 'fit' the participating individual to someone else's previously formulated definition of the situation. They are therefore necessarily 'taught' courses (Van Maanen and Schein, 1979), and do not presuppose the existence of any kind of reciprocal interaction or mutual learning. There is no attempt to conceal this fact, and the people attending such courses are left in no doubt as to why they are there: it is simply to hear and take on board the 'corporate message' and to be taught the core values (Alexander, 1987; Poulet and Moult, 1987; Cline, 1988; Murphy, 1989).

My own research provides a clear example. One of the organizations studied conducted a series of management seminars to accompany the change to a 'business-led' culture – nine days of marketing and strategic management training spread over a year, for all 120 of its business managers. The programme was designed and led by staff from a local university, but resourced mainly by people from within the company itself. On one level it was simply a course in marketing skills but at another, deeper, level it was a structured experience within which people were taught the 'basics' of the chairman's new cultural doctrine. Various documents written by the chairman or his top team were required reading, and the highlight of the course was the appearance of the chairman himself on the last day, the purpose of the visitation being to enable the participants – in his words – to 'put a face to the message'.

The guiding metaphors of the indoctrinative approach, like those of the aggressive approach, have a distinctly militaristic flavour. This time, however, the stress is more on the brain than the brawn, the idea being that managers need to provide strong and intelligent leadership and some tangible values for the 'troops' to follow. British Airways chairman Sir Colin Marshall, illustrates this point:

> In a sense, top management and corporate culture are interchangeable terms; for what top management perceives as useful and good, other managers will tend to emulate . . . A classic case is when an army changes a top commander. Whatever the merits of the argument about individual worth, when Montgomery replaced Auchinlech as the 8th Army's

commander in Africa in World War II, there was no question that the style, the culture and the modes of command changed very rapidly down to the combat units themselves . . . Top management has to make clear and explicit the values which will underpin the culture that it expostulates.

(1988: 36)

The case in point was the BA 'Managing People First' programme, a one-week programme for all 1,400 of its management personnel, aimed at removing the 'internal blockages' and 'converting' participants to Marshall's organizational values – caring, achievement, creativity, innovation and profit (Poulet and Moult, 1987: 64).

Another aspect of the indoctrinative approach is that, like the aggressive approach, it is distinctly Skinnerian, making use of 'cultural policing' (Peckham, 1976) to ensure that the appropriate responses to the corporate 'message' have been made – that people have begun to practise what has been preached. Dow Corning, for example, conducts 'surprise audits' on its employees to check that the ethical standards laid down in its codes are being obeyed (Murphy, 1989), and Blue Bell sends evaluation forms to course members' supervisors after a training programme has finished to assess the extent to which agreed action plans have been implemented and 'quantifiable improvements' in behaviour have occurred (Alexander, 1987: 47).

From Trice and Beyer's (1985) anthropological perspective, training programmes involve various kinds of 'rites'. Rites are organized and planned activities that have both practical and expressive consequences. The ones that are most relevant to this discussion are (a) rites of passage: new recruits learn the prescribed form of the new culture; (b) rites of enhancement: participants are repeatedly exposed to hypothetical situations (case studies, exercises etc.) which model and underwrite the 'new' cultural values – case studies serve as modern-day parables; and (c) rites of integration: lectures and discussions reaffirm the moral rightness of the new values and norms (some examples from the 'business seminars' above were entitled 'nobody owes us a living'; 'bigger profit means better service'; and 'responsible behaviour is meeting your bottom line').

I described these training programmes earlier as 'socialization' processes. Stronger terms would be 'indoctrination', 'cultural condition-ing' (Ochs and Schieffelin, 1984) or – more idiomatically – 'people-processing' programmes (Van Maanen, 1978: 19). Indoctrination is the extreme of one-way-only forms of learning, motivated primarily by a desire on the part of the corporate leaders to create a unified system of values throughout the organization (Chapter 3). The stress is on the communication of a complete *logical framework* or structure of thought (a doctrine), as opposed to a random assortment of separate substantive elements, and this is possibly the single most important feature of the indoctrinative approach. At a tacit theoretical level it reflects a commitment to the 'structuralist' position that form, not content, is the major source of meaning for people.

Forms expressing the 'new' culture come in a variety of disguises: credos, ethical codes, value statements, mission statements, and many more. What they all have in common is the ambition to make the *managerial* culture into the *corporate* culture (see Sir Colin Marshall's opening comment above). Bråten's (1973) apt phrase for this brand of cognitive imperialism is 'model monopoly' – the dominance of one world-view over the rest. The re-creation of the organizational culture in the leadership's own image has long been part of the management dream, indeed it is as old as management ideology itself.

No description would be complete without a reference to that exemplar of the indoctrinative approach, Disneyland. Strong culture organizations, like Disney, have made this approach their very own. The attraction is that it provides the perfect setting for turning leaders' fantasies into reality, a closely controlled environment within which language and symbols can be manipulated in order to implant the chosen meanings into the victims' minds! Van Maanen's fascinating, behind-the-scenes, view of the University of Disneyland (see Box 11.3) provides a suitable end to this section.

Box 11.3   The University of Disneyland (*Source*: Van Maanen, 1991)

Paid employment at Disneyland begins with the much-renowned University of Disneyland whose faculty runs a day-long orientation programme (Traditions I) as part of a 40 hour apprenticeship programme, most of which takes place on the rides. In the classroom, however, newly hired ride operators are given a very thorough introduction to matters of managerial concern and are tested on their absorption of famous Disneyland fact, lore, and procedure. Employee demeanour is governed, for example, by three rules:

First, we practice the friendly smile.
Second, we use only friendly and courteous phrases.
Third, we are not stuffy – the only Misters in Disneyland are Mr. Toad and Mr. Smee.

Employees learn too that the Disneyland culture is officially defined. The employee handbook puts it in this format:

Dis-ney Cor-po-rate Cul-ture (*diz'ne kor'pr'it kul'cher*) n 1. Of or pertaining to the Disney organization, as a: the philosophy underlying all business decisions; b: the commitment of top leadership and management to that philosophy; c: the actions taken by individual cast members that reinforce the image.

Language is also a central feature of university life and new employees are schooled in its proper use. Customers at Disneyland are, for instance, never referred to as such, they are 'guests'. There are no rides at Disneyland, only 'attractions'. Disneyland itself is a 'Park', not an amusement centre and it is divided into 'back-stage', 'on-stage' and 'staging' regions. Law enforcement personnel hired by the park are not policemen but 'security hosts'. Employees do not wear uniforms but check out fresh 'costumes' each working day from 'wardrobe'. And, of course, there are no accidents at Disneyland, only 'incidents'.

So successful is such training that Smith and Eisenberg (1987) report that not a single Disneyland employee uttered the taboo and dread words 'uniform', 'customer' or 'amusement park' during the 35 half-hour interviews they conducted as part of a study on organizational communication.

The university curriculum also anticipates probable questions ride operators may someday face from customers and they are taught the approved public response. A sample:

Question (posed by trainer): What do you tell a guest who requests a rain check?

Answer (in three parts): We don't offer rain checks at Disneyland because (1) the main attractions are all indoors; (2) we would go broke if we offered passes; and (3) sunny days would be too crowded if we gave passes.

Shrewd trainees readily note that such an answer blissfully disregards the fact that waiting areas of Disneyland are mostly outdoors and that there are no subways in the park to carry guests from land to land . . . They discuss such matters together, of course, but rarely raise them in the training classroom. In most respects, these are recruits who easily take the role of good student.

During orientation, considerable concern is placed on particular values the Disney organization considers central to its operations . . . Elaborate checklists of appearance standards are learned and gone over in the classroom and great efforts are spent trying to bring employee emotional responses in line with such standards. Employees are told repeatedly that if they are happy and cheerful at work, so, too, will be the guests at play. Inspirational films, hearty pep talks, family imagery, and exemplars of corporate performance are all representative of the strong symbolic stuff of these training rites.

Rationales

Changing culture at a deep-structural level

According to Peckham's (1976) theory mentioned earlier, cultural change occurs when the balance between directions and performance is disturbed – either because the directions change (aggressive approach) or because performance changes (corrosive approach).

To locate the indoctrinative approach within this scheme we have to introduce into the discussion a third element from his model: the notion of *meta-directions*. These may be thought of as the 'directions for issuing directions': they are the guiding principles, the founding or generating ideas – the philosophical as opposed to normative frameworks of organizational life.

If directions and performance are the 'content' and 'process' of culture, then the meta-directions are its 'form'. They give identity, wholeness and organization to directions and performance; they add the missing cultural ingredient to these more mundane aspects of life; they are the doctrinal and logical material from which particular normative directions are shaped. The directions act as their agents in the field, ensuring that philosophy is being translated into action at the various empirical frontiers of the organization.

The whole model of a cultural system therefore looks like this:

FORM		CONTENT		PROCESS
meta-directions	<———>	directions	<———>	performance
(philosophies)		(norms)		(action)

Unfortunately the diagram does not show the degree to which each can influence the others. My view is that changing the meta-directions will have a proportionately greater impact than changing either of the other two elements. The reason is that meta-directions are the 'frame' within which reality is defined. Change these and the whole definition of reality changes. The scale of this is therefore second order whereas change in 'performance' – the everyday enactments – tends to be of a more first order nature.

The indoctrinative approach might be seen as superior to the other approaches because it is operating at this level of meta-directions, devoting itself to changing the underlying frame of meanings and values, and leaving directions and performance to follow on naturally and developmentally behind.

This seems to be the gist of what a director was getting at when I interviewed him about his culture seminars:

If I can get my people on board to the basic idea of our new culture, the rest should follow. This is what our seminars are all about: give them the highway code and leave them to get on with the driving. As long as I can be sure they're out there following the rules of the road, I don't have to waste time checking up on them, or issue thousands of fancy instructions that they have no intention of carrying out.

If we now superimpose the four approaches on this conceptual scheme, we can see that the indoctrinative approach is located in the most strategic and influential area of all, at least as far as major, second order change is concerned:

META-DIRECTIONS	DIRECTIONS	PERFORMANCE
Indoctrinative	< ——— > Aggressive < ——— >	Corrosive and
approach	approach	conciliative
		approaches

(Note the position of the conciliative approach. This has not been discussed in relation to the model but it is felt that its pragmatic nature – its suck-it-and-see philosophy – would put it in the performance-led category along with the equally pragmatic corrosive approach.)

The theory is certainly very convincing, but what about the practice? Once again we find that it does not necessarily live up to expectations. The evidence from my research shows that while the indoctrinative approach may be in the right place for effecting major cultural change, there is considerable doubt as to whether, in its present form, it is actually capable of making any real mark on the meta-directions of an organization. The main weakness is that it has no theory of learning associated with it, only a theory of teaching, which is of course a very different thing. This point is taken up again towards the end of this chapter.

The fit between the indoctrinative approach and classic OD

The indoctrinative approach has one great claim to respectability, namely that it follows the teachings of mainstream organization development. It shows a perfect fit, for example, with Beckhard's (1969) classic definition of OD as (a) a planned and deliberate attempt to introduce change, (b) managed and led from the top, (c) introduced system-wide, and (d) based on an educational strategy, and is thus grounded in an explicit theory of change. Its success will therefore depend on the particular strengths and weaknesses of this orthodox change model when applied to *cultural* change.

One of the most criticized aspects of the OD model, however, is the notion of planned change, the problem being that planned approaches rarely seem to go according to plan (recall the fuller discussion of this in Chapter 7). This seems particularly true in the area of cultural change. As Dyer (1985: 222) has noted, cultural change occurs, as often as not, in spite of rather than because of any definite plan on the part of the leadership:

> The events that precipitated change in the cultures of the [five] companies studied were *not* planned. Unanticipated recessions, financial crises, and the illness or death of key leaders were instrumental in triggering cultural change in these companies. Serendipity and historical accidents played critical roles, and while it may be possible to anticipate such occurrences, managers' abilities to control these events are negligible.

The planning contained within cultural indoctrination programmes is subject to the same limitations. For example, the research suggests that few of the people attending courses swallow everything that they hear hook, line and sinker, or go through the 'conversion' experience that the leaders are seeking (Poulet and Moult, 1987). Even Disney would accept this:

> There is a limit to which such overt company propaganda can be effective. Students and trainers both seem to agree on where the line is drawn for there is much satirical banter, mischievous winking, and playful exaggeration in the classroom . . . it is difficult to take seriously an organization that provides its retirees 'Golden Ears' instead of gold watches after 20 or more years of service.   (Van Maanen, 1991: 67)

As we noted in Chapter 3, people are well able to make up their own minds about what they are prepared or not prepared to accept.

There is also doubt as to whether a change in the meta-directions, accompanied by appropriate training, always works through into the participant's day-to-day performance. Training of the kind described does seem to give participants what Giddens (1979) calls a 'discursive' kind of consciousness, that is a theoretical knowledge of culture, one that enables them to think and talk about it in an informed way. What it does not give them is a 'practical' consciousness of culture – a form of knowledge that they can actually use in their everyday life. One reason for this is that, despite the good intentions, there is rarely any comprehensive follow-up developmental activity beyond the initial programme. What is lacking is a protracted socialization process of the kind upon which the approach is modelled, e.g. mother–child, teacher–pupil, one which gradually establishes a bridge between concept and action, and grounds and embeds new meanings in the participants' personal reality.

To summarize, we might say that values training programmes in themselves do not seem capable of indoctrination and control, only communication and influence.

This is all quite consistent with Louis's (1989) suggestion that culture cannot be 'taught' on simple *information-giving* lines. Her point is that cultural learning must be active: it has to be 'sought' by the individual concerned following the reverse *information-seeking* principle. The passive recipients of disembodied cultural messages from the heavens hear little and learn even less; the message passes them by. To engage with it they must be switched into an active receptive mode; they need to participate in the kind of independent, self-directed, exploratory, responsible and active learning process that is absent from most indoctrination programmes.

If, as Louis is suggesting, cultural learning – and therefore cultural change – can only occur in routine, continuous, experiential and interactive settings, it follows that the unroutine, discontinuous, non-experiential and non-interactive setting of the indoctrination programme is not the place to be trying to achieve cultural learning and change.

Perhaps the villain of the piece is therefore the classic OD paradigm itself, its particular values and rationale having misled people into taking inappropriate action in the particular area of cultural change. For example, OD stresses being explicit whereas cultural knowledge is tacit and implicit, and cannot easily be 'stated'; much of OD is also acontextual (Pettigrew, 1985), whereas cultural knowledge is highly contextual (i.e. statements made about culture out of context may be meaningless and incomprehensible); OD stresses planned and systematic approaches to change, whereas cultural knowledge is informal and disorganized; OD stresses hierarchy and leadership, whereas cultural knowledge is shared and built up through processes of mutual exchange; and OD is ahistorical (Pettigrew, 1985) whereas cultural knowledge is emergent – statements made at a point in time lack a sense of historical development which may be important in applying the information (Louis, 1989).

In short, it may be that the kind of processes encouraged by OD are better suited to 'technical' rather than 'cultural' forms of learning, insensitive to the special characteristics and qualities of cultural knowledge, and incapable of providing the kind of conditions that a cultural learning process requires.

While intervention at the level of an organization's meta-directions would seem to offer one of the most promising routes for achieving cultural change, the field is still waiting for an approach that is capable of doing just this.

12 Evaluating different approaches to cultural change

The design parameters for cultural change

Looking back on the four approaches to change discussed in the preceding chapters, I am tempted to ask the same question that Henry Mintzberg (1979: 468) asked having spent more than 150 pages describing his five 'structural configurations': do they really exist? In addition to stealing his question I should also like to steal his answer: in one sense the four approaches to change do not exist at all. They are only words on pieces of paper (my words, at that), not reality itself. The problem with words is that they often become disconnected from their subject; like shadows they are simpler and sharper round the edges than the real thing.

However, just because they are not real does not mean they are not useful. As Mintzberg observed, 'there are times when we need to caricature, or stereotype, reality in order to sharpen differences and so to better understand it' (1979: 304). This is the point I would also make about my own work: I have overstated each description to make it clearer, and am not suggesting that an exact replica is ever likely to be found in an organization. The best way to regard each of the four approaches is as a 'pure' type, a primary colour with many shades. In this sense, therefore, it might be said that the approaches do exist, albeit in more complex and diverse forms.

Real approaches to cultural change in all but the most trivial organizations are enormously complex, far more so than any of these described here. The closest we can get to reality is to say that there are a lot of people out there trying to achieve cultural change with a wide variety of different – often fundamentally different – methods. The problem in the real world is that we are spoilt for choice – there are too many options to choose from. Selecting the best option is a daunting and by no means straightforward task.

So how do we know whether we are going about things in the right way, and how do people who are planning to embark on a programme of cultural change begin to put together an approach that will effectively meet their requirements? This brings us to the sticky question of what constitutes an 'effective' approach to cultural change – the main concern of the next two chapters.

At the start of this section I made it clear that the approaches to be discussed were not specific to cultural change but may be found in all types of organizational change. However, what is of interest to us here is finding a way of evaluating their effectiveness with particular regard to *cultural* change. This raises a number of fundamental questions: What indeed is 'effective' cultural change and how are people to know when they have achieved it? Are some approaches generally better than others, or will their effectiveness vary from situation to situation? If this is the case, what are the conditions for this? Then there is the question, 'effective' from what and whose point of view? These are difficult questions to which organization theorists have yet to provide convincing answers. With interest in the topic of changing the organizational culture running so high among practitioners it is unfortunate that there is so little guidance on these issues.

Further progress at the level of implementation depends very much on our ability to analyse cultural change attempts and develop some criteria against which they may be constructively assessed. From my own research data and a wide-ranging survey of the literature I have extrapolated what I believe are the core elements or components of any method for changing organization culture. They are not only evaluation criteria; they are also design criteria, the equivalent of Mintzberg's 'design parameters' – the basic elements to be used in the design of effective cultural change programmes. The reference to Mintzberg's work is deliberate: thanks to him we have design parameters for structure, now we need them for culture.

The design parameters hold the key to effectiveness in cultural change programmes. Their role is to help us find a method for getting from A to B without taking too many wrong turns or getting hopelessly lost along the way. They are like maps: while they do not actually tell us the best route to take they do show the various alternatives that are available and provide a focus for discussions about the right way to go. To put it another way, they offer a grid for decision-making about change. The aim of this chapter is to help an organization to select and prioritize its design parameters for cultural change.

The complication about the parameters in question – and what makes them different from maps – is that they have no fixed or universal value. What might be effective or appropriate in one situation may be ineffective or inappropriate in another. Take the example of 'expressiveness', the first of these parameters. In situations where second order transformational change is desired, 'expressiveness' is an essential ingredient of the change method, but where only first order cultural development is desired (i.e. more of the same) it is of less importance. 'Durability' is another example: using an approach that creates durability may be desirable when the culture in question is functional and dripping with unexplored potential, but undesirable when that culture is in decline. The same may be said of 'commonality': as we have seen, in some companies a strong set of shared values may be a source of strength whereas in others it may be a weakness, so the importance of commonality will vary. The requirements of an organization will also change over time – for example, expressiveness will be very important at the birth of a new culture, whereas commonality and penetration will be more important considerations when it is beginning to develop and grow.

Before examining the parameters in detail we must therefore stress that they are not fixed benchmarks for assessing the effectiveness of any approach to cultural change, nor ideal targets that cultural change designers should be aiming for. The key point to be grasped is that the weight, relevance and value of these will vary from organization to organization, and from period to period within the same organization. The very essence of the strategic process is one of subjectivity – of people struggling to arrive at their own conclusions about the importance of these dimensions and the weight that should be given to them with respect to their own organization. They have to make their own decisions, not let a book do it for them.

There are five design parameters. Each of these is a quality or characteristic of any approach to cultural change, a factor that should be taken into account when designing a change programme. The parameters are summarized below together with the particular aspect of organization to which they relate:

Design parameter	Aspect of Organization
Expressiveness (The ability of an approach to express a new core idea)	**The affective component** (feelings)
Commonality (The ability of an approach to create a unifying set of values)	**The social component** (relationships)
Penetration (The ability of an approach to permeate different levels of the organization)	**The demographic component** (numbers involved)

Adaptability (The ability of an approach to adjust to changing circumstances)	**The developmental component** (process)
Durability (The ability of an approach to create a culture that will be lasting)	**The institutional component** (structure)

I shall now define these in turn.

Expressiveness (the affective component)

This is the ability of a cultural change approach to:

- Initiate and express a core or founding idea, a symbol of sentience that has the power to 'move' people.
- Create a 'significant form': an idea or image that expresses something in a novel, symbolic way. Through symbols it articulates and presents concepts, enabling people to grasp something that was previously ungraspable, realize something that was previously unrealized, and comprehend something that was previously not comprehended. It is the essence of every art (Langer, 1953; the phrase 'significant form' was first coined by Clive Bell, the art critic).
- Express something known but not previously named.
- Capture people's attention; excite, energize, activate and disturb them.
- Create something irresistible, a compelling idea; it attains the status of a cognitive imperative (Oakes, 1980).
- Create a 'design concept', the basis for something completely new.
- Evoke a feeling and a picture.
- Arrest normal action: stop people in their tracks and set them thinking.
- Put across a message that can be digested easily.
- Encapsulate a big idea in a few words or a simple picture; 'communicate the big picture' (Carlzon, 1987: 98); put it all in a nutshell; hit the nail on the head.
- Communicate a simple idea that people can understand, one that illuminates, enables them to see things in a new way (even if they do not necessarily agree): 'We need at the end to have simplified to a stage where one sentence, almost a slogan, will describe what we believe, and what we can . . . work to. We aim to make the

simplifying process one of distillation and concentration . . . '
(Harvey-Jones, 1989: 56).

- Make previously unrelated thoughts and ideas fall into place: it is an
  organizing idea (Timasheff, 1965: 262), a systematizing and directing
  mode of thought; cf. Ibsen's 'Bedentungsfeld': a group of words that
  forms some kind of semantic unity (Miller and Johnson-Laird, 1976:
  237).
- Put things together in such a way as to create something that was not
  there before – something much more than the sum of the parts.
- Convert people: make them reject a previous view.
- Displace a previous 'ruling truth' (Allais, 1989): knock it off its perch,
  discredit it, make it passé or obsolescent. The important thing is that
  there is a substitution.

It should be noted that all of this adds up to something much more
than 'vision'. A 'vision', an overused term that has become a rather trite
and meaningless expression, is an attempt to articulate, as clearly and
vividly as possible, a desired future state (Belgard et al., 1988: 135). It is
mainly cognitive and rational, with the accent on producing a 'real'
picture in the mind (it shows us something), whereas a 'significant form'
is mainly affective (with the accent on producing an emotional truth) and
existential (in the sense of triggering an out-of-frame sensory experience
and a new quality of awareness). The quality of a significant form is that
it is enchanting and bewitching like a fairy tale. It is, in fact, just this – a
fiction, a confabulation, a myth which acts as the vehicle for the
communication of meaning (Bettelheim, 1977; Boje et al., 1982).

Producing these significant forms is probably the nearest one comes to
being an artist in an organization (Chapter 1). As described here, these
forms are the 'Music of the Spheres' (Kelly, 1990: 3), the beautiful
product of the left hemisphere of the brain, with its talent for developing
a melodic line, working in tandem with the right hemisphere of the brain,
with its talent for form and harmonic structure. We may not always like
what we hear, but it cannot be ignored; the tune is catchy: we find
ourselves humming it even when we hate it!

Not all visions have the sensate quality of significant forms, and not all
significant forms profess to having a clear view of the future. Visions are
imaginary and future-orientated, whereas significant forms are immediate and impactful, and very much in the here-and-now. Arguably, with
regard to gaining the necessary commitment for a change programme
significant forms are more important than visions because they engage
the heart as well as the mind – they gain the attention, and potentially the
commitment, of the full person to the core idea. Perhaps there is a place
for both. For example, Martin Luther King's powerful 'I have a dream'
speech was an exquisite synthesis of vision and expressiveness. Or

perhaps it is simply a case of restoring 'vision' to its richer, biblical meaning. Biblical visions were complete experiences and gripped mind, emotion and spirit. Since then the wholeness of the concept has unfortunately been cut down to fit modern Western rationality.

Whichever words we choose, the point is that expressive forms are structures of feeling as well as structures of thinking. The Apollo space project is a good example of this:

> By committing themselves to 'placing a man on the moon by the end of the 1960s', the leaders of the project took a stand. The clarity and conviction they generated touched people at all levels of the enterprise. One can imagine how much less spectacular the results might have been if they had adopted an alternative mission statement, such as 'to be leaders in space exploration'. Unfortunately such 'motherhood' mission statements are the norm for most organizations.   (Adams, 1984: 71)

However, recalling the introductory comments, not all approaches to cultural change will be seeking this quality. There is a time and a place for everything, including expressiveness: it would hardly have been appropriate if an inspiring idea like the 'man on the moon' had been followed shortly after by another equally inspiring, but different one. Too many engaging ideas are likely to cause confusion and ultimately cynicism. Another point is that not any old idea will do since different times will require different kinds of ideas.

Commonality (the social component)

Having a dream is one thing, getting others to want to share in it is quite another. No one person – not even a powerful leader – can create a culture single-handedly. Culture is a social product, produced not *by* people but interactively *between* people. For an idea to achieve cultural status it needs to be transferred from the individual to the group and recreated in the collective imagination of the whole community (Polanyi and Prosch, 1975), whether this be the whole organization or merely a part of it. This quality of commonality is the essence of culturalness. In such a situation:

- Individuals 'share the categories of their thought' (Douglas, 1987: 8).
- People think and feel alike: there is a 'thought collective' (Fleck, 1935: 41).
- They speak a common tongue – there is linguistic homogeneity.
- They are prepared to share responsibility for what happens and not undermine or subvert it.

There is

- 'Common ownership of the broad parameters of what the world may look like' (Harvey-Jones, 1989: 55).
- A sense of shared meaning, collectivity and common purpose.
- Solidarity, completeness of commitment and support.
- Comradeship and fellow-feeling.
- A unified system of values.
- Coincident meanings.
- Homogeneity and consistency of shared understandings (Louis, 1985).
- 'A cooperative community' (Douglas, 1987: 31).

This might be summed up by the word *intercommunion*:

> This concept refers to the fact that individuals are similarly affected by contact with the same organizing idea, that they spontaneously recognize the similarity of their mental states, and that in this manner they are induced to common action.   (Timasheff, 1965: 263)

Penetration (the demographic component)

Another factor to be considered in the design of a cultural change programme is how far one wants the change to spread throughout the organization. For example, if a complete organization-wide change is being sought (rather than say a change to the culture of the senior management group or a work group) one will be looking for an approach that has the quality of 'penetration'.

Another type of penetration is also significant, namely how deeply people are individually or collectively affected by the change. The term 'penetration' is used here in both of these senses. It refers to the extent to which the approach can:

- Permeate the organization and become entrenched in local systems of knowledge.
- Create a large constituency that 'votes' for the core idea, and a caucus of support to promote and champion it.
- Acquire legitimate status.
- Penetrate deeply into the individual and collective consciousness.
- Become part of everyday language and discourse – a talking point.
- Become incorporated into the organization's mundane methods of operating.
- Become actualized in everyday behaviour.
- Attain the quality of 'of-courseness' and the status of common sense.

- Become firmly anchored in people's minds.
- Achieve so high a profile that it cannot be ignored!

Adaptability (the developmental component)

Another question that must be asked is how adaptable we need our cultural change programme to be. Obviously all approaches must be adaptable to some degree, but this factor will be particularly important in organizations that are operating in turbulent, unpredictable environments, for example, an organization like British Rail (BR), which after a relatively long period of stability now finds itself on the verge of privatization and large-scale change. Whatever BR has today may not be appropriate for tomorrow. 'Adaptability' is the extent to which an approach to cultural change is:

- Capable of maintaining a steady rate of development within its own parameters.
- A mutant cultural form, capable of necessary reorientation but able to retain popular support.
- An evolving approach which, once initiated, develops by itself.
- Flexible enough to deal with the many unknowables in the environment (Quinn, 1982).
- Mimetically connected to the changing aspects of the situation.
- An 'intelligent' approach: one that questions its basic premises, can rethink its assumptions, and if necessary retrace its steps.
- Permissive: tolerant of deviance and experimentation.
- Continually striving to transcend itself, yet never believing in the attainability of an ideal state.
- Resistant to being typecast and becoming an 'ism' or dogma.
- Capable of self-parody, avoiding taking itself too seriously!

Durability (the institutional component)

Finally, there is the question of how durable we want the newly created culture to be. Again this will vary. For example, the desire to create something lasting is likely to be strong in the period following a major cultural upheaval. On the other hand, durability is an undesirable objective to be pursuing when the culture in question is in decline. As we shall shortly see, some approaches fare better than others in their ability to create a lasting culture, and it is up to those involved in masterminding the change to ask how important this is and choose their methods accordingly. A durable culture is one that:

- Has acquired momentum so that it cannot readily be halted or reversed (Miller and Friesen, 1980).
- Can withstand and manage conflict and opposition.
- Is supraindividual, transcending the individual(s) whose activities called it into being (like a work of art that outlasts its creator).
- Cannot be tampered with by individuals at will.
- Becomes institutionalized: the subjective idea takes on the character of external objectivity, acquiring firmness in a person's mind; it acquires its own 'reality': 'The institutions are there, external to him, persistent in their reality . . . He cannot wish them away. They resist his attempts to change or evade them. They have coercive power over him, both in themselves, by the sheer force of their factity, and through the control mechanisms that are usually attached to the most important of them' (Berger and Luckmann, 1966: 78).
- Gives rise to a governing structure of norms that give stability to the idea and allow it to be enforced.

Assessing the four approaches in terms of the design parameters

The above design parameters provide a basis for evaluating the effectiveness of any cultural change programme. For example, if we take the four approaches discussed in this section we can now analyse them and identify those areas in which they are strong and those in which they are weak. I have carried out such an analysis based on my own observations of these approaches (and their variants) in practice, and the results of this assessment are presented in Figure 12.1 opposite. Each approach has been given a simple rating of High (H), Medium (M), or Low (L) on each of the five design parameters, and from this an initial impression of its effectiveness can be gained. This is supplemented by a brief qualitative analysis within each box of the table.

This analysis provides a framework for the design of an effective approach to cultural change. An example and further discussion of this will follow in the next chapter.

Approaches to cultural change

Design parameters	AGGRESSIVE	CONCILIATIVE	CORROSIVE	INDOCTRINATIVE
EXPRESSIVENESS	**H** — Radical. Innovative. Idealistic. Deals in plain and simple messages. Confronts and discredits existing ruling ideas	**L** — The pursuit of pluralism and balance dilutes the message and makes it wishy-washy. Lots of detail but no simple core idea or ruling truth. Softly-softly approach: works with rather than against the existing order	**L** — Pragmatic – no strong guiding principles. Point is *not* to show your hand: the aim is to conceal rather than reveal. Sometimes deliberately obfuscate and put out mixed messages. Makes compromises for the sake of a deal	**H** — Specializes in communicating core messages, employs people specially trained to do this, and takes place in a situation removed from normal action, where people are more suggestible
COMMONALITY	**L** — Creates rancour, discord and disharmony among groups. Top-down method leads to resistance, and fails to gain common ownership of the proposed change	**H** — Highly participative. Operates on consensus principles and deliberately seeks to unite people in thought. Creates a trust culture of solidarity and comradeship	**L** — Self-interest prevails over common interest. Strong win – lose orientation. 'Mistrust is so deep that cooperation is impossible' (Douglas, 1987)	**L** — Promotes a cooperative community feeling, but only among a group that ceases to exist after the indoctrination programme ends!
PENETRATION	**M** — Widely marketed and merchandized, but does not necessarily affect everyday 'consumer behaviour'	**H** — Involves much time in the field talking to people, familiarizing them with the proposals and discussing the implications	**M** — Selective in its application, but where it does occur it is deeply embedded in everyday action	**H** — A structured learning experience designed to deepen understanding. A total immersion programme
ADAPTABILITY	**L** — Dogmatic, single-minded and inflexible. Messianic – set in tablets of stone. Suffers from belief in the instant solution: weak 'developmental orientation'	**H** — Open-minded, always willing to accommodate new views. Working constantly to achieve best fit with people's demands and situational requirements	**H** — Has a strong pragmatic orientation and is not rule-bound. Is demand-led: the informal power network is infinitely flexible and is continually responding to changing requirements	**L** — Everything is 'programmed'. Emphasis is on conformity and uniformity. No provision for experimentation or deviance: 'yes-men' preferred
DURABILITY	**L** — The Big Idea is everything; structural follow-up is neglected. Based on the cult of personality, rarely transcending the person who created it. Alienates certain groups who seek to undermine it	**H** — People are keen to preserve what they have painstakingly created together. New culture is grafted firmly onto established practices	**L** — Each 'deal' is struck according to the needs of the moment; corrosives resist any formal structuring that would reduce their ability to do this. Based on personal relationships that frequently change	**L** — Theoretical, and ungrounded in the local reality: the effect soon wears off back in the workplace. People do not feel compelled to defend and maintain what they have not helped to create

Figure 12.1 Evaluating the effectiveness of different approaches to cultural change according to certain key design parameters

13 Designing an effective approach to cultural change

However tempting it may be just to choose what seems to be the best of these approaches and slot it into your organization (especially one like the conciliative approach which scores highly on a number of factors), it is unfortunately not as easy as that. You do not tend to get an effective approach to change by simply taking something ready-to-wear straight off the peg. Unless you are very lucky none of the four approaches described is ever likely to give you everything you want, indeed you cannot even assume that a high-scoring factor is going to provide anything relevant to your own situation. It is far better to assume that you will have to build up your change programme piece by piece, tailor-making it to your own particular aims and requirements, using the design parameters as a guide.

You have to begin by asking yourself what are the appropriate design parameters for your situation. 'Effectiveness' is a function of selecting those criteria that are most relevant to what it is you want and what the situation requires. If cultural durability is the most pressing need, you obviously would not use an aggressive approach (at least not on its own). However, if it is second order change that you require there could well be a case for such an approach. As I say, you pick your approach according to your need.

This probably sounds obvious but the evidence suggests that people frequently do not do this. More often than not they merely apply the method they have always used in matters of change, cultural or otherwise. They select their approach uncritically and then they stick to it throughout. One problem with this is that the approach may of course be inappropriate from the start. Alternatively, what looks like a promising approach initially may become less and less appropriate as the programme unfolds.

The criticism that I would make of normal ways of implementing change is that on the whole they tend to be narrow and inflexible and to be framed with too little regard to the particular purposes for which they are required. To give this criticism more substance I would say that too many change programmes are:

- *Solitary* Each approach represents an independent province of meaning, structured in its own time and place (Schutz, 1967), and intolerant of promising, potentially complementary, approaches. The chosen change method tends to occupy the users' whole field of attention, having its own immanent and self-sufficient logic and mode of justification. This is typical of the 'either–or' mentality discussed earlier: people tend to go for one approach or another, rarely a combination of approaches.
- *Persistent* Having adopted a particular approach people tend to stick to it from beginning to end. There is no criss-crossing from one approach to another and no conception of changing the approach as the change process unfolds. Alternative methods or a sequence of methods are 'unthought of' (Wilkins and Dyer, 1988: 525) – out of sight and out of mind.
- *Generic* The chosen approach is the 'Man for all Seasons' – invariant, applied uniformly in all situations regardless of events or circumstances; it is not interactive with its environment.
- *Automatic* Approaches to change are not so much conscious strategies as a manifestation of different management styles. People tend to use them spontaneously, unreflectively and uncritically without deep consideration of the point or appropriateness of their activities. As far as change is concerned they simply do what comes naturally to them.
- *Ungrounded* Approaches to change rarely take account of the culture that is to be changed (Chapter 7). They tend to be stock methods, probably the same ones that will be used when a change in technology, structure or systems is being implemented.
- *Inflexible* People tend to get locked into a particular style and become incapable of responding to the changing needs of the cultural development process. A strong commitment to one approach reduces versatility and prevents exploration of the full range of options available.
- *Consonant* The approach to change is itself culture-bound – people tend to adopt a method of change that avoids dissonance with the existing culturally preferred method. 'Conciliative'–type cultures tend to adopt conciliative change methods, and 'aggressive'-type cultures aggressive ones. The result is that the existing culture is actually reinforced and sustained. The method becomes not so much a method of change as a method of order.

The above features are characteristic of a *morphostatic orientation*: people come to organizational cultural change with an approach whose underlying form is already fixed, and they stick with it throughout. The flaw in this is that a static approach is being applied to a dynamic process. As Whittle and others (1991: 3) have so rightly pointed out:

> Cultural change is not an event (although it may be achieved through events) but an ongoing sequence of changes – a journey rather than a destination.

This is very much in agreement with what I was saying in Chapter 7 about the notion of a cycle of cultural development. With this in mind, I believe that the morphostatic orientation needs to be abandoned in favour of a *morphogenetic orientation* (Smith, 1984; Lundberg, 1985) – a more fluid, change-orientated, environmentally sensitive model, one that allows different approaches to be used at different stages of a cultural cycle.

The basis of the morphogenetic approach is 'frame fluidity' (Wilkins and Dyer, 1988: 527), which in terms of my Figure 12.1 in the previous chapter means reading up, down and across the whole table, picking from the complete range of options, and not allowing oneself to be confined within the column of any one approach. Managers of change therefore need to build up a varied repertoire of approaches from which they can select the one that best aligns with the dominant activities of a particular episode within the change sequence. This, in turn, requires greater awareness of what the alternatives are, and the skills to recognize when a switch is needed, what the next approach should be, and how the transition can be achieved. At times it will also be necessary for people to nurture and protect those approaches that are not consonant with the existing organization culture.

The key issue in all of this is *appropriateness in time*: in deciding on the initial approach managers of change will have to put together something which reflects what is required at that moment in time, but that approach must be expected to change as the programme unfolds. Once the process is under way and the cycle of change begins to occur it will be necessary to modify the approach to match the particular stage in the cycle that has been reached – one approach has to give way to another. Because there is a limit to which one can plan ahead in these matters (see Chapter 7), people need to be opportunistic and take seriously to heart the principle of 'flexible design'.

Just as there is no one best approach, so there is no one best sequence or combination of approaches that can be prescribed for all situations. However, in this chapter I should like to recall the typical life cycle of culture described in Chapter 7 and offer one example of how different approaches may be used at different points in this cycle. This particular model would be appropriate for an organization whose culture is in decline and in need of radical transformational change. It begins with the birth of a new culture, after which its growth and development are nurtured from youth through to maturity.

It is not necessary to use any of the four approaches in their pure, undiluted form. There is no reason to restrict one's choice simply to these four, just as a painter would rarely choose to work only in the primary colours. Like the painter, one selects from a wide range of shades of the original colours in order to produce the desired effect. The important thing is that the colours should complement each other and add up to a pleasing whole. The painter must be aware of this and have a concept of the whole picture even while working on only one part of it. So, too, with the organization culture designer. In the following illustration I shall be working in both primary colours and shades of them.

A note of reservation: what follows cannot adequately capture the essence of this artistic process. Words on the page make the business of change much too clear and logical, and can easily give the impression that each approach is used separately from the others as part of a linear or episodic sequence. The reality, one that cannot be conveyed in words, is that there is much blurring around the edges, with the different approaches frequently overlapping, converging, diverging and intertwining with one another as the change runs its uncertain and unpredictable course. Furthermore, just as a colour will be repeated in different parts of a picture, so may a particular approach need to be repeated in different parts of the change process.

Another problem is the word 'organization' itself, a term that has probably been used much too loosely in recent chapters. It is important to state from the outset that the aim will almost certainly not be to change the whole of the 'organization culture' – this is probably neither possible nor even desirable. As I said in earlier chapters, one does not – and should not – set about the complete change of a culture (after all it would be a pity to throw the baby out with the bathwater), but should identify the specific mentalities or sets of mentalities ('isms') within it that need changing. It is therefore better to regard the model as applying to particular vicious circles of thinking rather than a culture in its entirety. Hence, the short-term 'organization culture' should be seen to refer to that particular aspect of the culture that one is seeking to change.

With these limitations in mind we can now introduce the model for second order cultural change and discuss how the different approaches are involved.

The *aggressive approach* has received a very mixed press to date. Nevertheless, it has to be said that it is probably the most expressive of all methods for changing culture, and the only one that is capable by itself of triggering a second order change. This or some variant of it is therefore arguably the best way to begin the process. (It does not have to be as brutal and heavy-handed as it often is. With certain modifications it could be redefined 'Progressive', and this would reflect the positive role it can play in the change process.) However, as we know, one of its weaknesses is that it often provokes negative reactions and unleashes forces that may prevent the change from going forward. Other problems are that it is weak on 'development', lacking follow-up and finish, and poor at handling the many interests affected by the change, and therefore has little use beyond the initial stage of the change programme.

The *conciliative approach* may be weak on expressiveness but it scores high on the other design parameters, especially commonality. It can therefore offer excellent follow-up to an aggressive beginning by providing the opportunity for everyone to argue and have their say, exert some influence and thereby gain ownership of the ideas. It also acts as a safeguard against any excesses on the part of the aggressors. In any case the intention is to phase out the aggressive approach as the conciliative approach comes into play; the latter approach, however, may well extend for the full duration of the change programme, running concurrently with other approaches, on account of its versatility – this can be seen in the large number of 'Highs' in its column in Figure 12.1. For example, apart from helping to create commonality, it is also able to give stability and permanence to any change that occurs, providing a level of durability that no other approach could give.

After a period of conciliation, some variant of the *indoctrinative approach* might be brought in to draw these emergent ideas together and enable them to be systematically incorporated within the participants' personal frames of reference. Including it at this stage in the programme reduces the danger of any single group imposing its own ideas on the rest and alienating them. With an emphasis on mutual learning and the sharing of ideas the process becomes one of socialization rather than indoctrination. Re-labelling the approach as 'educative' gets away from the associations with brainwashing. (This is a good example of using a 'shade' rather than the original primary colour.) Referring back to Figure 12.1, we also see that one of the strengths of this approach is penetration. If, as often happens at this stage, one is looking to spread the word to other parts of the organization and to deepen its penetration into the members' frames of reference, the approach may well provide an ideal vehicle in this regard.

After this the change programme can be handed over to the informal political processes of the organization, their unique contribution being to translate words (and ideas) into deeds, concretizing commitments and enabling them to be adapted for use in everyday life. Unfortunately, one of the problems with any *corrosive approach* is that it is impossible to control, and may just as easily undermine a change programme as reinforce it. However, placed here it does not enjoy the unfettered freedom to roam at will and do its own thing. Already there are parameters laid down – and around which a good deal of support will have been mustered (and not just from senior groups) – that contain and direct the informal system. Given these limitations on its freedom, and the fact that it is likely to be working in a positive way, the derogatory implications in the term 'corrosive' are no longer justified. 'Corrosion' suggests a weakening process, like rust eating away metal, whereas the approach in question is actually adding strength. It might therefore be more appropriate simply to label it 'informal networking'.

By carefully mixing and combining the approaches one moves towards the achievement of one's objective – a second order cultural transformation followed by a period of first order growth and development for the newly established culture. Of course the choice of approach is not the only issue. The broad conditions for change also have to be right (Chapter 7). However, what can be said with confidence is that the chances of attaining one's goals are heightened by the adoption of the approaches in combination rather than individually, showing once again the value of the 'both–and' philosophy.

So much for the synopsis. Let us now look at the details of the model, this time concentrating not so much on the approaches as the essential stages through which they take the cultural development process. Figure 13.1 gives a summary of this process, showing the various phases of change and the different approaches and design parameters relating to these. The model has been superimposed on the curve or cycle of cultural growth, development and decline that was discussed in Chapter 7.

First phase: deformative

In this first phase a qualitatively different construction or impression of reality is starkly presented, one that captivates people and moves them to experience their situation in novel, and often unanticipated, ways. Stravinsky's 'The Rite of Spring' was 'deformative' (Griffiths, 1978: 43), a savage and audacious force that destroyed most of the established conventions of music and left people reeling. Many condemned it as a barbaric annihilation of all that musical tradition stood for, while others praised it for doing precisely this. It produced a reaction – and this is the whole point about a new paradigm: love it or hate it, you cannot ignore it; you just have to respond to it.

In using such an approach deliberately, one is seeking to deliver some kind of shock to the system that will lead to a change of 'track' or 'orbit' (disengagement or reorientation), and trigger a process that will take the organization off in a new direction (Bate, 1978). 'Induced crisis', as this

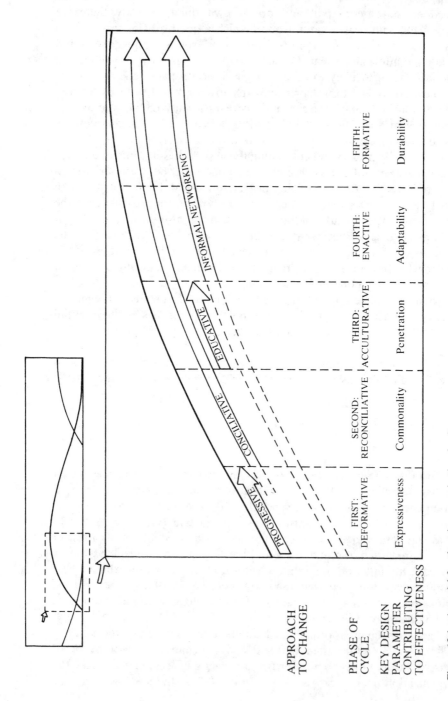

APPROACH TO CHANGE	PROGRESSIVE	CONCILIATIVE	EDUCATIVE	INFORMAL NETWORKING	
PHASE OF CYCLE	FIRST: DEFORMATIVE	SECOND: RECONCILIATIVE	THIRD: ACCULTURATIVE	FOURTH: ENACTIVE	FIFTH: FORMATIVE
KEY DESIGN PARAMETER CONTRIBUTING TO EFFECTIVENESS	Expressiveness	Commonality	Penetration	Adaptability	Durability

Figure 13.1 A model for changing organizational culture

is, is justified in situations where the existing 'glue' holding the culture together (Baker, 1980: 8) has set so hard that it requires an extremely powerful solvent to loosen it. Communist Eastern Europe is one obvious example. As John Simpson, BBC television's foreign correspondent, remarked about the events unfolding in this part of the world, 'A certain amount of violence is necessary to bring change about.' This all contrasts very sharply with piecemeal approaches such as gradualism and incrementalism: as I have already noted these get bogged down in politics and frequently end up going nowhere. The aggressive type of approach has no truck with this, and will resist any attempt by the old order to reassert itself or to continue to serve up 'more of the same'.

The use of shock tactics may sound rather heavy-handed but it is rooted in the belief that if one waits for people to initiate voluntarily second order change – and here we are talking mainly about those in positions of power with strong vested interests in the status quo – one may have to wait for ever:

> The mass of mankind wants its existing orientations reinforced, no matter how outworn and false they may be, for new ideas are uncomfortable and disturbing. The market for the exhausted and dead is limitless, the market for the new and the real is tiny and profitless. Only a fraction of mankind can endure either novelty or a little more reality than they are adapted to.
>
> (Peckham, 1981: 28)

The fact must be faced that most people prefer things to stay as they are, even if this is to their cost. If change must take place, then better to let it be first order, incremental, adaptive change and hope it will suffice. Johnson (1990: 187) has noted that such timidity and caution are particularly observable at the level of strategic change:

> There is typically a marked resistance to substantial change . . . as Grinyer and Spender (1979) show strategic change may take place readily within the constraints of what they call the recipe, but infrequently outside it.

It is this kind of resistance that change programmes have to overcome if they are to make any progress, and here is where aggressive tactics have the advantage. They 'punctuate the equilibrium' (Tushman and Romanelli, 1985), produce 'framing confusion' (Bateson, 1955), and introduce 'semantic discontinuity' (Peckham, 1985) into the situation. The pressure for change comes from the fact that people can only stand so much uncertainty before they have to do something about it. As Goffman once said: 'We tolerate the unexplained but not the inexplicable' (1974: 30).

As a result of 'dissolving the regnant constructs' (Peckham, 1985: 60), people are compelled to switch from an automatic processing mode (a routine, non-reflective way of thinking) to an active, 'consciously aware' mode of thinking and enquiry. This is absolutely essential, for as Parrett (1987: 22) has pointed out, most people rarely have cause to examine their values and beliefs:

> A person need not be conscious of holding a basic belief yet he is committed to it; he thinks and acts in accordance with such a basic belief as if it were true. But further, a person need not have to express explicitly his basic beliefs. Commitment to these beliefs is so fundamental that people usually go through life without needing the opportunity to express them explicitly.

The effect of moving people from the implicit and unconsidered to the explicit and considered is to render the existing paradigm susceptible to conscious thought and challenge, and to reveal to people what Peckham has called the 'culturally redundant absurdities' (1985: 174) of the situation – habits of mind which belong to an age gone by, which need to be weeded out and dispensed with.

A mode of thought is thus created which can no longer be accommodated comfortably within existing orthodox forms, and whose very presence now produces the tension or dialectic for a process of second order, frame-breaking innovation to occur (Watzlawick et al., 1974). Like Stravinsky's 'The Rite of Spring', this act of cultural rebellion mounts an assault on tradition and conventionality and undermines epistemological certainty; it alters the rhythms, tempos and bar lines of life, challenging what has always been counted on to be good, dependable common sense.

Common sense is one of the prime targets of the exercise because it is this which stands between people and change. It is the enemy of change; it discourages any kind of reflection, introspection or criticism, and above all it paralyses action. Arthur Koestler's account of what happened to him in the Spanish Civil War illustrates this point beautifully. Reflecting on his experience, Koestler asked himself why he had not done the logical thing and left Málaga before the enemy arrived, thereby avoiding his later imprisonment and sentence of death. He was in no doubt as to the cause – the problem had been 'common sense': the 'smiling voice' of common sense had persuaded him, against his better judgement, that he did not really need to go (see Box 13.1).

Common sense is a cultural system. Intervention in the common sense systems of an organization must therefore logically hold the key to cultural change. The whole point about beginning with an aggressive type approach is that this is precisely where it claims to excel. More than any other approach it is capable of putting the frighteners on the common

Box 13.1 The Smiling Voice of Common Sense (*Source*: Arthur Koestler (1937), *Spanish Testament*)

I was reminded of a scene from a play about the French Revolution by a German writer of the last century. Danton learns that Robespierre is going to have him arrested on the following day, and he flees from his house at night. He wanders blindly across the dark heath. It is cold and windy and suddenly he has a feeling that it is highly illogical to be wandering at night over a windy heath instead of sleeping at home in his good bed. Robespierre and the Convention seem to him unreal figments of the imagination, and the only common-sense thing to do seems to be to go home to bed and sleep. This he does. 'Even should we know in theory,' is the substance of his reflections, 'even should we know in theory of all the dangers that threaten us, deep down in us there is a smiling voice which tells us that the morrow will be just as yesterday.' The next morning he is arrested.

Deep down in us, too, on this last evening was that smiling voice that told us that the morrow would be just as yesterday.

The next morning at 11 a.m. we were arrested.

As Ernest Chausson the composer once remarked, 'Common sense always lands you in it' (Nichols, 1992: 44)!

sense beliefs of the establishment, and forcing people to think for themselves.

Therefore, to sum up, this first phase is a period when the forces of history and tradition are contested and a torrent of creativity and innovation is unleashed. It is not so much a time of solutions as a time of questions. It is a period when deviation meets head on with conformity, when people can be found 'going up the down staircase', and when efforts are being made to transcend the cultural protocols of the situation and make the organization more avant-garde in its tastes. It is the period when the ruling truths and conventions are challenged and discredited.

It may be a period of liberation but it is hardly a time of elation, for what people experience as the result of these aggressive interventions (sometimes following a brief initial period of euphoria) is a form of 'culture shock' (Brown, 1986: 35), a condition that may involve them in a good deal of stress and discomfort (such as occurs frequently among people who go to live abroad or move to a new organization). Adler has provided a good description of this condition:

> Culture shock is . . . a form of anxiety that results from the loss of commonly perceived and understood signs and symbols of social intercourse. The individual undergoing culture shock reflects his anxiety and nervousness with cultural differences through any number of defence mechanisms: repression, regression, isolation and rejection . . . With the familiar props, cues, and clues of cultural understanding removed, the individual becomes disoriented, afraid of, and alienated from the things that he knows and understands.   (1972: 8)

In spite of all this, it would be wrong to label this first phase as destructive. As Timasheff (1965) would say, it is as much an act of foundation as it is of termination. The process is one of deconstruction–reconstruction, not simply an act of demolition. The intention (no matter how naive) is that a phoenix, that symbol of cultural replenishment and renewal, will rise from the ashes of the fire that has been lit.

Whatever the moral objections to this approach – and there are many – it cannot be denied that it is a powerful learning process, one that is rooted in the age-old concept of sink or swim. Sensitivity is certainly not its forte – those operating in this mode would not deny this, but then again they would argue that a degree of *insensitivity* is precisely what is needed to get the change process started. Much better to leave it to those involved in the next phase of the process, the professional conciliators, to pick up the pieces and make something of the opportunities that have been created.

Second phase: reconciliative

One of the great myths currently circulating in the business world is that culture can be created by those in senior positions and imposed on the rest of the organization in a top-down fashion. Such a view is, I believe, seriously misguided. It is now widely accepted by academics from many disciplines that you cannot 'impose' a culture. Anthropologists, who after all were the originators of the culture concept, have always assumed this to be the case. As Meek points out,

> Most anthropologists would find the idea that leaders create cultures preposterous: leaders do not create culture, it emerges from the collective social interaction of groups and communities. (1988: 459)

The point that must be grasped by practitioners is that cultural change, as the above quotation states, is very much a collective enterprise; participation, involvement and dialogue are all essential. Cultures are produced interactively and therefore can only be changed interactively.

They are the product and property of the interactants of a given organizational community and are not readily susceptible to the influence of any single individual member. Like it or not, cultural change must always have at its core some kind of participative, communal activity. In this respect cultural change is the great leveller. In the area of culture no position or group is privileged. No one has a monopoly or even a majority shareholding in the ownership of culture. It remains outside the grasp of any one person and is remarkably unimpressed by rank or hierarchy.

Of course people at the top (or anywhere else for that matter) may come up with ideas and attempt to frame the situation for others, but this is not the same as creating a culture.

> Managing the deepest layers of culture requires a participative approach . . . because top management, with or without the help of consultants, cannot dictate changes in assumptions about human nature and the business environment, they can only set appropriate parameters.
>
> (Hassard and Sharifi, 1989: 12)

Management practitioners seem to have had some difficulty grasping (or should the word be 'accepting'?) this point. One way of persuading them of its merits is simply to remind them of what happens when the top-down approach is used. On the face of it change may seem to have been accepted, even welcomed. However, more often than not it is a classic case of people saying one thing but doing another. Hassard and Sharifi again:

> Top-down approaches yield changes that are relatively easy to bring about, but which are difficult to sustain; these approaches generally result in overt compliance to what is mandated, but not covert compliance.   (1989: 13)

Changing culture is all about changing meanings, but as I have argued repeatedly in this book the problem is that such meanings cannot simply be imposed; people will always end up producing their own meanings (in the informal system) despite what has been provided for them. In recent years this point has been made particularly strongly in the field of media and cultural studies, where the monolithic (Murdoch?) scenario of a ruling force producing mass culture through a medium like the press has now been discredited:

> Despite the power of ideology to reproduce itself in its subjects, despite the hegemonic force of the dominant classes, the people still manage to make their own meanings and to construct their own culture within, and often against, that which the industry provides for them.   (Fiske, 1987: 286)

What happens when you do not offer a participative phase is that a lot of people will almost certainly react against the planned change and go off and do their own thing. Remember that in our model there is, as yet, no sign of a 'new culture'. All that has happened so far as a result of phase one is that an attack has been mounted on the old culture and a new set of ideas has been presented. The peace has been shattered; shock waves are echoing around the organization. Inevitably the forces of resistance have begun to muster.

Which brings us to why the present 'reconciliative phase' is needed. The aim of this phase is to give the ideas social form and to bring about the necessary change from individualism to collectivity. The purpose is not so much to help the parties come to terms with the proposed change as to let them participate in the making of those terms, widening rather than narrowing the possible options open to them. The underlying theory, which may appear paradoxical but in practice is not, is that convergence is achieved by encouraging divergence – unity through diversity.

At this stage the prevailing emphasis on the ideas themselves therefore begins to fade and an alternative field of attention – centering on the issue of the politics of acceptance – comes into focus. The main task here is the management of pluralism: preventing the mobilization of potentially uncontrollable political forces and regaining the trust of the parties involved. This is a time for putting the reality back together, albeit in a different form; declaring a truce between the proponents of the old and the new, and getting them to sit down together; identifying and extending the zone of agreement between the parties and finding ways to unite them in thought.

It is now that we begin to see a move away from the 'dominant ideology' model normally favoured by the aggressives to one that emphasizes a decentred power struggle among conflicting discourses and institutions, and a commitment to radical eclecticism (Collins, 1989). This represents a switch in approach (though not as abrupt as it appears here) to one that provides the missing participative element in the change process. This is very much a second phase in the programme, and there should be no suggestion that the efforts of the aggressives are in any way discredited by this move (or accredited for that matter). The fact is that they are simply making way for an approach that is better suited to this phase, a conciliative type of method being the obvious choice because it is strong on the two design parameters most relevant to the task in hand, namely 'commonality' and 'penetration'.

New paradigms confuse and politicize things (Nicoll, 1984: 165). The role of the conciliator is to deal with this confusion and handle the politics of change. A process must be set in motion that will enable all aspects of the proposed change to be fully considered and allow a common interpretation of (though not necessarily agreement about) the 'new reality' to emerge. Individual meanings must be exchanged and fitted into bigger structures of collective meaning. Thus the task of negotiating a new order is begun – the stress being very much on negotiation and joint meaning-making rather than imposition and unilateralism.

Where there is no consensus of meaning there is no scope for further progress at a cultural level (remembering that consensus defines the boundaries of a culture or sub-culture). Obviously there is nothing to prevent people at this stage from trying to impose some of their ideas in the form of rules, but this of course then becomes normative change not cultural change, with those involved doing what is required of them not because of anything they have agreed but because they are obliged to do it.

There is nothing soft about this reconciliative process nor does it have much to do with the sort of 'consensus seeking' approaches we often read about in the organization development literature. The order is a negotiated order: people do not see eye to eye on everything, or even most things. As we have said many times before, culture is not a perfectly formed, monolithic entity but a loose package of diversities.

Those leading this part of the change programme therefore require a wide range of skills in order to tackle the many tasks that face them. These include creating a climate for argument and debate, taking account of alternative and oppositional positions, and coordinating the heterogeneous audiences; overseeing and mediating in the social interactions of the different stakeholder groups; in short, creating a 'productive community' for culture.

The target must be the establishment of a cultural democracy where the emergent culture is held and sustained in the form of a social contract: an agreed interpretation of reality based on a mutuality of meaning, shared understandings and reciprocity.

Third phase: acculturative

So where have we reached in the cultural development process? A core idea has been expressed, tossed around, stretched and distorted in a number of directions. Now we need to look around and take stock of the joint meanings that have accumulated. Like all creative activities, the reconciliative phase has been volatile and messy, affording little time for tidying things up and putting them in an intelligible order. We must begin to clarify and consolidate what has emerged, and to allow those affected by the changes to think about the new cultural meanings in a more personal sense and find ways of accommodating them within their existing frames of reference. Therefore the key factor in this next phase is 'penetration', and for this an indoctrinative type of approach is particularly well-suited (see Figure 12.1).

The first two phases might be summed up in Weick's (1979) aphorism that first you must capture people's *attention* (first phase) and then you must capture their *intention* (second phase). We must now move into a third phase, one which is concerned with communicating and ingraining the collective meanings that have been emerging, and gaining the *commitment* of those involved.

There is no quick-fix way of communicating the new message and getting it to stick. 'Dick Tracy' merchandizing methods are ephemeral – the product is likely to be thrown away with the wrapper. Deeper penetration of the message requires more than flirtations with fashion, glossy advertising and bland mission statements. If the focus of the previous phase was negotiation, the keynote of this one is learning. Learning is the basis of remembering. Organizations often suffer from 'corporate amnesia' because of their failure to initiate a learning process. In cultural matters there is always a need for a well-organized socialization and learning process ('acculturation', in cultural terms) and the *indoctrinative approach*, or rather a variant of it, provides the ideal vehicle for achieving this. Its role is crucial in turning the change process into just such a learning process.

During this phase the work of the conciliatives still continues, but an education programme is introduced to run in parallel with it (Figure 13.1). Its primary purpose is to organize, 'format' and diffuse the emerging meanings and values underpinning the new culture. As I have said, cultures are the result of social learning, and this phase provides a forum where learning the ways of the new culture can begin. It involves distilling and repacking the – by now highly complex – ideas, making them more accessible and coherent for people, and therefore easier to assimilate and retain in the memory. As a result the culture begins to take root in individual consciousness.

In contrast with the first two phases of this model, which might be said to involve opening up activities, this phase is concerned with narrowing down activities. This is the issue of 'orientation': we shield our minds from having to consider anything and everything that the reconciliative phase may have thrown up, and prevent excessive stimulation and overload. 'Orientation' is concerned with the framing of culture – providing a 'formative context' (Ciborra and Lanzara, 1990) which shapes the way people perceive, understand, make meaning, perform and get organized.

This phase also provides the opportunity for further negotiation of meaning by organizational members. It should be a far cry from the indoctrination activities described in Chapter 11. As we have seen, what normally tends to happen is that the leaders decide what the new corporate culture is going to be and immediately follow this up with indoctrination-type training programmes – effectively inoculating people with a strong dose of their way of thinking. My proposed model is very different. By following a period of participation and wider involvement, rather than coming hot on the heels of the first phase, the type of training programmes envisaged here no longer contain only the guiding values of the leaders but the negotiated and agreed views and beliefs of a much wider constituency of people.

In practice the formal, classroom-based programmes are no longer one-way 'teaching' forums, which exist for the sole purpose of relaying the message down from the top, but interactive milieux in which there is an exchange of views and *mutual* learning. The model of adult–child socialization, widespread but largely unsuccessful in the organizational context, is abandoned in favour of an adult–adult model, one in which meanings are no longer imposed from the outside, but jointly negotiated and agreed from the inside. In this sense everyone can be said to be contributing to the development of the emerging culture by way of a structured, but self-directed, learning process.

The intention is that people leave this particular phase with a framework of personal commitments and obligations (and rights, of course) which they themselves have helped to create and around which they feel a sense of ownership. It is important to have this because they are about to enter the 'hands-off' period in the growth of culture, a time during which they will be entrusted with putting these commitments and obligations into practice within the context of the informal or 'unmanaged' part of the organization (Chapter 3).

Fourth phase: enactive

The point has now been reached where all the 'pre-match' talk ends and the actual 'game' – the transference of the 'espoused' culture to the 'actual' culture – begins. The players are, as it were, ready to play. They know the overall game plan (first phase), they have put together a community of (broadly) like-minded people (phase two), and they have also learned and internalized the basic rules of engagement for the game itself (phase three). In short, they have reached the critical moment when they must now translate words into deeds and put to the test their ability to discharge their personal obligations and to achieve effective concerted action. This fourth phase can therefore be labelled the *enactive phase*.

It is the point at which the cultural meanings that have been forming in people's minds make contact with everyday behaviour – where they become *cultural practices*. It thus marks a significant shift from the 'thinking and talking' phase to a phase where abstract and generalized ideas are concretized in situation-specific action schema. A 'practical consciousness' (Giddens, 1979) of culture must now be acquired, as distinct from the 'discursive consciousness' aimed for in the second phase: people must relate what they have learned to day-to-day matters and develop the skill to use it to achieve practical outcomes. In Geertzian terms this is the embedding of the emerging culture in systems of 'local knowledge' (Geertz, 1983), and in Weickian terms, 'enactment' (1979), constructing and acting out the new culture within the context of everyday roles and practices. The stress now more than ever is on process – of a culture not made but still in the making.

If the change process is to develop further, it must now be given its head; its development must for the time being be handed over to the informal system, which will carry the new cultural meanings into the nooks and crannies of local practice, and allow them to permeate deep into the minutiae and mundaneity of daily organizational life. This will afford the opportunity for people to work through changes on their own 'patch', making whatever contracts are necessary in their own way. In other words we are talking about the method of 'informal networking' mentioned earlier (Figure 13.1), which relies on the notion of 'performance' leading 'directions' in order to advance the process of cultural change (Chapter 10).

If the new culture is to endure it must be able to satisfy local needs and requirements – it must be a contingent culture. To achieve this, the informal system must be granted all the freedom that it requires to allow for further improvisation, negotiation, accommodation and mutual adjustment to take place. Only the informal system can do this. It must become a legitimate and accredited part of the change process, not regarded (as it so often is by managers and policy-makers) as an unwelcome intruder into the organization's affairs. We have reached the stage where the detailed politics of cultural change need to be addressed. Formal systems can deal with issues of authority, but only the informal system can deal with the raw issues of power and power relationships.

The informal political processes precipitated by any programme of change are usually highly unpredictable, and left to themselves with nothing to guide them they may do little to advance the change programme – in fact they may seriously undermine it. There is virtually no way of preventing such processes since they are an inevitable feature of organizational life. Indeed, they will have already been operating continuously since day one of the change programme – and before. However, the conciliators should have been able to minimize the risk of the informal system reacting negatively and dismissing the proposed change before it has been given the chance to prove its worth (or otherwise). Thanks to their sterling efforts, those currently involved can now afford to take a fairly relaxed view of the informal processes and have sufficient confidence that they will make a positive contribution to the programme. People may have autonomy (indeed, as we have seen, always will have autonomy in cultural matters), but what the previous phases have helped to ensure is that this will be 'responsible autonomy'.

This may sound rather like the manipulative system of self-control which was criticized in Chapter 3, but the difference in this case is that it has not been a single management group making the rules but a wide constituency of different interest groups. In my model, managers may manage change but it is not they who exclusively decide on what that change should be.

Responsible autonomy is manifested in two forms of enactment: first there is 'personal enactment', which is what the individual undertakes to do in order to make the culture live in an everyday sense, and second there is 'collective enactment', what people resolve to do together in order to ensure that this happens.

To illustrate what is meant by the first type we can refer to the cultural transformation that has been taking place in the UK supermarket industry since the early 1980s – a case to which the model outlined in this chapter would be well-suited. This has involved an attempt to shift the culture of the supermarkets from a 'best price' ('pile 'em high, sell 'em cheap') culture to a 'best value for money' (though not necessarily cheapest price) kind of culture. In addition to this, it has also involved commitments to customer care and Marks and Spencer-style service – the total quality concept (Ogbonna and Wilkinson, 1988).

The broad core idea for the new culture has been enacted through a great number of specific initiatives taken at the local, supermarket level: for instance, a rapid expansion of product lines to cater for a wide range of tastes; the extension of shopping hours into evenings to make shopping more convenient for customers; the siting of new superstores away from city centres to make parking easier; the provision of restaurant and child care facilities, and so on.

However, most of the onus for achieving genuine cultural change has fallen on the shoulders of the individual employees themselves. It is in the actual roles they play that we will be able to discern whether or not cultural change has occurred – in the personal enactments of the agreed cultural direction. A customer-caring culture only exists in reality when front-line supermarket staffs display something more than just a superficial courtesy and act in a manner that is responsive to customers' needs – behaviour more often associated with an airline steward(ess) than a store employee.

The mention of the airline stewardess takes us back to an earlier discussion in Chapter 3 and reminds us that the important thing is that employees 'smile' because they want to do it, not because, like the air hostesses at Delta and the employees at Pizza Hut, they have been told to do it. This again is why the previous stage of actually involving employees in the formulation of a culture is so important. Unless there is this, a gap between the espoused culture and the actual culture will always exist.

One recalls all too painfully the sight of a bored British Rail catering employee slopping anaemic-looking tea into several cups at the same time while a long thirsty queue of impatient customers looked on, and a huge sign above them – the latest cultural initiative from the marketing department – proclaimed 'BR: Putting Its Customers First.' A perfect example of a good idea that had failed to materialize in the role enactments of the actors themselves.

There is, of course, always the problem of what to do with the newcomer, the person who has not shared in the authorship of the culture and therefore does not own it in the same way that longer-serving employees might do. There is no easy way of getting round this problem, but if we remember that cultural change is not a one-off event but a continuous process it should be one in which new employees can join and participate at any point. A commitment to enfranchising them to do this is the important thing. There must be a continuous participative process in which they can influence and share in the making of meaning – formally and informally.

The issue of enfranchisement brings us to the second form of cultural enactment – 'social enactment'. Seattle's Seafirst Bank is a real-life example of a business that has followed a programme of change very similar to the model proposed here, and which has paid particular attention to the issue of enactment. It all began with the realization in the mid 1980s that the bank was suffering from a bad case of 'cultural lag' (Chapter 7) and that dramatic changes were needed in order to bring it up to date and make it more relevant to the environment in which it was operating. Mr Luke Helms, the bank's president, stated the problem in blunt terms: 'We discovered we were offering exactly what the customer *didn't* want and doing a good job of it. We were trying to push people into cash machines – but they wanted to deal with human beings. We were trying to push people into pre-packaged products – they wanted choices' (1988: 69).

The existing culture was seen to be seriously flawed. A whole new cultural paradigm was required, one that recognized banks as retail and distribution businesses which therefore needed to be customer-driven. The company began by devising a new strategy to create a sustainable sales and service culture at Seafirst (the first 'expressive' phase of my model). They saw the weaknesses in trying to impose such a culture and decided the only way forward was to have extensive dialogue and involvement (second phase). It also became apparent early on that training was going to be one of the biggest challenges and as a result of this the Seafirst College was created in partnership with the University of Washington. In line with normal university practice, the emphasis was to be on learning, not indoctrination (third phase).

Which brings us to the present phase of enactment. Helms and his colleagues drew exactly the same conclusions that I have drawn: that the only way to ensure an effective transfer of the new cultural meanings into specific cultural practices was to hand over the change programme to the participants themselves and let them jointly decide how things should develop from here on. The employees in the bank's 164 branches were turned into 'franchisees' and given 'local ownership' of their businesses. The reasoning was simple:

> We felt that our employees in Yakima knew more about Yakima than headquarters in downtown Seattle did. Why not leave them alone, we reasoned, and let them 'own' the business? (1988: 70).

The franchise had no legal standing; its role was purely symbolic: it stood for trust, autonomy, respect, responsibility and initiative. As with all symbolic acts, a certain amount of hype and ceremony was in order: 'We held ceremonies in each branch in which we gave the branch manager a certificate of "ownership".' (The certificate in question is reproduced in Figure 13.2 below:)

Although this does come dangerously close to the 'hoopla' and gimmickry I was poking fun at in an earlier chapter, its justification in this case is that it actually gave people much more than a mere piece of

Figure 13.2 Tides change at Seafirst

paper: it gave them the freedom to create their own self-governing cultural principalities within the larger organization state. Furthermore, the ceremony was a recognition not so much of the leader's value system (although to avoid this impression it might have been better to leave Helms's bust off the certificate), as of a value system created (and continuing to be created) by a wide range of individuals and groups. The franchise encapsulated the ideal of a cultural democracy; it made the informal system legitimate, and initiated a process whereby people became jointly responsible for the making of a local culture within the agreed national guidelines. Recalling an earlier phrase, it was a 'productive community' for culture in every sense of the word.

Fifth phase: formative

In this book culture has been defined as a variety of things – a strategic orientation, a process, a set of practices, a structure. The implication is that if we are to 'change culture' we must therefore work on changing all of these things. This in a way is what this illustrative model has been about: finding a way of changing cultural orientations (phase one), cultural processes (phases two and three), cultural practices (phase four), and now cultural form. The model has remained faithful to the initial perspective. The final phase we now move into is concerned with the last of these aspects: the structuring of culture and the creation of form.

It will be recalled from Chapter 2 that the structuring of culture requires a synthesis of art and design – this being captured in the phrase the 'architecture of meaning'. The basis of this activity is to make the 'invisibles' in the organizational culture – the ideas, orientations, under-standings, processes, intentions – visible. This is the essence of all art, the notion of giving an idea form. It is precisely what I was getting at in Chapter 2 when I wrote the following: 'Organization design should be elevated to an art form, its aim being to achieve what any work of art would be broadly seeking to do, i.e. symbolically represent reality, capturing and freezing a message or idea in structural form, and creating an illusion of life – a truth rather than the truth . . . The aim of organization design should be to produce a work of art.'

Burke once said 'Talk is everything'. He would no doubt approve of my change model, which it must be admitted does involve an awful lot of talk! Unfortunately Burke was wrong. Talk – at least in matters of change – is not everything. What it lacks is permanence and conse-quence. Like a tent, it blows away in the wind, leaving no residue or trace. This last phase of the model is here to ensure that instead of a tent we end up with something more like a solid piece of architecture, not necessarily complete but at least reasonably secure and well founded. In other words we are looking to satisfy the last of the design criteria for a cultural change programme, namely 'durability'.

In the literature the giving of constitutive form to a change process has many labels, the most common being normalization, stabilization, objectivation, institutionalization or anchoring (Berger and Luckmann, 1966; Meyer and Scott, 1983; Pettigrew, 1985; Scott, 1987; Zucker, 1987, 1988; Hennestad, 1991). Any one of these could be applied to the fifth phase of this model.

Probably the single most important feature of my model for cultural change is that it is based on the concept of post-structuring: structure follows process – 'design' follows 'development' – not the other way round. Most change programmes seem to do these things in reverse, placing structural change at the beginning of the process (structure-led change), and using a top-down 'Mafia' model of organization design (Stebbins and Shani, 1989) to implement it. In such cases, structuring exists not to liberate action but to frame it, not to widen dialogue and choice but to narrow them – a case of locking the door *before* the horse has bolted! In my model, letting the horse bolt is actually an essential part of the change process.

The underlying argument is that structure creates nothing. Creation will already have occurred by the time this final structuring activity takes place, in a process that has been unfolding ever since the start of phase one. The role of structure (and here we would also include systems – for example appraisal, reward and recruitment systems) is simply to capture, reflect, reinforce and consolidate the product of this protracted creative process. This as I have said is 'poststructuring' not 'restructuring', an activity that stems from the conviction that *organization* does not precede the process of *organizing* but follows it. It marks the end of a programme that began with an act of dissolution and now finishes with an act of resolution.

The structuring activity is not only a consolidating force but also a stabilizing force. In the words of Peters and Waterman (1982: 315), it is the 'stability pillar' that every organization requires, the simple, consistent, underlying form that maintains broad yet flexible enduring values.

Normally, when restructuring occurs at the start of a change programme it does exactly the opposite – it is a destabilizing force, precipitating a good deal of disruption and upset. This is not surprising. All new structures are intrinsically meaningless, and they contain few directions for performance. They are empty frameworks waiting to be filled with meaning. In contrast, phase one of this model contains lots of meaning and little form. The poststructuring process of the final phase seeks to provide the framework for that meaning, and thus bring stability to the organization – that is, until such time as the process needs to begin all over again!

What I have described here has been just one model of change among many. The range of possibilities is enormous, and the configurations of the five design parameters for culture infinite. People must now put together their own models of change. However, in concluding this chapter I should like to add a comment about the spirit in which they should approach this endeavour.

The message of this chapter – indeed of the whole book – is that cultural change requires special knowledge and skills over and above those required in the area of change in general. The tendency today is still for most people to think of organization in terms of the 'physical dimension' – the creation of the product, the running of trains in a service, and so on. Within that world one starts with the blueprint and then turns it into something. The initial idea may go through a number of development stages but these usually occur elsewhere, involving relatively few people, and only when the finished plan is finally approved do the workers actually begin making the product. This is the classic system of performance follows directions. Unfortunately, the system tends to be universally applied on the assumption that whatever rules apply to physical life apply to everything else as well – the rules for making TV sets are the same as the rules for making culture.

This view is incorrect. The same rules do not apply. In the world of cultural design there are no knobs to turn and no levers to pull; there are no controllers and none of the normal lines of command. The cultural world is a different dimension of organizational life, in which cultural form (the norms and institutions) grows out of the actions: it only begins to emerge when 'everybody's doing it' – cultures are produced interactively. This is a powerful argument for acknowledging that the cultural dimension of organizations is quite distinct from the physical dimension. Because it is there it needs managing, and because it is different it needs managing in a different way.

14 Leading cultural change

It is now time to fit the faces to the phases and ask who is to lead the cultural change process, and how are they to do it. In view of my previous remarks about leaders not being able to create cultures, it may seem bizarre even to be contemplating a chapter on 'leading cultural change'. As usual, it all boils down to definitions, in this case what is meant by the term 'leadership'. My earlier comments were intended to refer to leadership as it has traditionally been defined and practised – the conventional 'thinking and doing' of leadership – and in this regard I still stick by my original claim.

However, the question I now wish to pose is this: is there another conception of leadership – different, perhaps even radically different, from the one to which we have become accustomed – which comes much closer to fulfilling the ambition of a managed or directed process of cultural change? My view is that there is, and the intention is to find a form of words to describe it. This will involve challenging many of the taken-for-granted views that have grown up around leadership in an organization setting, especially those that have given a false impression about 'leading change'. In their place I shall be offering new metaphors of leadership, some of them provocative, others, on first impressions, preposterous.

The subject of attention is not the only thing I want to change. I also feel it is important to switch 'voices', from what up until now has been a broadly modernist form of writing, with its accent on coherence, rigour and comprehensiveness, to more of a 'postmodernist' (Tyler, 1986) or 'surrealist' (Clifford, 1988) one, in which all of the fragmentation and incompleteness in our knowledge of cultural change is revealed. A text turned inside out – a kind of Pompidou Centre on paper.

The inspiration for this is not some perverse desire to reveal my own intellectual gaps, nor is it a devious plan to avoid having to draw some hard-and-fast conclusions. It stems simply from the conviction that final chapters should studiously avoid anything that smacks of the 'last word'. To seem to have it all figured out and sewn up is not a virtue but a deception, especially in this line of work. Better that ends are not ends at all but beginnings, opening up a subject rather than closing it down, offering future avenues to explore and revealing the juxtapositions and interplay of ideas rather than some mythical finished jigsaw.

Ends should be all about loose ends: they should draw attention to the things that simply do not add up or are not finished off. They should be outrageously jagged and eclectic, and resist the pressure for textual order, congruity and continuity. The justification for this fragmentation is that it cannot be otherwise: life is itself fragmentary, not at all organized. There is a 'whole' of course, but that whole is emergent; rather than being assembled and then handed over on a plate by some know-all, see-all author, it is allowed the space and freedom to grow in the mind of the reader. For every reader there will therefore be a different whole, constructed from what he or she has chosen to focus on and considered to be of significance.

Despite the odd lapse back into modernism, the text that follows tends to place the stress more on the 'images' than the 'facts' of cultural leadership, evocations rather than representations, snippets (Stravinsky called them 'squibs') rather than finished works – a text so polyphonic that no one (not even the author) is allowed to have the last word. The central mechanism is one of collage, an assemblage of items cut rudely from their contexts and pasted roughly together in the form of a newspaper – synthetic rather than actual truths, fictional rather than real-life creations, the products of a scattering of different correspondents rather than a single author. The ambition of such a collage is to give freedom from the restrictions of one's own frame of reference, allowing unthought-of comparisons to flourish, and novel ideas to emerge. In an area like leadership, where the same ground has been worked over time and time again, any attempt to break out of the frame must surely be welcome.

Another reason for this change of voice is that I wish to resist the temptation to present some kind of overarching blueprint for the management of cultural change. The whole thrust of my argument has been that people have to decide things for themselves (and between themselves), not to let outside saviours – writers, consultants, business gurus, experts or whoever – do it for them. It is essential that change comes from within:

> You cannot buy a distinctive organizational culture and you cannot copy it from someone else. You must grow it.   (Wilkins, 1989: 16)

As I interpret it, my role as one of these outsiders is to provide some of the raw materials and supplies for your journey, tips and helpful hints for getting from A to B, wherever that may be. What you finally choose to use and how you use it is your decision; you make the meanings, not I. This is very much a pick-and-mix model, in which you choose the elements to suit you and your own particular situation.

Someone once said that the meaning of the text is the sum of its misreadings. In view of what I have just said, what is so bad about that? After all, misreadings are subjective interpretations, and subjective interpretations, being the necessary precursors to action, are precisely what one is trying to encourage at this point.

This last chapter is therefore offered to you as a scrapbook of propositions, aphorisms, conceptions, facts and prejudices about the leadership of change. Like a newspaper it has sections and headlines, but within these sections various images have been allowed to run riot.

It begins, however, in fairly sober and conventional fashion with the equivalent of an editorial.

Re-thinking leadership

The first thing we need to get clear in our minds is what we are supposed to be leading and what it is we are trying to change. In this book cultural change has been broadly conceived as the process of giving an idea form, the unfolding of the human spirit (the German word *Geist* is much better) and its ultimate realization in new collective practices and a different quality of 'between-ness' between the members of an organization community. In this context we may define 'leadership' as any activity that assists in guiding, influencing or directing the passage of the idea or spirit through the life-course of the cultural production process. To put this more simply, cultural leadership is about helping to create or develop a particular way of life (form) and way of living (process) for an organization and its members.

I have identified a number of dimensions to the cultural process (mirroring the multidimensionality of life itself), each pertaining to a different aspect of that life and each requiring a particular and very different kind of stewardship or leadership:

1   An aesthetic dimension

The leader assists in the creation, expression and communication of a new idea or system of ideas.

2   A political dimension

The leader assists in 'writing' or inscribing those ideas into a body of socially agreed meanings – fitting them into or supplanting existing frames of reference.

3   An ethical dimension

The leader assists in developing and imparting to others a framework of moral standards governing the expression and development of these meanings and ideas.

4   An action dimension

The leader assists in the process of transmuting the agreed cultural meanings into concrete cultural practices.

5   A formative dimension

The leader assists in structuring these meanings and practices into some kind of rationale or framework.

This perspective calls for radical rethinking about the nature of leadership, requiring us to recognize that:

- Culture is a multidimensional phenomenon which needs a multi-dimensional process of leadership (as outlined above). Goethe once said that truth was a 'jewel with many facets'. Leadership is just the same, and for that matter so is culture.
- In each dimension the conception and purposes of leadership are very different. Basically, you need different leaders for different parts of the cultural change process. The scope for new models of leadership is immense. There is room for the poet, the storyteller, the rebel, the magician, the explorer, the architect and many more. For too long they have been kept out by the 'men in grey suits' brigade, the product of narrow and oppressive twentieth-century rationalist philosophies. My view is that an enrichment of these role models and philosophies would lead directly to an enrichment of organization culture itself.
- It is the way in which leadership is exercised in each of the dimensions, and the interrelationships between them, that will dictate the direction and outcome of the change process. Therefore

the choice of leader depends on the kind of culture you want. Leadership is a question of blend and balance. Different blends of leadership will produce different kinds of cultures. If any one dimension is dominant it will show up in the culture (for example, if dimension 2 is dominant you get 'power cultures', whereas if dimension 4 is dominant you get 'action-man cultures', and so on).

- Leadership is a collective not an individual activity. The idea of a single leader creating culture is a nonsense. Despite the impression they frequently give, individual leaders do not 'make it happen'; it is groups or networks of leaders that do. It is unreasonable to expect things of a single leader that he or she cannot actually deliver. The reason why there are limits on what any one person may accomplish is that culture is a social not an individual phenomenon: socially created, socially maintained and socially transformed. The image of the leader as a striking figure on a rearing white horse crying 'follow me' is rather an unfortunate one. While there is still a need for the Alexanders, Caesars, Napoleons and Churchills, in matters of cultural change they must learn to be good followers as well as good leaders. One nineteenth-century British prime minister grasped the point perfectly when he remarked, 'Where are my men? I am their leader. I must follow them.'
- We need leaders at many levels of the organization, not just at the top. The concept of leadership needs to catch up with the realities of the democratic age. One of those realities is that people lower down the organization have been practising informal leadership for years. As Edmund Burke once said, 'I have never yet seen any plan which has not been mended by the observations of those who were much inferior in understanding to the person who took the lead' (quoted in Williams, 1965: 332). We have to face up to this fact, and begin to search for ways to draw the informal leaders into the cultural change process. In this regard, official leaders can take comfort from the fact that they would not be giving up anything they had not lost already!
- Leadership is about process, idea and form. None of these is privileged over the others. Each acquires its meaning and significance through and with reference to the others:

Form isn't an overcoat flung over the flesh of thought . . . it's the flesh of thought itself. You can no more imagine an Idea without a Form than a Form without an Idea. (Julian Barnes, *Flaubert's Parrot*, 1985: 36)

Returning to the five dimensions I have outlined, we can say that, roughly speaking, cultures develop down the 'chain' from 1 to 5 (see Chapter 13 for details), although once triggered each dimension tends to remain active for some time. Just as the character of the cultural process changes, so too must the character of leadership. In broad terms I believe this signifies an important progression from leadership as art to leadership as craft, from 'painting' to 'architecture', from subjectivity to objectivity, from individualism to collectivity, from right-brain to left-brain thinking, and from idealism and romanticism to rationalism and realism.

The reality is most definitely 'both–and' since the cultural process requires 'scientific' leaders *and* 'artistic' leaders, and design as well as development experts – and will be all the poorer if any one of these is missing. The overall image of leadership is one of different sets of 'helping hands' performing various tasks on the emerging culture as it moves along the production line. The role of the leaders is to see that the process is successfully completed and the correct blend and mix of operations is achieved for the particular kind of change being contemplated.

Hence, in the early stages of cultural transformation, the spotlight will be on the 'aesthetic leader', the person who has a talent for capturing hearts and minds with a new image or representation of reality, an idea that soars above form and frees itself – and those influenced by it – from existing reality. In the later stages, however, the emphasis on 'ideas' in preference to 'form' is reversed, and there is a growing call for a 'designer leader', someone who can shape the emerging meanings into a well-founded and visually pleasing piece of cultural architecture. A former rather than a transformer, a builder rather than a demolition expert.

This is not to say that only one kind of leader is ever active at any one time. As I have stressed repeatedly, we are not talking about organization culture in the singular but cultures in the plural. Cultural meanings are constantly being produced and worked on, all of them at different phases in their life cycle and all of them calling for a particular kind of leadership at a given moment in time. No matter what type of leader you are there will always be plenty for you to do in your particular area of cultural change and development.

'Leadership in crisis! Leadership in crisis! Read all about it!'

There are ominous signs that leadership itself has become the victim of cultural lag, cloaking itself in a 'mythos' that is now out of date, and out of joint with modern-day realities. Certainly in its present form it has little chance of producing the kind of intelligent cultural change envisaged here. The aim of the following is to dispel certain myths that are retarding its development, and to put in place some new conceptual foundations for the leadership of cultural change.

- Leadership is not a person but a system: (the Myth of the Single Leader)

People normally equate the term 'leadership' with 'the leader'. This is partly the result of the 'cult of personality' that has been gaining ground in our society as a whole, and partly the result of a growing business hagiography, which over the past decade has lionized (or in some cases self-lionized) such figures as Jan Carlzon, Lee Iacocca, Anita Roddick, John Sculley and John Harvey-Jones (Bryman *et al.*, 1992: 2). The effect has been to make us think that they, and they alone, have been the culture-makers, and that somehow the future of these cultures rests solely in their hands. I believe this to be pure myth. Initiators – yes, perhaps; influencers – certainly; but creators and changers – most definitely not. I wish to challenge the 'Great Person', 'Charismatic', 'Heroic', 'John Wayne', 'One-Man-Band' theories of leadership that have become so popular in recent times, and argue that they have only limited validity in the world of culture and cultural change.

People have made the mistake of overexaggerating the contribution of individual leaders to changing culture. The fact of the matter is that in this area individual leaders, even those at the pinnacle of an organization, cannot actually lead, and it is time we stopped pretending that they can. The reasons are hard political ones. The powers of symbolic and situational definition are (and probably always have been) too diffuse to assume any one person is or can ever be in control of the cultural process.

We must therefore concur with Bennis (1989) and Krantz (1990), who have said that there is a growing 'crisis of leadership' in society and organizations, where the people at the top (including people at the very top like world leaders, economic ministers and international peace-makers) have begun to realize that they no longer have the power to determine opinion or make things happen, at least not in the way they would like. As Bennis states, the existing pluralism within the culture of the organization conspires to prevent leaders from 'taking charge and making change'. They are powerless in the face of the gigantic, enormous, multi-legged octopus we call culture and perplexed (though few would admit to it) by the whole issue of how to intervene in, influence or change it. Given these problems, they may even have begun to wonder whether we have entered a new, post-leadership age.

The problem with trying to lead today, at least in the old-fashioned sense of the word, is that there are just too many unknowns, too many things requiring attention, too many forces and counterforces pulling in different directions, too many things to get done and too many different demands on human ingenuity and skill for any one person to be expected to shoulder on his or her own. Without the help and support of others, top leaders invariably end up the victim of their organization culture –

or, to be more specific, the kind of paralysing vicious circles of thinking described earlier.

We are in urgent need of a sea change in the way we think about and practise leadership, and I believe the culture perspective might help us to achieve this. What it does is depersonalize and decentre the leadership concept, so that we start to perceive leadership as a cooperative or collective enterprise spread throughout the organizational network or system, a property of the system rather than of any single individual. Clearly, there are still individual leaders participating in, even initiating, the process of change, but now they are no longer portrayed as omniscient or omnipotent, but as links in a much bigger chain or 'network of leadership' (the unit of cultural production). The culture perspective does not therefore rule out individualism, but makes it part of a bigger joint endeavour. From this viewpoint leadership thus moves from the singular to the plural, from the personal to the systemic, from a privilege exercised by the few to a function exercised by the many. Change becomes a collective effort. Krantz (1990: 52) puts it in a nutshell:

> In systems terms, leadership is a property of the overall system and stems from the ongoing process of interaction among the important elements of the system. From this perspective, leaders and followers mutually co-produce overall system leadership.

The leadership of cultural change fits this conception perfectly. The essential requirement here is to build a system of leadership in the organization which involves different leaders looking after different parts of the change process (a 'division of labour' with regard to leadership), while at the same time using various mechanisms to achieve the necessary coordination within the overall unit of cultural production. The key words to be stressed are interdependence, mutuality, relatedness, coalition, dialogue, collaboration and community.

Let us be clear: this new image of leadership derives not from an ethical imperative for more participation or workplace democracy (although this does make its own legitimate claim), but from a political imperative which accepts that organization members, no matter what their level, do have the power to avoid or resist cultural domination, and will exercise that power if they see fit (Chapter 3). That is precisely why we have sub-cultures and counter-cultures operating in our society and corporations today.

It seems inconceivable to me that groups wielding such power and attracting such loyalty should continue to be disenfranchised from the formal leadership process. Bennis predicts that things will rapidly change in this regard, indeed are already doing so:

Leadership (and its companion, decision making) will become an increasingly intricate process of multilateral brokerage . . . The idea of a relatively small group of 'movers and shakers' who get things done is obsolete. Increasing numbers of citizens and stakeholders, and even those who are only indirectly involved in an issue, have interested themselves in its outcome – and when the decision goes the 'wrong way', very noisily so. This state of affairs has led one writer to describe the organization of today as a 'jungle of closed decisions, openly arrived at'.   (1981: 16)

This notion of cultural leadership as multilateral brokerage in a jungle of meaning is precisely what I am trying to evoke in this chapter.

- Leadership is not a static but a dynamic phenomenon: (the Myth of Leadership as a Constant)

Much of the talk in the literature in recent times has been about the need for leaders to become more 'context-sensitive', that is, more responsive to the changes that occur in the external environment (Pettigrew and Whipp, 1991; Bryman *et al.*, 1992). This point is well made, but there is also an important related point that should not be overlooked: at the same time leaders will have to learn to be more 'process-sensitive', that is responsive to the shifting concerns and requirements of the internal change process. Both points stress the need to move away from the flat, fixed view of leadership that has dominated our thinking up until now (a view that was probably formed when leadership was all about maintaining order and holding the line) towards one where both the internal and the external dynamics of the situation are taken fully into account by the leaders.

The point is simply that cultural change is a dynamic process that requires a dynamic conception of leadership. No longer can it be assumed that leadership is fixed for all time. It has to be more adaptive. A uniform, homogeneous view of leadership must give way to one of dynamism, diversity and heterogeneity, in which all the necessary roles are brought into play to effect cultural change. Different kinds of leadership will be needed at different stages of the change process. The challenge lies in putting together a leadership process that reflects the changing requirements of the cultural process, where individuals and groups resource and service these requirements in a variety of ways.

As long ago as 1979, Weick argued that we should not be talking about 'organizations', which was much too static and dead a term, but processes of 'organizing'. A similar case now needs to be made with regard to culture and leadership: we should have 'organization culturing' instead of organization culture and 'leading' instead of leadership, both of them implying continuous change, of a culture constantly in the making. Not until we alter these basic labels will we be able to achieve the processual-dynamic view of culture and leadership that is required for the change activity.

- Leadership is facilitation not manipulation: (the Myth of Control)

The traditional notion of leadership is that it is all about 'control' – control exercised by the privileged few we call leaders in the apparent interests of the many we call followers. As Krantz (1990: 51) puts it, leadership is generally regarded as something that 'comes out' of the senior person or group, and then cascades in top-down fashion to the rest of the organization. Granted, in these more enlightened times there is less talk of orders and more talk about participation and involvement, but still there is no question of leadership itself being shared or given away. Allan Flanders, the industrial relations academic, once made a perceptive comment about the participative leadership movement when he said that 'the only way to regain control is by sharing it'. Thus, even in a participative organization, leadership tends to remain as it has always been, the right and privilege of those people we choose to call leaders. They may give control away, but only in order to get it back again.

The recent interest in 'cultural change' has shown not a single modification to this traditional approach to leadership. Whether contemplating changing the cultures of an airline, a computing company or a motor manufacturing plant, the basic assumption is the one that has always applied: that it is the leader and his or her close senior colleagues who will decide on what the new culture will be. In other words, the culture of the company is to be the culture of its leaders. Cultural change will continue to 'come out' of the leaders as surely as smoke comes out of the papal chimney.

James McGregor Burns, the leadership theorist, once made an important observation: 'To control things', he wrote 'is an act of power, not leadership, for things have no motives. Power wielders may treat people as things. Leaders may not' (1978: 20). His comment has particular validity in the world of culture. Top leaders cannot treat cultures as 'things', as commodities that they can produce and alter at will and distribute around the system in a way that they decide. Organization culture is not an outgrowth of a controlling elite, but a complex social process in which people at all levels will demand some involvement and if this is not forthcoming will simply help themselves to it. They will not be content to be consumers; they will also insist on being producers. And if these demands are not met, they will resist, or simply go off and make their own cultural product. There is no doubt about this, for even in the most intolerant and repressive of regimes we find this to be the case.

The top-down conception of leadership is unworkable in cultural terms. As I have said repeatedly, you cannot impose a culture on an organization. Culture is not the property of any individual or group, but of a social system. It follows that all leaders can do is create the conditions for the potential energy or momentum already present in the system to be released, and then try to do something constructive with it. Their role is therefore not one of manipulation but facilitation, not because this is ethically more correct (which it most certainly is), but because it cannot be otherwise.

Leaders cannot control or manipulate culture, much as they might like to – and much as the old model might say they can. What they can do is initiate, influence and shape the direction of the emerging culture, making its birth as painless and troublefree as possible. Perhaps in matters of cultural change there are therefore no leaders, only managers. Or there again, perhaps what we are saying is that everyone is a potential leader.

The five dimensions of culture leadership

Dimension	Leader as*
The Aesthetic	The Bringer of New Meaning
The Political	The Bringer of Common Sense
The Ethical	The Bringer of Enlightenment
The Action	The Bringer of Reality
The Formative	The Bringer of Order

I do not intend to give a detailed examination of all five. It is mainly in the first two dimensions that the biggest difference can be seen between the culture perspective on leadership and other more familiar perspectives, and for this reason I have decided to give most space to these. Another reason is that arguably they present the greatest challenge for the leaders of cultural change. The remaining three dimensions will be dealt with more briefly.

The Aesthetic Dimension (the sensate, the ideational and the idealistic; the 'spices' of culture)

In virtually every example of cultural change we can discern the emergence of a 'movement', a spontaneous and voluntary coming together of people in the pursuit of a joint or collective endeavour, whether this be a big major event like the overthrow of a tyrannical

* With apologies to Gustav Holst's 'The Planets'

regime or a small major event like the fight to retain one's local real ale pub. The essence of such a movement, as the term implies, is that people are sufficiently 'moved' by something – a feeling, an idea, an ideal, or sometimes all three – to want to get together and create the necessary critical mass for change. The simple point is that to get a movement you need to move people.

Leaders in this dimension of cultural life are the people who provide the impulse or stimulus for this 'moving experience'. They are the activators of human energy and momentum, the animators of the spirit, the stirrers and protesters who lead the call to arms. 'Movement' also implies action and change, the leaving of one cognitive domain in search of another. Leaders are movers in this sense, too, disengaging people ('liberating' or 'emancipating' would be stronger words) from their familiar symbolic world ('cultural prisons') and transporting them to a new one: 'setting them free from their normal embodiment and revealing a new sort of truth' (Langer, 1953: 50). They are the people who are in constant rebellion against what they see as a stagnant and dehumanizing world.

The leaders we are talking about here are, in Carlyle's (1795) sense, the 'homo symbolicus' of the organization, the bringers of new symbolic meaning:

> The great man is the one who, by experiencing within himself the failure of old symbols, perceives that new symbols must be created.
>
> (Peckham, 1981: 185)

Burns (1978) calls them the 'transforming leaders', the inspirers, those who through their own power as personalities and through the exciting, energizing force of their vision, inspire others to passion, commitment, energy and excitement about a shared purpose. The adjectives he uses to describe such people – elevating, mobilizing, exalting, uplifting, exhorting, evangelizing . . . 'a crescendo of harmonious voices, an epiphany of human effort' – would not be out of place in a cathedral, never mind a factory.

Let us now develop a metaphorical conception of this particular aspect of leadership.

Master metaphors

● **Leader as Artist**

Moving people is basically what the arts are all about, indeed the very thing they strive for. It is also something at which they excel:

> The arts can move us more deeply than ordinary 'real' events can because
> they associate their thematic content with the artificial features of a frame.
> (I.A.Richards (1936), art critic)

Hence, the leaders of cultural change are first and foremost artists. Their commission is to create a work of art – a painting (image) or sculpture (model) – for the organization. As any artist would, they put a frame around their subject, and within that frame strive to create a new representation of reality, smaller than life yet larger than life, that others will look at and be moved by. At one level the picture is a picture of an object or scene, a vision, something cognitive, but at another level it is affective, a 'structure of feeling' (Williams, 1973) – feeling frozen in a frame; an engager of heart and mind.

In management circles we hear plenty of talk about the need for 'cognitive-focused strategies', patterns of thinking that help achievement and personal effectiveness. What we do not hear much about is the need for 'affective-focused strategies', patterns of *feeling* that will support a new organizational direction. This is a major omission, since feelings are driven by thoughts, and thoughts by feelings. The two are interdependent.

> It's often been said in philosophy and elsewhere that reason must rule the
> passions; it has been said by David Hume, that reason 'is, and ought to be,
> the slave of the passions'. Both of these views are dangerous. To divide the
> human soul into reason and passion, setting one against the other in a
> struggle for control, one to be the master, the other the slave, divides us
> against ourselves, forcing us each to be defensively half a person, instead of a
> harmonious whole. There is no problem of reason versus the passions. There
> is only the problem of who we are and would be through our passions and
> on reflection.   (Solomon, 1976: 20)

Never, it would seem, is the both–and philosophy far from our text. Perhaps what we therefore need is not one kind of strategy or the other, but one that embraces both feelings and thoughts.

The quality of art lies in its expressiveness, the ability to communicate an idea and imbue others with feeling, to stir up the spirit and to provoke a reaction. The quality of expression and the quality of thought are inseparable:

> I don't believe you can possibly separate expression from thought in an
> imaginative work. The better a thing is expressed, the more completely it is
> thought.   (Virginia Woolf, in Nicolson (ed.), 1977: 201)

Therefore, if you want to improve the quality of thought in an organization, start by improving the quality of expression, and find a leader capable of doing this. Get the priorities right: 'Expressiveness is more important than technical competence,' says Peter Vaill talking about organization leadership in his book *Managing as a Performing Art* (1989: 110).

Art is not merely a faithful recorder or reproducer of reality; it actually creates something, puts something there that was not there before. That synthetic 'something' may be fictional but it is still well capable of moving people:

> A work of art is more than an 'arrangement' of given things . . . Something emerges from the arrangement of tones or colors, which was not there before, and this, rather than the arranged material is the symbol of sentience.
>
> (Langer, 1953: 40)

In this sense, the artist – the leader of cultural change – is more interested in the 'truth-value' than the 'fact-value' of his or her creation, for, as is frequently pointed out, artistic value has absolutely nothing to do with what is factual or what is real. 'Good' cultural leadership in this dimension is not therefore good because it has discovered 'the facts' (i.e. the solution, the key, or the best-way) but because it has succeeded in creating its own truth: it has expressive power regardless of its factual accuracy, and can and does exist and move people independently of its factual content. In other words, it does not have to be 'true' to become an engaging and persuasive 'truth'. After all, as Geertz (1984: 10) states, to be moved by someone like Macbeth, you do not have to ask whether there really was a man like that. Some things move us whether or not they are actually real. The created illusion substitutes for, ultimately becomes more powerful than, reality itself.

It is strange that organization leaders devote so much time to presenting the 'facts', when facts by themselves make so little impression on us. Perhaps it is time they took a lesson from the artists and stopped trying to paint things as they are, and concentrated instead on producing the more seductive and alluring illusions of life. After all, 'An artist is judged by how well he communicates his visions in his works of art' (William Butler Yeats), not by how accurate, or even prophetic, they finally turn out to be. The stress should be on making things conceivable rather than factual.

Some artists are not merely indifferent to cold reality, they are opposed to it. They wish to displace it. Picasso was one:

> The painter takes whatever it is and destroys it. At the same time he gives it another life. For himself. Later on for other people.
>
> (quoted in Arianna Stassinopoulous Huffington's *Picasso*, 1988: 118)

To him and many artists like him, creation was destruction and destruction was creation.

Art inhabits the world of imagination, not the world of reality. It expresses not what exists but what could exist: 'An artistic problem is the imaginative anticipation, not of unknown facts that do exist, in some sense, in nature, but of a fact of the imagination – of a poem or a painting that could exist' (Polanyi and Prosch, 1975: 99). The leader working in this dimension therefore fuels the imagination of people so that they are alerted to, even tantalized by, the possibility of change. Through the visions, inventions and fictions he or she creates, they are able to see an alternative world and feel themselves drawn inside it. If this happens, then the leader can truly claim to have produced a work of art:

> To produce a work of art is to make something never before seen but grasped in a vague way by powers of anticipation. (1975: 98)

Art, like leadership, also suffers from the cult of personality. However, despite what this cult would have us believe, art is not an artist sitting in glorious isolation working on his inner psychic genius, but a socially embedded and socially responsive process. Artists themselves are acutely aware that if their works are to be impactful they must resonate with feelings and sentiments already present in their audience. They cannot create in isolation, but need to trigger or evoke a response which is latent within the audience. It is not the stimulus but the response that brings their picture to life:

> A picture only lives through the one who looks at it. (Picasso)

Hence, the paradox is that the act of creating begins with an act of responding (taking account of), in which existing cultural meanings are used as the springboard for change:

> Cultures change when individuals can articulate a need that most people in society have vaguely felt but have not explicitly recognized.
> (John Gillan, anthropologist (1948), quoted in Wilkins, 1989: 84)

To be successful, leaders must therefore 'get on the same wavelength' as their audience and learn how to project their voices and 'play to the gallery'. Only by working with the sentiments embedded within the community are they able successfully to implant the seeds of their own imagination into the collective imagination:

> The artist works with his audience's capacities – capacities to see, or hear, or touch, sometimes even to taste and smell, with understanding . . . Art and the equipment to grasp are made in the same shop.   (Geertz, 1974: 118)

In this sense artistic leaders in organizations are not elitists but populists, people who must become adept at lighting the blue touch paper in the hearts and minds of their followers. What happens after that is not really their concern, for as we shall see a very different kind of leader is needed for the firework display itself.

Leaders should take note: contrary to the mythology, artists have little time for overarching visions and abstract ideas, preferring instead to work with mundane, everyday objects – a casserole, for example:

Box 14.1: Any old casserole

I want to tell something by means of the most common object: for example, a casserole, any old casserole, the one everybody knows. For me it is a vessel in the metaphorical sense, just like Christ's use of parables. He had an idea, he formulated it in parables so that it would be acceptable to the greatest number. That's the way I use objects. I will never paint a Louis XV chair, for example. It's a reserved object, an object for certain people but not for everybody. I make reference to objects that belong to everybody; at least they belong to them in theory. In any case, they're what I wrap up my thought in. They're my parables. (Picasso, quoted in Gilot and Lake, 1964)

Or as Weick (1979) might have said, 'Any old casserole will do, so long as it gets you moving'. (Perhaps it should be 'cooking'!).

- **Leader as Poet**

Poets in many societies are influential people. They attack, criticize and preach, and people listen to them (Geertz, 1974: 114). Not so in organizations, unfortunately. While we may talk about the need for visionary leaders, we conveniently choose to ignore those whose profession is dedicated to the making of visions: the poets. (DeWitt Parker once said the poet's business was to 'make us dream an interesting dream', and what is a dream but a vision?) We talk about the need for people who can 'sell' their vision, and yet we turn our backs on the people who do just that for a living. We talk about the need for practical people, yet we fail to find a place for those whose time is largely spent giving the unlikeliest of dreams an air of reality. And we talk about the need for good 'communicators', yet we have no room for the people who know and use just about every rhetorical trick in the book to achieve their effect – the poets.

Language occupies a place at the very heart of organization processes. It is the main thing we use when we want to get things done. As a number of writers have pointed out, we generally prefer to use language as a substitute for raw power or brute force in organizations, and because of this preference language has come to be the main vehicle through which most of our activities take place. If this is the case, who could be better qualified for the job than those masters of language the poets and prose fiction writers?

If the language of organizations is impoverished, and there are grounds for believing this to be the case, then so too must be their cultures, their thinking and their action. And if Vico was indeed right when he said that minds are formed by the character of language, not language by the minds of those that speak it, then the sooner we bring in the professional poets and prose writers – the language-makers – the better.

Perhaps we can look forward to the day when the following ad appears in the vacancies column of our newspapers:

Wanted: CORPORATE POET
Extensive experience of words and visions required.
Applications (in rhyming couplets) to the Personnel Manager . . .

Other metaphors of leadership include:

Leader as Rebel and Bohemian
Leader as Adventurer
Leader as Virtuoso
Leader as Jester
Leader as Utopian
Leader as Inventor
Leader as Illusionist (i.e. capturing in two dimensions – page or canvas – features of the world that are three dimensional. All great artists have to be great illusionists.)

Each of these represents a different way of expressing the 'anti-role' (Peckham, 1976) in organizational life, its function being to expose, provoke, exploit and ultimately transcend the prevailing cultural conventions. Take the case of the jester, for example, that person in times gone by who, by wearing the fool's cap, found the perfect way of criticizing the system and spreading a subversive message:

Mockery was his forte. He ridiculed the wooden solemnity with which the courtiers performed their duties, and the purse-lipped earnestness with which each court office-holder regarded himself as the most vital cog in the ceremonial machinery. He mercilessly laid bare the nature of the royal household, which was no more than the reflection of princely will – like the moon reflecting the light of the sun and producing none of its own . . . Where even powerful courtiers were condemned to silence the fool could speak his mind. (Amelunxen, 1991: 3 & 8)

Some if not all of these role images are implicit in what follows.

The guiding philosophies of the aesthetic leader
There are many:

- *Fictionalism*
- *Impressionism*
- *Irrealism*
- *Expressionism*
- *Individualism*

But above all there is —

- *Romanticism*

Without romanticism there would be no anthropology, and without anthropology there would be no culture perspective. For what we need to appreciate is that the culture concept was born out of the 'romantic rebellion' against science (Shweder, 1984). One can therefore no more imagine culture without romanticism than science without rationalism. Romanticism is a must for anyone who has ambitions to 'think culturally' about organizations and organization change. To put it more directly, if you don't like romanticism, you shouldn't be using the culture paradigm. The worst thing you can do is graft culture on to the alien paradigm of rationalism and treat it as a scientist would treat it, namely as a variable or a thing.

As an aspiring romantic leader you need to know exactly what you are letting yourself in for, and what particular qualities you are expected to express. Let us begin in one of the pleasantest and unlikeliest of places: the romantic garden. Over to Mr. G. Rose (sic.) our gardening correspondent. He describes the features of a romantic garden as follows:

> It excludes reason and appeals directly to the senses . . . creates a spiritual and other-worldly atmosphere, a world of fantasy . . . it plays with the effects of light and shade on an intimate scale . . . it captures the imagination . . . it presents reality in a charming and idealized way . . . it is an assault on the senses – brilliant, kaleidoscopic, vast, extravagant, over-the-top . . . it appeals to emotion rather than to reason . . . it is escapist, a therapeutic distraction from such mundane worries as work and how the bills are ever going to be paid . . . it fosters noble contemplation, even cathartic melancholy . . . it loves creating mystery and uncertainty. As Oscar Wilde once said, 'The very essence of romance is uncertainty'. (1988)

A 'romancer' in the original, medieval sense was one who dealt in extravagant fictions; a fantastic liar. And that is what the romantic leader must be, a truly talented person who contrives to make us ignore the world outside and believe that the impossible is readily attainable. That person – to return to Mr. Rose and his garden for a moment – is someone who 'leads us down an enchanting track to an idyllic corner of Arcadia' (1988: 8).

Now, take a look at late eighteenth-century romantic art. What does it express? Over to our art correspondents Charles Rosen and Henri Zerner (1984): Romantic art is essentially a matter of emotion . . . it celebrates the superiority of inspiration and judgment over tradition, rules and skill, and the 'by eye' approach over objective mathematical measurement . . . it is also vigorously anti-order and anti-establishment . . . romantics take a passionate pride in being 'out': 'It is a genealogy of rebels that Romanticism founds' (p. 13) . . . their art is extreme, often appearing as an act of provocation . . . they want to shock: 'Now I have been attacked by the government, by the priests, and by the newspapers. It's complete. Nothing is lacking for my triumph' (Flaubert in a letter of 1857 after the publication of *Madame Bovary*).

And how about romantic music? Waiting in the studio is the *Sunday Times*'s own music correspondent, Paul Driver (1990). Consider, he says, the romantic piano pieces of Schumann – 'their fluid, unpredictable but subtly manipulated formal structures [that] initiate musical irony'; or 'the music's improvisatory spirit and quizzical, allusive nature'. Of Liszt – 'Everything was pure dancing suggestion, glinting colour, bitter-sweet irony . . . strength held ever in reserve.' And of Brahms – 'The sheer coruscation of texture, the unbridled display of virtuosity . . . Brahms the Progressive.'

The same philosophy runs through them all – music, literature and art itself:

– A philosophy that rejects reason

Over briefly to our academic correspondents:

> Romanticism is the 'revolt from reason' . . . life is a matter of emotion and judgement. (Peckham, 1970)

'Logic won't quite do' (Gregory Bateson, quoted in Capra, 1989: 78), or 'there's more to thinking than reasoning or evidence' (Shweder, 1984):

> A central tenet of the romanticist view holds that ideas and practices have their foundation in neither logic nor empirical science, that ideas and practices fall beyond the scope of deductive or inductive reason, that ideas

and practices are neither rational nor irrational but rather nonrational.
(1984: 28)

The romanticist counterpoint to rationalism is the disparagement of reason and the glorification of intuition.

Heightened energy of the soul, that romantic overflow of feeling, rather than discursive reasoning. (Our history correspondent, J.L. Talman, 1967: 156)

Now back to our philosophy correspondent:

In this new way of thinking, it was the irrational forces that were given their due . . . The world was no longer viewed as predetermined and orderly; it was an aimless rush of possibilities, and the imagination of a man could not stretch far enough to envision the future insanities that might lie in store.
(Solomon, 1976: 117)

The last word is reserved for the artist writers themselves. According to Alfred de Musset, romanticism is the 'alliance of the mad and the serious'. As to change itself, the key to this is not using reason but finding a way of losing it! Robert Frost's poem 'Directive' captures this point marvellously. It is about a confusing journey into the back country of New Hampshire and the mind. One line of the poem reads,

You're lost enough to find yourself now.

If you want to find your way out of vicious circles, find a way of 'losing' their logic.

– A philosophy that rejects order and authority

. . . awakening the mind's attention from the lethargy of custom and directing it to the loneliness and the wonders of the world before us.
(Coleridge, quoted in Talman, 1967: 165)

Freedom from the restrictions of order, pattern, convention and perfection.
(1967: 136)

NB Despite the modern connotations of the word, there is nothing soft, dreamy, sentimental, hopeless or sickeningly sweet about romanticism. It is, in fact, a movement with barbs, well able to draw blood and powerful enough to overturn regimes. As Picasso put it, 'A good painting is one that bristles with razor blades.' But most important to this book, romanticism is —

– A philosophy that embraces change

The romantics' agenda is constant change, change for change's sake – 'The Permanent Revolution' – a state of perpetual becoming, never to be completed . . . The history of romanticism is a history of redefinitions, always incomplete and unstable, fluid and expansive (Rosen and Zerner, 1984).

An aversion towards the 'fixities' and 'definities' of life, and a restless drive for revolutionary change (Talman, 1967).

The issue of change lies at the centre of romanticism . . . it opposes uniformity and changelessness . . . change becomes a positive value not a negative value . . . romanticism is the record of a process . . . it expresses life in motion . . . it is about growth, development and evolution (our American academic correspondent, Morse Peckham, 1970).

What better philosophy could there be for the leadership of cultural change in organizations than one that is indigenous to culture and dedicated to change?

Nevertheless, eyebrows might be raised in contemporary management circles about using a philosophy that died, in the arts at least, more than 150 years ago. But the message for the fashion-conscious is – don't worry: romanticism has been enjoying a comeback in recent times, and in the most unlikely of places at that – in management writings themselves. In the writings of the best-selling business authors to be exact.

Books like *In Search of Excellence* and the whole genre of books it has spawned are, in my view, essentially romantic novels – romances about organizations, escapist fairy-tales, confabulations about success, call them what you will. They are books that admire passion (cf. *A Passion for Excellence*) and imagination above all other attributes and despise the rational models of managing (for example, see Peters and Waterman's devastating attack on rationalism: 'Right enough to be dangerously wrong', 1982: 29). They encourage rule-breaking and urge experiment and change, development and evolution. They petition us to put the human element back into this dehumanized world, and to replenish our lives with meaning and vitality. They remind us about the infinite possibilities of organizational life, of the limitless depths and imponderable magic of being a cultural leader.

The similarities to what we have described are too numerous to be a coincidence, and we must therefore conclude that popular management has at last discovered romanticism – albeit 200 years on. This delay is hardly surprising given the perception that the best way for it to achieve respectability was to gain recognition as a science (rather than an art). Times, as they say, may well be a'changing. Better late than never.

In the opening chapter of this book I made clear my intention to steer clear of the 'guru' writers, whom I described rather dismissively as the KISS bunch (keep it simple, stupid) – a title which, in fairness, they had also given to themselves. Now, and very much in keeping with the fine traditions of romanticism, I am pleased to announce, in this regard at least, a reconciliation. There is a happy ending. Thanks to romanticism we have at last found something on which we can agree.

A thesaurus for the romantic leader

> Passionate, destructive, expressive, moving, cruel, devious, inspiring, paradoxical, aggressive, primitive, bombastic, self-centred, childish, tactless, humourless, conflictual, irresponsible, escapist, radical, utopian, individualistic, eccentric, extravagant, avant-garde, organic, brutal, violent, exciting, magical, ironic, flexible, improvisatory, quizzical, vivid, demonic, spectacular, exotic, other-worldly, secretive, enigmatic, intangible, elusive, distant, blurred, messy, obtuse, iconoclastic, volatile, unpredictable, brilliant, intuitive, extravagant, nonconformist, nonrational, antiestablishment, heretical, energetic, insensitive, rebellious, honest, courageous, adventurous, weird, self-questioning, idealistic, restless, innocent, naive, natural, seductive, alienated, inchoate, complicated, immoral, muddled, exasperating, brooding, haphazard, unstable.

And most definitely not a team person!

Role models

Picasso, Wordsworth, Browning, Schonberg, Keats, Schumann, Wittgenstein, Byron, Scott, Chateaubriand, Manzoni, Tennyson, Hugo, Delacroix, Blake, Shelley, Dumas, Berlioz, Brahms, Wagner, Rousseau, Chopin, Beethoven, Hazlitt, Coleridge, Lamartine, Rosa, Poussin, Lorraine, Liszt, Gandhi . . . and Admiral Lord Nelson —

> it was also his engaging human weakness, his passions, flamboyance and vanity, his willingness to stretch the rules of personal morality and professional discipline.   (source unknown)

But don't panic: you will not be expected to attain the dizzy heights that these people have reached. They are the exceptions. The rest of us are the rule. Organizations are perfectly capable of flourishing with mediocre, second- or even third-rate romantics like you or me. After all, organization culture is not high culture; there is a difference between painting a Mona Lisa and making breakfast cereal.

The Political Dimension (putting the idea into words, and giving the ownership of that idea to the organization community)

A word fitly spoken is like apples of gold in pictures of silver.

(Proverbs 25: 11)

And so we turn from the glitterati to the literati, from the image-makers to the storytellers and word merchants, from the rarified atmosphere of the idea to the 'messy human stuff' of organizational life, and from the power of an idea to the power of the spoken word. For the main difference between these first two dimensions of leadership is that aesthetic leaders are good with ideas, whereas political leaders are good with words. They are the language experts, the people who possess the silvery tongues and the gift of the gab, whose philosophy is not the normal MBWA – Management by Walking Around – but MBTA, Management by Talking Around, or even MBCI, Management by Chattering Incessantly! They are, in short, that much maligned group of people, the organizational wags and gossips.

It is not all idle chat, however, for the role they play is absolutely crucial to the whole change programme. This consists of giving leadership during the critical period in which individual meanings are converted into social meanings; when something that was originally a psychic phenomenon (an idea in someone's mind) is transformed into a fully fledged cultural phenomenon (a socially embedded meaning system), and as a result becomes the property of the community rather than a single person. Language holds the key to this transformation, for it is language that gives birth to meaning, language that gives birth to culture, and linguistic invention that ultimately gives rise to cultural change. By translating the idea into words the leader is able to liberate it from its original creator and make it live socially and culturally in people's mundane thoughts, conversations and interactions. This is a major test for any cultural change programme and its leadership: getting the new aesthetic established as a 'collective speech act' within the realm of everyday language, and having it accepted by those involved as just good, plain 'common sense'.

What we have to be clear about is that a work of art, the product of the first dimension of leadership, is not a culture. All it is is an individual creation. What makes it cultural – and this is where this particular phase of leadership comes in – is the recreation of the idea in the collective imagination of a community through the medium of its language. It is the 'sharedness' of the idea that makes it cultural. This being said, it may never actually make it! In fact, the odds on its 'catching on' culturally are about as high as a theatrical production in the provinces reaching the West End or Broadway, for most artistic ideas suffer the equivalent of getting closed down at the end of the first week. Obviously the role of the leaders is to try to prevent this from happening, though always recognizing that no one, not even the most energetic marketing person, can make a cultural success out of a bad idea.

The dominant metaphor for this second dimension is 'leader as rhetorician' or 'linguist': the one who puts the idea into words; the one who writes the script 'based on an original idea by . . . '. The reason why this kind of leader will always be needed is that artists are generally unwilling to talk about their art, a case of 'whereof one cannot speak, thereof one must be silent'. And even if they were willing, we cannot assume they would be any good at it. How often, for example, have we seen business leaders coming up with a brilliant idea and then killing it stone dead at the briefing with an absolutely dreadful presentation?

If the first dimension of leadership is the art of fiction, the second is the craft of rhetoric – a skill whose importance has been consistently undervalued in organizations up until now (Conger, 1991).

> While we have learned a great deal about the necessity of strategic vision and effective leadership, we have overlooked the critical link between vision and the leader's ability to communicate its essence. In the future, leaders will not only have to be effective strategists, but rhetoricians who can energize through the words they choose. The era of managing by dictate is ending and is being replaced by an era of managing by inspiration. Foremost among the new leadership skills demanded of this era will be the ability to craft and articulate a message that is highly motivational. Unfortunately, it seems that few business leaders and managers today possess such skills. To make matters worse, our business culture and educational system may even discourage these skills. (Executive overview, Conger, 1991: 31)

While this is all true, we must never forget that there is a good deal more to words than actual messages. 'Words', Crescimanno tells us, 'are the wings of meaning' (1982: 15). This is why we also need to have in mind the image of the 'leader as meaning maker'. Perhaps in this sense the leader has a lot in common with Humpty Dumpty!

> 'When I use a word,' Humpty Dumpty said in rather a scornful tone, 'it means just what I choose it to mean – neither more nor less.'
> (Lewis Carroll, *Alice Through the Looking Glass*, 1873)

Language processes are a symbolic system: the language that we use helps to determine what meaning life will have for us and for other people. As Humpty says, the language-maker is not just the communicator but also the meaning-maker.

Language is the key to change. Putting it rather crudely, if you, as leaders, want to change the way people think, you do it by changing the way they talk – their linguistic conventions. You feed them new scripts and draw them into new kinds of language games; you try to improve the quality of the dialogue around the ideas that are in circulation; you endeavour to shape intellectual and symbolic structures by giving people new topics of conversation to debate, gossip and fight about; and you give them new stories and myths to tell and retell to each other. You activate them mentally by energizing them linguistically.

This is all made possible by the fact that linguistic structures are also mental structures – we think 'through' (i.e. by way of) language, the important implication being that the quality of organizational thought will always depend on the quality of its language:

> What we think is conditional upon the language in which we think . . . no communicable thought is possible independently of language.
>
> (Sturrock, 1986: 1)

> The limits of my language are the limits of my world.   (Wittgenstein)

> La pensée et la parole sont un magnifique synonyme. (Joseph de Maistre)

The theory of change is therefore actually quite a simple one: if we can unfreeze and restructure language we can unfreeze and restructure thought. This is 'linguistic restructuring', a process which involves 'interpreting, re-framing, extending, blueprinting, translating, transacting, packaging and writing – in short using different rhetorical means for inscribing the idea into words' (Bate, 1991).

These activities come together in a variety of overlapping leadership roles, which again can best be conveyed using metaphor.

Master metaphors: first role cluster – meaning making
This cluster comprises four main roles

- Leader as Storyteller and Raconteur.
- Leader as Novelist and Impersonator.
- Leader as Myth-maker.
- Leader as Gossip.

- **Leader as Storyteller and Raconteur**
Basically, the aesthetic leader comes up with the idea, whereas this type of leader comes up with the story to go with it. He or she creates the narrative to tie experiences, views and interpretations together. The storyteller leader is skilled in dealing with two main issues: (1) narrative probability: providing a coherent story, which is free of contradictions and which hangs together well; (2) narrative fidelity: telling something

which 'rings true', with which people feel they can identify (Weick and Browning, 1986: 249).

Stories and storytelling are a crucial aspect of organizational life:

> stories and storytelling are not just diversion. Stories connect facts, store complex summaries in retrievable form, and help people comprehend complex environments.   (1986: 255)

They are also the basis of cultural change since they do not simply carry culture but may also create it:

> Stories are not a symptom of culture, culture is a symptom of storytelling.
>   (1986: 251)

Similarly conversation:

> Conversation itself has real consequences that endure. Face-to-face conversation builds, reaffirms, and can change the pattern of organization. Managers should not take conversation for granted, because what they say and to whom they say it creates the working structure of the organization.   (1986: 255)

- **Leader as Novelist and Impersonator**

Leaders can create culture through the spoken word or the written word. If it is the latter, their role becomes one of organization novelist or prose fiction writer. Given the pluralistic nature of organization and the bewildering diversity of intersecting dialects, idioms and professional jargons within it (what Mikhail Bakhtin (1953) called 'heteroglossia'), they might well feel that the most appropriate genre in which to do their writing is that of the 'polyphonic' novel.

> The polyphonic novel is . . . a carnivalesque arena of diversity . . . a utopian textual space where discursive complexity, the dialogical interplay of voices, can be accommodated. In the novels of Dostoyevsky or Dickens he values precisely their resistance to totality, and his ideal novelist is a ventriloquist – in nineteenth-century parlance a 'polyphonist.' 'He do the police in different voices,' a listener exclaims admiringly of the boy Sloppy, who reads publicly from the newspaper in 'Our Mutual Friend'. But Dickens the actor, oral performer, and polyphonist must be set against Flaubert, the master of authorial control, moving godlike among the thoughts and feelings of his characters.   (Clifford, 1988: 46-7)

However, if Dickens, Dostoyevsky or Flaubert strike you as being a bit on the heavy side, then try the management writers like Peters and Waterman. Their book *In Search of Excellence* (1982) is the polyphonic novel *par excellence*. The authors are themselves skilled 'ventriloquists' (I would prefer the term 'impersonators'): they 'do' the business leaders in different voices. Just count the number of quotations given verbatim from practitioners and you will see what I mean. They actively promote a diversifying discourse instead of trying to narrow it down, they revel in encouraging open competition between different ideologies, and they seem to be completely undaunted by the huge amounts of detailed data with which they have to juggle. They do not mind that things are not neat, nor do they mind showing us the joins in their writing. Now compare this 'carnival' of voices with the dry, one-sided, cleaned-up reports we tend to find circulating around organizations today, and ask yourselves which is the more valuable and persuasive of the two? The case for having more organization polyphonists is certainly a strong one.

- **Leader as Myth-maker**

Another way of seeing leadership is in terms of 'myth-making'. With myth, like the make-believe, fairytale world it creates, anything and everything is possible. Myth provides:

- a vehicle for change:

> The most constructive approach that we, as agents of transformation, can take may be to become identifiers and teachers of the new myths . . . We need to ferret out the ways old myths dominate us. We can teach people in organizations what we are beginning to understand about myths and how they affect us, and we can help them to recognize and identify their own operational myths. (Stephens and Eisen, 1984: 189–190)

Myths are the means of extending, moving and re-shaping the boundaries of reality. Through them we make the world appear in this or that disguise.

> Change consists of inventing new myths: Myth is invention. To invent means to extract from the sum of a given reality its cardinal idea and embody it in imagery – that is how we get realism. But if to the idea extracted from the given reality we add . . . the desired, the possible and thus supplement the image, we obtain that romanticism which is at the basis of myth, and is highly beneficial in that it tends to provoke a revolutionary attitude to reality, an attitude that changes the world in a practical way. (Gorki, source unknown)

Myths contain the 'rules of thought'. If you want to change the way people think, you must change the rules of thought, and that means the myths. Myth-making is change-making.

– a compelling definition of 'reality':

> A myth is a good story that grips you, creates a world, and, to some significant degree, transforms and interprets the 'real world'. Working with or in a given myth is like living in a good novel. The difference is that you can't put the myth down. A myth not only reflects life, it becomes life.
>
> (Stephens and Eisen, 1984: 217)

Wilkins (1983) has drawn attention to the fact that people are much more ready to believe something that is enshrined in myths. Myths act as 'vehicles for conception', embracing within them complex explanations and thus providing 'cognitive short cuts', and also communicating the 'vision of the organization's mission or role'.

– a shared or joint outlook:

> Myths are collectively valued objectives, socially approved and jointly endorsed constructions of reality. Myths contain all the ideas that have been taken into social ownership.
>
> Myths are the concrete expression of the collective imagination.
>
> (Berlin, 1980: 53)

– a mode of control:

> Organization control can be exercised through the generation and propagation of myths; they are a symbolic mode of manipulation, a highly persuasive form of language game. They provide 'authority' for a situation. The power of a myth is that it makes equally good sense whether it is based on fact or not. As A. J. Ayer (1985) once said, the world (and the organizational world is no exception) can exist perfectly well without facts. What is left once they are removed are the myths.

With myths 'the universe is infinitely suggestive'. (Roland Barthes, quoted in Sturrock 1986: 91).

• Leader as Gossip (but not quite of the usual sort)

Gossip forms a huge part of the life of any organization. Everyone does it, and everyone at some time or other has been the victim of it. But what part, if any, does this highly distinctive language game play in the affairs of an organization, and why mention it here?

Gossip is about order not change, about reinforcing and sustaining the existing culture: 'Gossip contributes to system maintenance because it communicates rules, values, and morals by dwelling on failures to satisfy them. Gossip is a way to diffuse traditions and history' (Weick and Browning, 1986: 250). At best it is disinterested, disengaged talk – idle talk, talk for its own sake (Peckham, 1985: 42). Certainly the idea of actually changing things, of removing the problem being gossiped about, is not something that would normally occur to the person doing the gossiping. In fact, for many people gossip is merely an outlet, not so much a way of drawing attention to a problem situation so that it can be resolved, as simply a way of living with that problem situation, while at the same time distancing oneself from it.

If leaders want change, they must find a way of countering the conservative tendencies of the gossip system. One way is to encourage gossipers to get off their backsides and do something about the problem that is exercising them: propose a new rule that says if you talk about something, you have an obligation to do something about it. Leaders can also use gossip as a means of gathering information about problems on which they need to take some action. Their aim should not be to stop the gossip, which would be an impossibility, but to intervene in it and give it both an action and a change orientation. By introducing new ideas into the gossip system they can get people thinking, talking and speculating about them, which is exactly what is needed if they are to acquire social meaning and significance. The goal should not be wholehearted acceptance of the ideas (which may not always be a good thing), but the prevention of outright rejection, and a full and proper examination of what is on offer.

All the above roles have one thing in common: the interruption, interrogation and transformation of language (Silverman and Torode, 1980). This is no coincidence, for intervention in language is a prerequisite to cultural change, the simple, two-step logic behind this statement being that (1) language is the primary cultural form in social and organizational life; therefore (2) if you want to change culture, you must find a way of changing language, i.e. the prevailing modes of discourse. Cultural change *is* linguistic change. By the same reasoning if you want cultural development, you need to be aiming for some kind of linguistic development, for example new myths and stories that extend and elaborate existing values.

The medium of language opens up a world of abundant opportunity for constructing and reconstructing the organizational reality. Where this particular dimension of the cultural process is concerned, language can be used in many different ways to improve, refine and extend the original idea. For example, language can make that idea:

– Clearer

   Words amplify an idea, making it more audible

     Without language, thought is a vague, uncharted nebula. There are no pre-existing ideas, and nothing is distinct before the appearance of language.   (Saussure, 1974: 112)

– More accessible and tangible

> The real power of Martin Luther King was not only that he had a dream, but that he could describe it, that it became public, and therefore accessible to millions of people. This dual capacity . . . to make sense of things and to put them into language meaningful to large numbers of people gives the person who has it enormous leverage. (Pondy, 1978: 95)

Things are often known but cannot be named. The leader provides the name or label, which people can then use as a handle to get in touch with their own ideas and feelings. Words possess the capacity for formulation; they act as the grammar for an idea.

– Logical

The narrative of a story or myth is an ingenious way of developing a logic around an idea, and of presenting that logic in a form that people can grasp and absorb without pain or difficulty.

– Real

Words give ideas the air of reality; they turn fictions into facts, truths into 'the truth'. Take the case of the myth:

> The mark of a genuine myth is its power to impress its inventors as literal truth in the face of the strongest contrary evidence and in complete defiance of argument. It appears to be so sacred a truth that to ask in what sense it is true, or to call it a figure of speech, seems like frivolity. For it is a figure of thought, not merely of speech, and to destroy it is to destroy an idea in its pristine phase. (Langer, 1953: 81)

– Authentic

Authenticity comes from repeated tellings of a story:

> C. E. Montague, in a chatty but thoughtful book called *A Writer's Notes on his Trade*, remarks on the odd phenomenon that in fiction past happenings seem to gain authenticity by being retailed at second- or third-hand, told by some character who may even claim to have the story from another: "I'm only tellin' ye what 'e told me."
> (Langer, 1953: 293)

– Special and select

> Impressionist tales when told in the flesh possess something of the provocative, sweet, secretive glitter of conspiracy. They are told to select audiences in select ways. When, where, and how stories are told reveal patterns of intimacy. Like gossip, the telling of impressionist tales implies closeness.
> (Van Maanen, 1988: 108)

– Irresistible

> Words turn ideas into common sense statements and imperatives. Language confers authority on an idea.

In view of what has been said, one might wonder why this aspect of cultural leadership has not been labelled the *linguistic*, *social* or *semantic* dimension. Quite frankly, any of these would have done. However, I chose to call it the *political* dimension so as to emphasize an even more important cluster of roles that cultural leaders must play (in combination with the first cluster). These relate to the 'politics of meaning negotiation' in the organizational change process.

The whole thrust of my argument up until now has been that cultures must be negotiated not imposed. If this is so, then the leader needs to be striving continually to establish the conditions in which people, as a result of hard-bargaining, will reach the point where they are prepared to 'buy in' or 'contract in' to the emerging culture on a voluntary basis. The goal is one of achieving 'semantic convergence', a negotiated order, which is not so much complete agreement as a state in which everyone knows, accepts and understands the new culture – where, as I have already said, there exists a set of 'common sense' understandings about the new reality, and a contractual undertaking to defend and uphold them. It is because of this that I referred originally to these leaders as the *Bringers of Common Sense*.

An organization is a space filled by many voices which even at the best of times is difficult to keep in order. Introduce a new idea into this space and the difficulties increase manyfold. The voices rise to a clamour and arguments break out in different parts of the hall as people struggle to shout down the others and get their opinions heard. The leaders at the front of the hall may well view the unfolding scene with some ambivalence because they see the difficulties of getting something meaningful out of the process increasing by the minute, yet at the same time they know that such verbal energy and involvement are essential if any kind of change is to take place.

The challenge is to find a way of accommodating (mollifying if not fully satisfying) the various parties present, and emerging with some kind of agreement about the best way of proceeding and moving the process forward. The skill is to encourage expression and avoid suppression, because the last thing one wants is to alienate a group of people so that they go off and do their own thing – which will invariably mean trouble further along the line. Again, the responsibility for achieving a successful outcome falls upon words, since it is these, rather than guns, that organizations on the whole still prefer to use (with notable exceptions). In this context, words provide the 'unifying story', the text within which the discursive complexities are accommodated.

The leader's goal is therefore to create a unity of discourse between the different groups. To achieve this, he or she may be expected to play many of the following roles.

Master metaphors: second role cluster – meaning negotiation
- Leader as Activator
- Leader as Messenger and Go-between
- Leader as Mediator
- Leader as Negotiator
- Leader as Conflict-handler
- Leader as Pathfinder
- Leader as Rule-maker

These leadership roles will probably be more familiar than the first group, and therefore do not require the same amount of elaboration. A general introductory word might be in order, however. The core image is one of 'transactional' leaders (Burns, 1978) working in a process of meaning negotiation, slowly piecing together a cultural order from the various materials that people have brought along. Their task is to identify the stakeholders involved (one of whom will be themselves) and attend to them as people, responding to their needs and aspirations in as positive and constructive a way as possible. The stress is on accommodation ('live and let live') rather than obliteration ('live and let die'): searching for an integrating definition that allows for the many separate individual acts to be fitted into a meaningful joint act (i.e. a system of shared cultural understandings).

The leader is neither neutral nor impartial in this process (what third parties ever are?), but this should not prevent him from doing whatever he has to do: eliciting responses to the initial idea, helping people to clarify their own agendas, and above all working to make the idea more palatable. In short, acting as the Mediator of Meaning.

The emerging images are therefore of the:

• Leader as Activator
Leadership mobilizes the silent majority and turns the apathetics into actors:

> The leadership of men like Lenin, Gandhi, and Mao brought literally hundreds of millions of men and women out of political isolation and into a new kind of political participation.   (Burns: 137)

The role of the leader is to enfranchise people in a cultural manner of speaking.

- **Leader as Messenger, Intermediary or Go-between**

The leader is Hermes, the Mercurial Entrepreneur (Bird, 1989), the lord of the pathways and all who use them, the cunning and street-wise messenger (who is not averse to opening and tampering with the messages), the one who engages in shuttle diplomacy, acting as the tireless go-between for the parties involved. The goal: conciliation (from the Latin *conciliare* – to unite the parties in thought).

- **Leader as Mediator and Power Broker**

From the Latin *mediare* – to occupy the middle position. From this position the leader manages the power relationships between the parties, making suggestions and recommendations about the way the core system of ideas might be developed. The aim is to achieve a synthesis of the various viewpoints: 'Strategic change is not so much an analytical, deductive process as an open-ended, inductive, synthetic process' (Normann, quoted in Hennestad, 1991: 253).

- **Leader as Negotiator**

The cultural order is a negotiated order; there can be no culture without negotiations. From a cultural perspective, negotiation is an interactive process in which the parties merge parts of their individual 'cognitive domains' into a common – cultural – domain. They do this by trading and bartering ideas and interpretations, and in addition embellishing and reinterpreting ideas brought to the table from outside (by aesthetic leaders for example).

In the negotiation model of change, culture has to be worked at. It is not the kind of thing you can design, build, implement and then forget. The order is never a permanent order. The cultural understandings resulting from negotiation all have temporal limits, for in time they will inevitably be reviewed, reevaluated, revised, revoked or renewed (Strauss, 1978: 5).

Leaders therefore have to be flexible and responsive, and they must be prepared to rework the original idea until such time as agreement is forthcoming – or, in the event of failure, be willing to abandon the idea entirely. This should be seen as a sign of strength not of weakness, for an idea without agreement is like a ship without a sail.

The ideal person for leading the process of meaning negotiation is someone 'who responds to various criticisms and affirmations by adding to, emphasizing, playing down, and eliminating selected elements of the original visions. This reworking makes the new doctrine more acceptable to special interest groups' (Anthony Wallace, quoted in Wilkins, 1989: 85).

- **Leader as Conflict-handler**

It is helpful if the leader has some sympathy with the Hegelian philosophy of perpetual pluralism: seeing opposites, then reconciling them, then on the basis of that reconciliation seeing new opposites, and so on. He or she

> must have the capacity to endure over long periods problem exposure and solution postponement, the preference for tension rather than for tension reduction, the capacity to tolerate tension, the ability to tolerate disorientation and the desire to seek disorientation actively, a sensitivity to cultural incoherence, a capacity for self-validation which in other circumstances would be condemned as arrogance, and an ability to exist without the constant flow of validation which is so constant and pervasive.
> (Peckham, 1976: 308)

The leader is not merely a conflict-handler but a conflict-user as well:

> Leaders, whatever their professions of harmony, do not shun conflict; they confront it, exploit it, ultimately embody it.   (Burns, 1978: 39)

A point echoed by Sir John Harvey-Jones:

> A high degree of constructive conflict is almost essential in this process [of gaining commitment to the direction in which the company must go] and I should perhaps quote the comments of a wise manager I worked for at one time, who pointed out that in industry the optimum level of conflict is not zero; just as no friction or one hundred per cent friction immobilizes movement in a mechanical sense, so total absence of conflict or one hundred per cent conflict will immobilize movement in a company. The seeking of business success is far too difficult and serious a matter to be done in a cosy way. Of course one wants to avoid situations where the conflict reaches excessive levels and actually gets in the way of running the business, but if the right decisions are to be taken it is essential that conflicting views are heard and thrashed out.   (1989: 40–1)

- **Leader as Pathfinder**

The objective is to find a way of getting the parties through the jungle of meaning and into the clearing beyond, with as few casualties as possible. This needs a leader with a good sense of direction, an ability to spot traps and dead-ends, and an intimate knowledge of paths and short-cuts leading to the final destination. He or she also needs to be a good 'pacemaker', able to set a speed which allows everyone to keep up.

- **Leader as Rule-maker**

We began with the animators (first dimension) and end with the regulators, the rule-makers, the people who lay down the standards and procedures for the conduct of the negotiations. These leaders are, you might say, the *referees of meaning*: they make sure people are playing the right 'game' and following the correct rules, in both a behavioural (what people do) and linguistic (what people say) sense.

The guiding philosophies of the political leader

- *Socialism*

  From each according to his ability, to each according to his work.

The goal is the democratization of culture: taking cultural production into public ownership and establishing a system of joint regulation for the management of change. The leader takes care in this process to ensure that the weaker parties are given a voice in the everyday affairs of the organization, and not exploited by the stronger ones (the notion of a regulated market). Since every person and every interaction is potentially important to the outcome of this process, the leader's working principle is: 'No opportunity is too small, no forum too insignificant, no audience too junior' (Peters and Waterman, 1982: 83). By refusing to defer to hierarchy, power and privilege, the leadership of the political dimension may often be in conflict with that of other dimensions.

- *Fictionalism*

A philosophy that sees change as 'fictionally based'. Fiction is more important than fact in organizational life because it is interpretations, myths, stories, not 'real' things as such, that determine the way people think and act. It is therefore in the fictional dimension that a change programme – especially a cultural change programme – needs to be anchored. From this perspective, the leader's role is to create an imagined world, a virtual reality, an illusion of life that people are prepared to accept for a while as their operating reality. To this extent, the leader is providing what the philosopher Whitehead once called 'useful fictions' – designer fictions, porkies with a purpose!

And what about the issue of change? According to this philosophy, an organization is an arena of competing fictions. What the leader must do is enter this arena and bring about a synthesis of the various interpretations present — words being his only weapon throughout this skirmish. These are used to 'frame' the story, the super-fiction, that version of reality that will supersede the other versions and thereby enable the organization to move forward.

But above all there is –

- *Pluralism*

which has already been extensively discussed in this book (and therefore needs no further comment), and —

● *Relativism*

which has not. In this philosophy there are no absolutes or certainties in life, no definitive version that tells us how things 'really are'. Reality is arbitrary. The only meaning it has is the meaning we put around it – our frame of reference. The world of organization is constituted by a multiplicity of such frames, each one different and each claiming to have the monopoly on truth (the notion of heterodoxy). Relativism is happy to accept the co-existence of different, even contradictory, frames. In this regard it is very much in favour of 'both–and' as opposed to 'either–or' thinking, and therefore fits well with the broader thrust of this book. For example, it would claim that to talk of something being 'right' *or* 'wrong' is meaningless because it can quite easily be right *and* wrong – it is all a matter of perspective.

> Thus . . . it is meaningless to ask, for example, 'is abortion right or wrong'; the meaningful question is 'within what frame is abortion right and within what frame is abortion wrong?'   (Shweder, 1984: 45)

What this particular philosophy offers to the leader is the idea that in order to bring about cultural change, he or she must find a way of changing people's frames of reference – what is normally referred to as 'reframing':

> All-important is the frame placed around experience; alter the frame and you can radically alter the meaning of the experience.   (Smith, 1984: 271)

The process of reframing is rooted in a dialogic structure, a verbal marketplace in which different interpretations and accounts are bartered and exchanged and various working truths arrived at. The relativist philosophy lays down some solid ground rules for the conduct of this process:

1. No frame or discourse is privileged – even though its owners may be! No matter who is saying it or how persuasively it is being argued it is still only one voice and one interpretation among many.
2. All viewpoints are of potentially equal validity.
3. There are no such things as facts, only theories. In life nothing is determinate, definite or complete. Nobody has it all worked out, despite what he or she might think.
4. Trying to prove something is a waste of time. For every fact there is always another one to contradict it.

Simple though they are, these rules can dramatically change the quality of organizational dialogue. One result is that the dialogue becomes more geared to 'how things seem to be' than 'how things are' – subjective and interpretive rather than quasi-objective and explanatory. Another is that people show a greater tolerance of other viewpoints and more willingness to grant them a fair hearing. Their awareness of language itself also increases, as they become more sensitive to the nuances of the discourse in which they are engaged.

A thesaurus for the political leader

Articulate, literate, political, sociable, diplomatic, credible, accessible, acceptable, responsive, flexible, resilient, adaptable, authoritative, non-judgemental, likeable, humorous, down-to-earth, engaging, participative, egalitarian, empathetic, cosmopolitan, pluralistic, kaleidoscopic, classless, broad-minded, open, versatile, optimistic, keen, active, involved, vigorous, loquacious, painstaking, patient, understanding, unflappable, tough, complicated, determined, tireless, tenacious, firm, fearless, alert, blunt, direct, coherent, understandable, wily, canny, conspiratorial, shrewd, protective, trustworthy, acceptable, fair, reassuring.

Truly a leader for our postmodernist age: one who is radically eclectic in outlook, whose tastes stretch from Unamuno to U2, from Springsteen to Spinoza, and from Mahler to Madonna.

Role models
Hermes, Arachne, Kissinger,

John Harvey-Jones —

I believe that, in deciding where you would like to be, you need a great deal of discussion and a great deal of development of new thinking and new processes. The idea of doing this through the planning department, or through a paper on strategy presented to the board, seems to me to be quite inadequate. This process involves large amounts of time and constant discussion with those involved lower down the line who will actually execute the strategies on which the whole picture relies. This sort of circular debate, frequently widening out to involve others within and without the company, goes on until all are satisfied that the result is as good as they are going to get . . . In a free society you are unlikely to get . . . commitment without a high degree of involvement.   (1989: 38/40)

Henry V —

O! now who will behold
The royal captain of this ruin'd band
Walking from watch to watch, from tent to tent,

Let him cry 'Praise and glory on his head!'
For forth he goes and visits all his host,
Bids them good morrow with a modest smile,
And calls them brothers, friends and countrymen.

(*Henry V* IV: Chorus 28–34)

Or better still, a combination of the two: A little touch of Harvey in the night.

And now for the rest of the news in brief . . .

The Ethical Dimension (cultural change as a guided learning process)

> Today our main job is to lift the individual spiritually, respecting his inner world and giving him moral strength. We are seeking to make the whole intellectual potential of society and all the potentialities of culture work to mold a socially active person, spiritually rich, just and conscientious. An individual must know and feel that his contribution is needed, that his dignity is not being infringed upon, that he is being treated with trust and respect. When an individual sees all this, he is capable of achieving much.
>
> (Mikhail Gorbachev, 1987: 30)

So it must also be in organizations. The job to which Gorbachev refers is one for which leaders in the 'ethical dimension' must take responsibility.

So how are these leaders to be distinguished from the previous ones? First there were the glitterati, then the literati, and now – the cognoscenti: the *Bringers of Knowledge and Enlightenment*.

And what is their particular contribution to the cultural change programme? Changing culture is not only a creative process (Dimension 1) and an interactive process (Dimension 2), but also an educational and learning process. Education and learning are the core responsibilities of the leaders in this dimension.

What does it involve? If the first dimension of leadership was about ideas and feelings, and the second one about words, this one is about ethics and praxis – the reflective, questioning and consciousness-raising stage of the cultural change process.

Master metaphors

● **Leader as Teacher, Educator and Pedagogue**

> The great eras that did have a cultural policy (even if not conceived or described as such) always concentrated on the subjective factor: the education of the individual.   (Simmel, quoted in Lawrence, 1976: 251)

The whole basis of cultural development in a civilized society is education. Civilized organizations should be no different in this regard. Unfortunately, they all too often are. A criticism I would make is that there are too few outstanding teachers and educators and too many 'DJ-type' leaders – people whose sole purpose in life seems to be to provide the flashing lights, frenzied music and stirring pep talks at employee training events. This is not education but indoctrination. The two are as different as chalk from cheese:

> education and propaganda work in two entirely different registers, even if they are confused in practice. Education appeals to reason and critical thinking, while propaganda works on the emotions and the need for identification and certainty.   (Gagliardi, 1986: 118)

Education is about self-control not manipulation, about stimulating the critical senses not numbing them. The leader's role is to create the opportunity for reflexivity so that people examine the emerging culture and ask, why are these things happening, why are they happening to me, what am I thinking, how am I feeling, and why am I acting and reacting in this way? Education involves giving people the chance to explore their subjective positions, including any contradictions and conflicts that may exist between their 'personal culture' and the 'organizational culture'. If this is what 'education' means, it would appear that organizations are not currently providing anything that even approximates to it.

This is a serious omission in today's rapidly changing world, where it is no longer a case of finding one's way within a particular cultural context, but of learning how continuously to learn emergent contexts (Vaill, 1989). Continuous cultural change requires a continuous process of learning. In other words, no learning, no change.

Leaders can contribute to a programme of cultural change by providing several different types of learning process (apart from the normal classroom setting). For example:

● **Leader as Coach**
Coaching, like education, is facilitation not manipulation, enabling others to take control of the situation and their own lives.

> Coaching is the process of enabling others to act, of building on their strengths. It's counting on other people to use their own special skill and competence, and then giving them enough room and enough time to do it.
> (Peters and Austin, 1985: 328)

> To coach is largely to facilitate, which literally means 'to make easy' – not less demanding, less interesting or less intense, but less discouraging, less bound up with excessive controls and complications. A coach/facilitator

works tirelessly to free the team from needless restrictions on performance, even when they are self-imposed.   (1985: 326)

● **Leader as Mentor**

Mentoring has a valuable role to play in both the construction and transformation of organization culture:

– Construction

> Values and meanings are abstract; and many organizational values and meanings are tacit, ambiguous, shifting. Mentors enable their proteges to identify, observe and internalize these in various ways. (Collin, 1992: 13)

– Transformation

> [Mentoring] plays a significant part not only in the development of individuals but also in the process of making meaning and so transforming the organization.   (1992: 1)

> We also found that mentoring breeds mentoring within an organization. So a mentor who may be 40 to 50 years old typically mentors someone who is in their 20 to 30s, these proteges will then start mentoring at a very much earlier age. Mentoring can therefore begin to change the culture of an organization and could be used for this purpose. (Scholefield, 1989: 139)

The guiding philosophies of the ethical leader

● *Asceticism*

● *Humanism*

But especially,

● *Scepticism*

> The aspects of things that are most important for us are hidden because of their simplicity and familiarity.   (Wittgenstein)

Scepticism, in the early Greek sense of the word, is a philosophy which is indisposed towards automatic acceptance of anything that presents itself as obvious or 'common sense'. As readers will recall, common sense is the product of the previous dimension of leadership. This effectively makes the leader in this dimension an overseer of the previous one, a person who scrutinizes the product to ensure that anything coming through in the name of 'common sense' is good sense rather than bad sense or nonsense. In short, the role involves putting the frighteners on common sense – and its champions.

Common sense, as I observed in the previous chapter, can frequently 'drop you in it'. This is undoubtedly true, but it is also a fact that we cannot live without it. It is the basis of cultural life – a case of no common sense, no culture. The trick is to have it but not get trapped by it. This is why the process needs ethical leaders. They are the ombudsmen of the obvious, the people whose role in life is to remind us that what we need are fewer common sense theories and more theories about common sense itself.

It will not have escaped the reader's attention that every philosophy of cultural leadership mentioned so far has carried that dreaded suffix, the 'ism'. This is worrying. It means that, left to its own devices, any one of these philosophies might deteriorate into dogma and end up as a 'vicious circle' of thought, obstructing rather than facilitating the process of change. The philosophy of scepticism is important precisely because it has the capacity to prevent this from happening to the other leadership philosophies, as well as to itself. It is critic, interrogator and whistleblower all rolled into one, a disturbing force that will not permit any of these philosophies to rest on its laurels or take itself too much for granted.

In view of this, some new leadership roles might be usefully added to those already mentioned:

- Leader as Whistleblower
- Leader as Critic
- Leader as Interrogator
- Leader as Devil's Advocate
- Leader as Internal Cultural Auditor

A thesaurus for the ethical leader

Intellectual, approachable, knowledgeable, moralistic, contemplative, caring, committed, supportive, encouraging, appreciative, introspective, insecure, uncertain, selfless, giving, critical, sceptical, uncommonsensical, civilized, discriminating, insightful, unconventional, heretical, contramundane, demythologizing, iconoclastic, academic, cerebral, philosophical, believable.

Role models

Mentor (the friend to whom Ulysses entrusted the care of his young son before embarking on his epic voyages); Plato; Aristotle; and, of course, not forgetting Bum Phillips, the New Orleans Saints coach:

The main thing is getting people to play. When you think it's your system that's winning, you're in for a damn big surprise. It's those players' efforts.

(Peters and Austin, 1985: 326)

The Action Dimension (converting cultural meanings into cultural practices – and back again)

Leaders in this dimension occupy the strategic ground between cultural *meanings* and cultural *practices*. Their role is to mediate between the two, ensuring that the 'espoused' culture (the formally agreed culture in theory) and the 'culture in use' (the informal culture as it is actually practised) are kept in rough alignment with each other, and where this is no longer the case to take whatever actions are necessary to make it so.

Typically, the absence (or failure) of such leadership will be reflected in divergence or 'drift' between the rhetoric and the action of culture, with the organization finding itself in a position of saying one thing but doing another (e.g. espousing a customer-friendly culture but in practice treating the customer like something the cat has just brought in!). This 'culture gap' or 'cultural contradiction' is extremely common in organizations, and is a sure sign of a failure of leadership in this area.

The change processes in which these leaders get involved are of two sorts:

1. Transmuting meanings into practices ('directions'-led change): in which case the role will be one of
    - Leader as Advocate
    - Leader as Champion
    - Leader as Salesperson
    - Leader as Implementer

    } of the 'official line'

Or the reverse:

2. Transmuting practices into meanings ('performance'-led change): in which case the role will be one of
    - Leader as Scout (reconnoitring at grass roots level in order to spot local trends and deviations).
    - Leader as Explorer (making contact with indigenous 'tribal' cultures to find out what the rest of the organization might learn from them).
    - Leader as Reporter (communicating information about them to the relevant parties).
    - Leader as Implementer (diffusing local cultural practices in both a lateral and vertical direction).

Leaders in this dimension are firmly committed to fixing culture in life – they have a strong action bias. However, they should not be confused with the 'action-man' leaders, those unfortunate and pathetic souls who

- like to fill their days with activity, and revel in fire-fighting;
- dash quickly and spontaneously from one activity to another;
- talk much more than they listen;
- hog the limelight, wishing to be at the centre of activity and attention;
- are dominated by immediate events (Logan and Stuart, 1986).

Leaders in this dimension are the complete opposite of action-man leaders. Their key quality is the ability to 'act thinkingly' (Weick, 1981) – to combine action with insight, to look before they leap:

> When we say that an action is done thinkingly, we mean that the act is done with attention, intention, care, interest, pertinacity, patience, initiative, alertness, resourcefulness, cunning, concentration, and self-coaching. For the sake of manageability, this list is shortened to attention, intention, and control. When people act thinkingly, they pay close attention to what is happening, they try to impose order on the setting and their actions in it, and they correct their performance when it strays from reference standards.
>
> (1981: 226–7)

The notion of thinking in the service of action.

The guiding philosophies of the action leader

- *Pragmatism*

Pragmatism is a doctrine that estimates any assertion solely by its practical bearing upon human interests. Everything else is either 'fluff' or 'guff'. Not surprisingly, pragmatists tend to be short on words and long on actions.

- *Realism*

> Therefore let us try and see things as they are, and not try to be cleverer than God.　　　　　　　　　　　　　　　　　　　　　　　(Flaubert, 1853)

Leaders in this dimension have their feet planted firmly in the 'real world', and for this reason they rarely count relativist leaders (dimension 2) or impressionist leaders (dimension 1) amongst their friends. Their ambition is to capture or portray things as they 'really are', in black and white, without distortion or embellishment – even if this does cause upset and embarrassment:

One evening at a dinner party, it is said, a lady turned to Degas and asked him aggressively, 'Monsieur Degas, why do you make the women in your paintings so ugly?' and he replied, 'Because women are generally ugly, Madame'.
                                                    (Rosen and Zerner, 1984: 155)

As you can see, leaders in this dimension are never averse to calling a spade a spade.

A thesaurus for the action leader

Independent, enterprising, adventurous, direct, practical, realistic, factual, energetic, pushy, noisy, active, instrumental, restless, opportunistic, improvisatory, undomestic, intuitive, canny, pragmatic, determined, certain, blinkered, impatient, honest, up-front, sociable, solutions-oriented (as opposed to problems-oriented), self-sufficient, enthusiastic, strong (mentally and physically), tough, down-to-earth, hands-on, forceful, single-minded.

Above all, this leader must be 'enactive' (Weick, 1979).

Leaders in the first dimension may 'shake' the world, but these leaders have the ability to 'make' the world. They are the enactors of their environment, people who do not simply respond to reality but go out and create it. People, in fact, who don't believe in 'circumstances':

People are always blaming their circumstances for what they are. I don't believe in circumstances. The people who get on in the world are the people who get up and look for the circumstances they want, and if they can't find them, make them.
                                                    (George Bernard Shaw)

Role models

If not George Bernard Shaw, then how about Anita Roddick, founder of The Body Shop and enactor extraordinaire? She describes her own leadership philosophy as being:

– Field-centred (MBWA)

We made it our business to walk about everywhere and chat to everyone; we poked our noses into every corner, barged into meetings and made sure everyone knew we were around.   (1991: 148)

– Deviant

I think Gordon [her husband] provides a sense of constancy and continuity while I bounce around breaking the rules, pushing back the boundaries of possibility and shooting off my mouth.   (p. 235)

– Direct

[If there is a problem] get hold of the area manager and insist on getting some answers . . . Grab him by the lapels and say, 'What the hell's going on here?'   (p.235)

– Optimistic

In the Body Shop . . . we possess . . . a further secret ingredient: an extraordinary level of optimism, almost amounting to euphoria . . . We are incurable optimists – and incurable optimists believe they can do anything.   (p. 226)

– Instinctive

I never want to be psychoanalysed because I have a horror that if I start annotating and scientifically dissecting what I do I'll lose everything that goes with a sense of instinct – the ideas, the sense of not knowing how big this company is or not wanting to know. Ever since I had an instinctive feeling when I was a child that my 'uncle' was my father I have learned to trust that instinct; when you go through something like that nothing budges you from clinging to your instinct.   (p. 236)

The Formative Dimension (the architecture of culture)

Having started as a struggle 'against' form, the cultural change process now ends in a struggle to 'make' form – before beginning all over again. Make and break, break and make; a process in which ends become beginnings, and beginnings never end.

> No permanence is ours; we are a wave
> That flows to fit whatever form it finds:
> Through day or night, cathedral or the cave
> We pass forever, craving form that binds.
> Mould after mould we fill and never rest,
> We find no home where joy or grief runs deep.
> We move, we are the everlasting guest.
> (Hesse, 1984 [1943]: 399)

Up until this point we have had:

Culture as Ideas	(Dimension 1)
Culture as Interaction	(Dimension 2)
Culture as Learning	(Dimension 3)
Culture as Practice	(Dimension 4)

Now, finally, we have

Culture as Form   (Dimension 5)
- the structure of culture
- in process terms, culture as 'forming' or 'structuring'
- the development of culture as a process of institutionalization
- in short, the 'architecture of culture':

Corporate change – rebuilding, if you will – has parallels to the most ambitious and perhaps the most noble of the plastic arts, architecture. The skill of the corporate leaders, the ultimate change masters, lies in their ability to envision a new reality and aid in its translation into concrete terms. Creative visions combine with the building up of events, floor by floor, from foundation to completed construction. How productive change occurs is part artistic design, part management of construction. (Kanter, 1983: 278)

The function of leadership in this dimension is to construct a piece of architecture that will 'house' and protect the meanings emerging from the other dimensions of the change process. The aim is to set the meaning in stone – to make it manifest, to materialize the immaterial, to objectify the personal and the subjective, to freeze the flow, to turn understandings into norms, to structure culture, and to raise meaning from the individual to the supraindividual level so that people may freely come and go without fear of the whole structure collapsing about their ears. All of this may apply in a literal sense with the construction of a new building or facade (e.g. an office block, sculpture) which symbolizes the culture or key aspects of it, or, as is more usual, in a metaphorical sense with the creation of a normative structure, such as an organizational chart or set of role descriptions.

The images of leadership that emerge within this fifth dimension of the cultural change process therefore include

- Leader as Architect
- Leader as Designer
- Leader as Draughtsman
- Leader as Builder
- Leader as Stonemason
- Leader as Sculptor

Most of these have already been described in the literature and therefore require little additional comment from me. However, there are some things that have been written with which I wish to take issue. Take the stonemason and architect, for instance.

There is a story management writers never seem to tire of telling about the two stonemasons who, while working on the same project, were asked what they were doing. The first replied: 'I am cutting stone'; the second: 'I am building a great cathedral.' Through the story the writers are seeking to point out that leaders should have the same aspiration as the second of the two men. They must be able to articulate an organization's 'mission' and communicate it in ways that 'religiously' inspire others to higher purposes (cf. Conger, 1991: 31).

This fills me with great unease. I believe it is a case of metaphor no longer being a vehicle of explanation, but a vehicle of moral persuasion, a parable on the virtues of the 'strong cultures' ideology. Certainly, the conception of leadership contained within it holds true only if you believe in the strong cultures ideology – which I do not. I stated my reasons in Chapter 3, the most notable of these being that the concept of the 'organizational church' is a highly dubious one, and has become increasingly so as strong culture companies like IBM continue to lay-off large numbers of their congregation because of the recession!

My choice of leader is therefore different. I would elect the first man, the humble stonemason, not the cathedral builder. My reasoning is simple: organizations are not cathedrals. They are not places to look at but to work in – places of work not places of worship. The comparison being drawn in the story is a false one. While I would not discourage the aesthetic leaders up the road from dreaming about their cathedrals and grand hotels, I would much rather the architects and stonemasons downtown were working on more functional structures – the 'vernacular' as opposed to the 'polite', office blocks rather than obelisks: in other words, the architecture of the everyday. Although by no means blind to appearance and quality of life issues, such people would concentrate on building something that fulfilled the purposes for which it was intended – the principle of 'form follows function'.

In this regard their role models are not Sir Christopher Wren or Michelangelo, but lesser known figures, the Invisible People like Edward Gimson, the architect and furniture-maker, whose doctrine was: 'the functional is the basis of the beautiful'. In other words, no frills, no ornamentation, no china for Sundays only, no unused space (it was Gimson who coined the revolutionary tenet 'death to the drawing room' during the 1920s).

The metaphor of leadership I am proposing for this dimension of the cultural change process is therefore much closer to the 'ordinary man' than the 'Divine Being'.

> Who built the seven towers of Thebes?
> The books are filled with the names of Kings.
> Was it Kings who hauled the craggy blocks of stone?
> In the evening when the Chinese Wall was finished
> Where did the masons go?
>   (Bertolt Brecht, *Questions of a Literary Worker*)

With luck, they went straight home to their 'ordinary' families, not even stopping on the way (like the Honda worker) to double-check that their newly laid blocks were perfectly aligned.

The guiding philosophies of the formative leader

● *Classicism*

Classicism is a philosophy that is altogether dominated by form. Its ideals are harmony, perfection, functionality, regularity, unification, serenity, resolution, integration, comprehensiveness and truth. What is important for the followers of these ideals is that things 'add up' or 'hang together'.

> In such a system, the architectural, aesthetic perfection, the achieved harmony and completeness of the edifice is regarded as proof of its objective correctness, the proof that existence has been truly grasped and comprehended in its entirety. This is the final culmination of the principle of form, for it makes intrinsic formal perfection and completeness the ultimate touchstone of truth.   (Simmel quoted in Lawrence, 1976: 235)

Despite first impressions, classicism is not only a philosophy of order but also a philosophy of change. It is only bad classicism that means formality, rigidity and pedantry. Good classicism means improvisation, flexibility and creativity – using structure as a springboard to higher and better things.

Take 'classical' music as an example.

> True, in the heyday of classical music, most of it was written in the traditional forms, mainly the sonata form. This was comparatively new and young; it was a good frame, firm enough yet flexible enough; and it had evolved for good reasons. The great masters did not need to bother further about these forms, for they had plenty to say, plenty to fill the frames anew and anew with their original, personal ideas; so much so that they unwittingly kept contributing to their further development, modifying them, deflecting them, bending them under the will of their individual genius.   (Toch, 1977: 154)

Similarly, the 'great masters' of organizational design need to be firm yet flexible, always prepared to stretch and bend their structures to accommodate new cultural meanings and ideas.

Just as classicism is not about rigidity, neither is it about symmetry and perfection. For as Stravinsky once said, 'To be perfectly symmetrical is to be perfectly dead' (Stravinsky and Craft, 1979: 20).

The concept of form or structure is organic, and to some extent ad hoc. In terms of the earlier architectural metaphor, the cultural building must be allowed the freedom to grow like Topsy. There will always be 'work in progress', as old parts of the building are knocked down and new wings, annexes and extensions added – not as part of some grand plan, note, but as a pragmatic response to the immediate need for more space. In this sense, classicists are more interested in 'forming' than they are in 'form'.

- *Rationalism*

    Reason is divine. (Aristotle)

    That glimmer of divine light . . . Man calls it Reason. (Goethe)

Leaders in this dimension are also rationalists, that is to say they

1. Guide their working lives by reason: 'Human reason is the ultimate authority' (Zijderveld, 1982: 31).
2. Seek empirical evidence on what causes what. 'Have all the facts and counsel necessary – then decide and stick to it' (Bill 'Montana' Marriott, Marriott Corporation).
3. Use reason as a universally applicable standard for judging validity and worth.
4. Try to adapt their behaviour to the demands of the environment.
5. Strive for consistency in their beliefs and practices by creating then following rules and principles.
6. Pursue their goals by engaging in such activities as gathering information, evaluating evidence, estimating likelihoods, making predictions, drawing inductive and deductive inferences, and constructing explanatory theories (Shweder, 1984: 80).

As one would expect their models of change are also highly linear and rational: they perceive change as a process that should pass through a number of fixed and discreet stages, for example:

- Unfreezing —> Moving —> Refreezing
- Evaluation —> Initiation —> Implementation —> Routinization
- Development of concern —> Acknowledgement and understanding of the problem —> Planning and acting —> Stabilizing the change

Left to their own devices they would therefore no doubt try to lead the complete cultural change process through a similar sequence of events, yet we know that cultural change does not happen in this way. This is not to say there is no place for rational leaders. Where their particular strengths are most appropriate, indeed invaluable, is in the last phase of the process, the refreezing, routinization and stabilization of culture.

Their involvement elsewhere would almost certainly bring them into conflict with leaders in other dimensions, particularly with leaders in dimension 1, who have a 'non-rational' model of change: i.e. a 'garbage-can' view of organization, which stresses chaos, uncertainty, randomness, unpredictability, haphazardness and unbroken flow in the change process. And it also brings them into conflict to a lesser extent with leaders in dimension 2, who have a 'bounded rational' model of change: i.e. a model that says that organizations are too complex to understand by reason or by any other means for that matter; things are more non-linear, chaotic, and sloppy than pure rationalists would have us believe. Their approach is not to have grand plans that ignore complexity but small plans that reduce the complexity to manageable sizes and proceed slowly and cautiously toward their goals.

Nevertheless, this is not sufficient grounds for excluding rationalist leaders (or any of the other leaders for that matter) from other dimensions of the change process. There is no place for demarcation and turf issues in this area of human endeavour. In any case, why should we assume that conflict would necessarily be a bad thing? Leaders do not have to see eye to eye in order for successful cultural change to occur. Indeed one might argue the opposite, that a friction between philosophies is not only inevitable but essential if the necessary 'heat' for change is to be generated. Rationalist leaders, like any other leaders, should therefore be allowed to roam the dimensions at will, just so long as they realize that the formative dimension is their 'home ground'.

A thesaurus for the formative leader

> Clear, cool, detached, impersonal, objective, logical, unemotional, literal, instrumental, traditional, formal, controlled, controlling, disciplined, cautious, conventional, systematic, normative, precise, analytical, mathematical, geometrical, technical, factual, observant, mechanical, numerate, hard-headed, sensible, solid, dependable, linear, reasonable, scientific, legalistic, calculating, 'either-or', puritanical, respectable, austere, arrogant.

And usually bureaucratic:

> One is dead only after the physician has filled out and signed the appropriate forms.   (Zijderveld, 1982: 32)

Role models

Descartes, Leibniz, Vico, Socrates, Plato, Aristotle, Augustine, Aquinas, Kant, Spinoza, Schopenhauer, Hegel, E.B. Tylor, J.G. Frazer, Barbara Hepworth, Chomsky, Lévi-Strauss, Hobbes, Goethe ('that paragon of rationality and good citizenship', Solomon, 1976: 127).

Robert McNamara, Harold Geneen, Dr 'find a need and fill it' Wang of Wang Laboratories.

Prime Minister John Major and Mr Spock (both, of course, crew members of the Starship Enterprise).

That concludes the description of the five dimensions of cultural leadership. All that remains for me to do is to find a way of finishing this chapter and ending the book. This is not easy, because thought processes, like cultural processes, have a nasty habit of going on for ever.

The details have been provided. What is needed now is a broad steer with regard to the formulation of a strategy for the leadership of cultural change. The image with which I would like to leave you is of a pentagon of leadership: an elastic pentagon that is stretched and distorted into different shapes by the pulling forces of the five different types of leader located at each of the five points (Figure 14.1). The organization culture is the space between these points, the product of these pulling forces, an entity in constant tension and flux.

What change-makers need to do is increase their awareness of these pulls in respect of their own organization, find out roughly where the current 'centre of gravity' lies and begin to argue amongst themselves as to where it should be. It is the searching not the finding that is important, for it is this which provides the whole dynamic of the cultural change effort.

There is no universally correct shape for the cultural pentagon: each organization will require a different balance of pulling forces for different tasks and different environments. With regard to tasks, for example, a think-tank may need a culture that is stronger on dimension 1 (ideas) than dimensions 4 and 5 (action and structure), whereas an organization hired to put out oil fires in Kuwait may need a culture that is stronger on dimension 4 (actions) than dimensions 2 and 3 (words and ethics). Clearly these are extreme examples, but they do illustrate the contingent nature

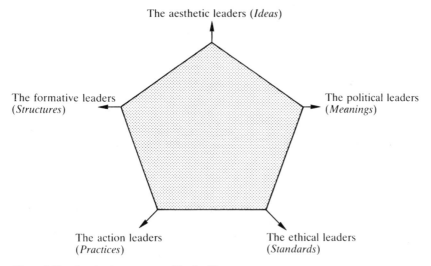

Figure 14.1   An elastic pentagon of leadership

of strategy, the need to find a system of leadership that will produce the kind of culture that the situation calls for. Even here one has to be cautious, because what is required may well change as the situation itself changes. For example, the think tank may need to become more practically orientated as its ideas get taken up, in which case aesthetic leaders must be ready to take a back seat in favour of the action leaders. The centre of gravity of the pentagon is very much a moving point.

With regard to different environments, these too will require their own particular kinds of culture, and therefore different kinds of leadership process. For example, dimension 1 leadership is likely to be less important in a stable environment; the same is true of dimension 2 in a homogeneous environment, dimension 3 in a routine, simple environment, dimension 4 in an intellectual or spiritual environment, and dimension 5 in a dynamic or turbulent environment. Again the position is unlikely to remain fixed for any length of time: organization environments change, and so therefore must their cultures and their leadership processes.

Any generalizations must, it seems, be made with extreme care, since for every case that fits the rule there is likely to be one that breaks it. Certainly, there are no hard-and-fast rules in this area, indeed given the number of possible exceptions one might even be tempted to say that there are no rules at all.

However, we do not need to leave things as much in the air as this. Rules are one thing, but danger flags are another. What I believe *is* possible is to issue some general warnings that will apply to any organization irrespective of the situation in which it finds itself. There are three warnings in particular:

1 *Be careful about missing out a dimension entirely*: Each dimension has its own special qualities and its own contribution to make to the overall process of cultural production. We can demonstrate this by imagining what the situation would be like without any one of them:

- A culture that is lacking an aesthetic dimension is a culture that is often stagnant and bankrupt of ideas. Labour organizations and political parties that have been around for a long time are particularly prone in this regard.
- If the political dimension is missing you tend to get schismatic 'secret society' cultures that do not talk to each other, but proceed to do their own thing and promote their own parochial interests under the same roof.
- When the ethical dimension is missing you may get 'dirty tricks' cultures, whose leaders are driven by paranoia about competition and win-at-all-costs mentalities. This may also produce 'single-loop'

cultures which are incapable of learning anything and frequently suffer bouts of corporate amnesia.

- Without an action dimension the culture becomes an endless 'talking shop', constantly debating ideas but never getting round to putting them into practice.
- If the formative dimension is missing you get 'come and go' cultures, dissolving almost as soon as they appear and leaving no memory trace.

2 *Be careful not to be attracted by the notion of balance for balance's sake*: Invariably the point in the middle of the pentagon will be a 'dead position', a doldrums in which the organization can easily get caught. It is a position where all of the leadership pulls are effectively cancelling each other out, where the matrix of forces has led to inertia.

What we need to appreciate is that there is absolutely no virtue in the notion of balance or equality between the dimensions. Indeed, a perfect balance produces a static situation starved of energy and direction. It is the continual interplay of competing forces that provides the life-blood of culture and cultural development. As the different forces mingle so new and exciting possibilities are opened up, such as the case of Disney where romanticism has merged with rationalism to produce a new breed of person called the 'imagineer'. This could be just the beginning. Who knows where we may end up as a result of further collisions between different cultural dimensions and philosophies?

Confuscianist principles simply do not apply in the field of culture. Depending on the situation, an organization will want to give primacy to one dimension or probably at most a hybrid of two dimensions – the notion of 'major' and 'minor' leadership processes, alternating as the cultural change process unfolds.

Rather than balance, therefore, there should instead be a leading edge or pivotal point in our pentagon, an area around which energies converge, at least for a time. The important thing is that leaders recognize when they are on this leading edge and when they are not, and when they should hand over the initiative to another dimension of leadership.

3 *Be careful not to overemphasize one dimension to the exclusion of the others*: Since so much of the culture perspective is about myths and mythology, it seems appropriate to end the book with reference to just such a myth. Lévi-Strauss (1972) tells the story of the Honey-Mad-Woman, who devours honey with total disregard for all the rules about its correct usage. In native thought the search for honey represents a kind of return to Nature in the guise of erotic attraction transposed from the sexual register to that of the sense of taste, which, if it is indulged in for too long, undermines the very foundations of the culture.

The myth is a parable about the dangers of excess in cultures – about excess undermining culture and returning it once more to nature and the wild. In my opinion this must also include organization cultures. Each corner of our pentagon is a potential hiding place for excess, a place where, if left unchecked, action cultures can turn into mindless 'gung-ho' cultures and political cultures can become ruthless Machiavellian cultures. Throughout this book we have dealt with this issue of cultural excess under the banner of the 'ism'. The important thing to recognize about an 'ism' is that it is not a passion but an obsession. The difference between these is huge: the former generates energy and creativity, the latter narrowness and dogma.

The best check against excess is the presence of other countervailing forces, just as the best safeguard for democracy is the absence of too large a majority for the ruling party in Parliament. And so we must make room in our cultural parliament for the rationalists and the romantics, the poets and the pragmatists, the sceptics and the structuralists. All are needed if we are to avoid extremism and keep the organization on an acceptable course. And so we end where we began, with the both–and philosophy. Having travelled all the way with us, it seems only right that it should be permitted the last word.

References

Adams J. D. (1984) *Transforming Work*, Miles River Press, Alexandria, Virginia

Adler P. S. (1972) Culture shock and the cross-cultural learning experience. *Readings in Intercultural Education*, **2**, Intercultural Communication Network, Pittsburgh, 8

Alexander G. P. (1987) Establishing shared values through management training programmes. *Training and Development Journal*, **41**, 45–7

Allaire Y. and Firsirotu M. E. (1984) Theories of organizational culture. *Organization Studies*, **5** (3), 193–226

Allais M. (1989) The economic science of today and facts. A critical analysis of some characteristic features. Paper presented to the Norwegian School of Management, Sandvika, 28 February

Amelunxen C. (1991) *Of Fools at Court*, de Gruyter, Berlin

Ashburner L., Ferlie E. and Pettigrew A. (1991) Organizational restructuring and the new health authorities: continuity or change? Paper presented to the British Academy of Management Conference, University of Bath, September

Ayer A. J. (1985) *Wittgenstein*, Wiedenfeld and Nicolson, London

Baburoglu O. N. (1987) The stalemate paradox: interpreting the dynamics of a system in transition. Paper presented to the Organization and Management Theory Division at the annual meeting of the Academy of Management, New Orleans

Baker E. L. (1980) Managing organizational culture. *Management Review*, **69** (7), 8–13

Bakhtin M. (1953) Discourse in the novel. In *The Dialogic Imagination* (ed. M. Holmquist), University of Texas Press, Austin, 259–442.

Barnard C. (1938) *The Functions of the Executive*, Harvard University Press, Cambridge, Mass.

Barnes J. (1985) *Flaubert's Parrot*, Picador, London

Bate S. P. (1978) Cultural analysis, confrontation, and counter-culture as strategies for organization development. Paper presented to the 19th International Congress of Applied Psychology, Munich, 28–31 July

Bate S. P. (1984) The impact of organizational culture on approaches to organizational problem-solving. *Organization Studies*, **5** (1), 43–66

Bate S. P. (1990) Using the culture concept in an organization development setting. *Journal of Applied Behavioural Science*, **26** (1), 83–106

Bate S. P. (1991) Reading the popular business texts from a cultural perspective. An examination of the role of folk theory in contemporary management discourse. Paper presented to the 8th International SCOS Conference on Organizational Symbolism and Corporate Culture, Copenhagen, Denmark, 26–28 June

Bate S. P. (1993) *Thinking Culturally* (manuscript in preparation)

Bates T. R. (1975) Gramsci and the theory of hegemony. *Journal of the History of Ideas*, **36**, 351–66

290 Strategies for Cultural Change

Bateson G. (1955) A theory of play and phantasy. *Psychiatric Research Reports*, 2, American Psychiatric Association, New York, 39–51

Bayley J. O. (1980) Structure versus unity. In *Structure in Science and Art*. Proceedings of the Third C. H. Boehringer Sohn Symposium, Kronberg, Taunus, 2–5 May 1979 (eds Sir P. Medawar and J. H. Shelley), Excerpta Medica, Oxford, 86–95

Beckhard R. (1969) *Organization Development: Strategies and Models*, Addison-Wesley, Reading, Mass.

Beckhard R. and Harris R. T. (1987) *Organizational Transitions. Managing Complex Change*, Addison-Wesley, Reading, Mass.

Belgard W. P., Fisher K. K. and Rayner S. R. (1988) Vision, opportunity, and tenacity: three informal processes that influence formal transformation. In *Corporate Transformation. Revitalizing Organizations for a Competitive World* (eds R. H. Kilmann, T. J. Covin and Associates), Jossey-Bass, London, 131–51

Bennis W. (1981) The artform of leadership. In *The Executive Mind: New Insights on Managerial Thought and Action* (ed. S. Srivastva and Associates), Jossey-Bass, San Francisco, 15–24

Bennis W. (1989) *Why Leaders Can't Lead: the Unconscious Conspiracy Continues*. Jossey-Bass, San Francisco, CA

Berger P. L. and Luckmann T. (1966) *The Social Construction of Reality*, Penguin, Harmondsworth

Berlin I. (1980) *Vico and Herder. Two Studies in the History of Ideas*, Chatto and Windus, London

Bettelheim B. (1977) *The Uses of Enchantment: the Meaning and Importance of Fairy Tales*, Vintage, New York

Bibeault D. B. (1982) *Corporate Turnaround. How Managers Turn Losers into Winners*, McGraw-Hill, New York

Bird B. (1989). The mercurial entrepreneur. A Jungian look at the venture process. Paper presented to the 4th International SCOS Conference on Organizational Symbolism and Corporate Culture, INSEAD, Fontainebleau, France, 28–30 June

Black P. (1972) *The Biggest Aspidistra in the World*, BBC Publications, London

Boje D. M., Fedor D. B. and Rowland K. M. (1982) Mythmaking: a qualitative step in O.D. interventions. *Journal of Applied Behavioural Science*, **18** (1), 17–28

Bonavia M. (1985) *Twilight of British Rail?* David and Charles, Newton Abbot

Brass D. J. (1984) Being in the right place: a structural analysis of individual influence in an organization. *Administrative Science Quarterly*, **29**, 518–39

Brissy J. F. (1989) Leadership in the courtroom: a Belgian experiment in 'Responsive Law'. Paper presented to the 4th International SCOS Conference on Organizational Symbolism and Corporate Culture, INSEAD, Fontainebleau, France, 28–30 June

Brockner J. (1992) The escalation of commitment to a failing course of action: toward theoretical progress. *Academy of Management Review*, **17** (1), 39–61

Brooks I. and Bate S. P. (1992) The problems of effecting change within the British Civil Service. In The Challenge of Change: the Theory and Practice of Organizational Transformations (eds M. Bresnen, A. Davies and R. Whipp), *Management Research News*, **15**, 5/6, full paper to appear in *British Journal of Management* (forthcoming 1994)

Brown H. D. (1986) Learning a second culture. In *Culture Bound. Bridging the Culture Gap in Language Teaching* (ed. J. M. Valdes), Cambridge University Press, Cambridge, 33–49

Bryman A., Gillingwater D. and McGuinness I. (1992) Leadership and organizational transformation. Paper presented to The Employment Research Unit Annual Conference, 'The Challenge of Change: The Theory and Practice of Organizational Transformations', Cardiff Business School, 9–10 September

Bråten S. (1973) Model monopoly and communication. *Acta Sociologica*, **16** (2), 98–107

Burke P. (1987) Introduction. In *The Social History of Language* (eds P. Burke and R. Porter), Cambridge University Press, Cambridge, 1–20

Burke, W. W. (1987) *Organization Development: A Normative View*, Addison-Wesley, Reading, Mass.

Burnham, J. (1971) *The Structure of Art*, George Braziller, New York

Burns, J. M. (1978) *Leadership*, Harper and Row, New York

Business Week (1984) Who's excellent now?: Some of the best-sellers picks haven't been doing so well lately. *Business Week*, November

Business Week (1989) Innovation in America. The challenge we face. What must be done. *Business Week*, Special Issue, August

Capra F. (1989) *Uncommon Wisdom. Conversations with Remarkable People*, Flamingo, London

Carlzon J. (1987) *Moments of Truth. New Strategies for Today's Customer-Driven Economy*, Harper and Row, New York

Chapman P. (1988) Changing the corporate culture of Rank Xerox. *Long Range Planning*, **21** (2), 23–8

Child J. (1984) *Organization: a Guide to Problems and Practice*, 2nd ed, Harper and Row, London

Ciborra C. U. and Lanzara G. F. (1990) Designing dynamic artifacts: computer systems as formative contexts. In *Symbols and Artifacts: Views of the Corporate Landscape* (ed. P. Gagliardi), de Gruyter, Berlin, 147–65

Clegg, H. A. (1975) Pluralism in industrial relations. *British Journal of Industrial Relations*, **13**, 309–16

Clifford J. (1988) *The Predicament of Culture. Twentieth-Century Ethnography, Literature, and Art*, Harvard University Press, Cambridge, Mass.

Cline A. D. (1988) Can corporate culture be changed? *Communication World*, **5** (January), 30–3

Collin A. (1992) The role of the mentor in transforming the organization. Paper presented to The Employment Research Unit Annual Conference, 'The Challenge of Change: The Theory and Practice of Organizational Transformations', Cardiff Business School, 9–10 September

Collins J. (1989) *Uncommon Cultures. Popular Culture and Post-Modernism*, Routledge, London

Conger J. A. (1991) Inspiring others: the language of leadership. *Academy of Management Executive*, **5** (1), 31–45

Connolly W. E. (1974) *The Terms of Political Discourse*, D. C. Heath, Lexington, Mass.

Cooke K. L. (1979) Mathematical approaches to culture change. In *Transformations. Mathematical Approaches to Culture Change* (eds C. Renfrew and K. L. Cooke), Academic Press, London, 45–79

Crescimanno R. (1982) *Culture, Consciousness, and Beyond*, University Press of America, Washington

Crick M. (1976) *Explorations in Language and Meaning. Towards a Semantic Anthropology*, Malaby Press, London

Crozier M. (1964) *The Bureaucratic Phenomenon*, Tavistock, London

Czarniawska-Joerges, B. (1989) Leaders, managers, entrepreneurs on and off the organizational stage. Paper presented to the 4th International SCOS Conference on Organizational Symbolism and Corporate Culture, INSEAD, Fontainebleau, France, 28–30 June

Dalmau T. and Dick R. (1991) Managing ambiguity and paradox: the place of small groups in cultural change. Paper presented to the 8th International SCOS Conference on Organizational Symbolism and Corporate Culture, Copenhagen, Denmark, 26–28 June

D'Andrade R. (1984) Preview: a colloquy of culture theorists. In *Culture Theory. Essays on Mind, Self, and Emotion* (eds R. A. Shweder and R. A. LeVine), Cambridge University Press, Cambridge, 1–24

Darmer P. (1991) Paradoxes – the stuff that culture thrives on. Paper presented to the 8th International SCOS Conference on Organizational Symbolism and Corporate Culture, Copenhagen, Denmark, 26–28 June

Davis K. (1965) *Human Society*, Macmillan, New York

Davis S. M. (1984) *Managing Corporate Culture*, Ballinger, Cambridge, Mass.

Deal T. E. and Kennedy A. A. (1982) *Corporate Cultures. The Rites and Rituals of Corporate Life*, Addison-Wesley, Reading, Mass.

DeLisi P. S. (1990) Lessons from the steel axe: culture, technology and organizational change. *Sloan Management Review*, **83** (Fall), 83–93

Denison D. R. and Mishra A. K. (1989) Organizational culture and organizational effectiveness: a theory and some preliminary empirical evidence. Paper presented to the Organization and Management Theory Division at the annual meeting of the Academy of Management, Washington DC

Dent J. F. (1990) Reality in the making: a study of organizational transformation. Paper presented to the Workshop on Strategy, Accounting, and Control, Venice, 25–26 October

Douglas M. (1987) *How Institutions Think*. Routledge and Kegan Paul, London

Driver P. (1990) Where the piano is king. *Sunday Times*, 18 February

Duenas G. (1991) Fractured organizational cultures. Paper presented to the 8th International SCOS Conference on Organizational Symbolism and Corporate Culture, Copenhagen, Denmark, 26–28 June

Dunphy D. C. and Stace D. A. (1988) Transformational and coercive strategies for planned organizational change: beyond the O.D. model. *Organization Studies*, **9** (3), 317–34

Dunsing R. J. and Matejka K. (1987) Macho management: what HR professionals should watch for. *Personnel*, **84** (July), 62–6

Dyer W. G. (1985) The cycle of cultural evolution in organizations. In *Gaining Control of the Corporate Culture* (eds R. Kilmann, M. J. Saxton, R. Serpa et al.), Jossey-Bass, San Francisco, 200–29

Dyer W. G. (1986) *Cultural Change in Family Firms: Anticipating and Managing Business and Family Transitions*, Jossey-Bass, London

Ebers M. (1985) Understanding organizations: the poetic mode. *Journal of Management*, **11** (2), 51–62

Feenberg A. (1986) *Lukács, Marx and the Sources of Critical Theory*, Oxford University Press, Oxford

Feldman S. P. (1986) Management in context: an essay on the relevance of culture to the understanding of organizational change. *Journal of Management Studies*, **23** (6), 587–607

Feyerabend P. (1987) *Farewell to Reason*, Verso, London

Fiennes G. F. (1967) *I Tried to Run a Railway*, Ian Allan, London

Financial Times (1991) BT plugs into a cultural revolution. 27 March, 12

Finney P. B. (1989) Even at Big Blue, the corporate culture had to change. *Business Month*, **133** (2), 69–70

Fiske J. (1987) British cultural studies and television. In *Channels of Discourse* (ed. R. Allen), University of North Carolina Press, Chapel Hill

Fleck L. (1935) *The Genesis and Development of a Scientific Fact*, University of Chicago Press, Chicago

Foster R. N. (1986) *Innovation: The Attacker's Advantage*, Summit Books, New York

Foucault M. (1972) *The Archaeology of Knowledge*, Tavistock, London

Fox A. (1966) Industrial sociology and industrial relations. Royal Commission on Trade Unions and Employers' Associations 1965–1968, Research Paper No. 3, HMSO, London

Fox A. (1973) Industrial relations: a social critique of pluralist ideology. In *Man and Organization* (ed. J. Child), Allen and Unwin, London, 185–231

French W., Bell C. H. and Zawacki R. A. (1983) *Organization Development: Theory, Practice, and Research*, rev. edn, Business Publications, Dallas

Frissen P. H. A. (1989) Bureaucratic culture and informatization: an institutionalist perspective. Paper presented to the 9th EGOS-Colloquium, Theory and Practice of Organizational Transition and Transformation, Berlin, 11–14 July

Fromm E. (1963) *The Fear of Freedom*, Routledge and Kegan Paul, London

Gabriel Y. (1991) On organizational stories and myths: why it is easier to slay a dragon than to kill a myth. *International Sociology*, **6** (4), 427–42

Gabriel Y. (1992) The organizational dreamworld: workplace stories, fantasies and subjectivity. Paper presented to the 10th International Aston/UMIST Conference, Organization and Control of the Labour Process, Aston University, England, 1–3 April

Gagliardi P. (1986) The creation and change of organizational cultures: a conceptual framework. *Organization Studies*, **7** (2), 117–34

Gagliardi P. (ed.) (1990) *Symbols and Artifacts: Views of the Corporate Landscape*, de Gruyter, New York

Gagliardi P. (1991) Designing organizational settings: the interplay between physical, symbolic and social structures, Paper presented to the Symposium, Consumption-Artifact-Culture, Vienna, Austria, 18–20 September

Garsombke D. J. (1988) Organizational culture dons the mantle of militarism. *Organizational Dynamics*, Summer, 46–56

Geertz C. (1973) *The Interpretation of Cultures. Selected Essays*, Basic Books, New York

Geertz C. (1974) From the native's point of view. On the nature of anthropological understanding. *Bulletin of the American Academy of Arts and Sciences*, **28** (1), ch. 4

Geertz C. (1983) *Local Knowledge. Further Essays in Interpretive Anthropology*, Basic Books, New York

Geertz C. (1984) Preview: a colloquy of culture theorists. In *Cultural Theory. Essays on Mind, Self and Emotion* (eds R. A. Shweder and R. A. LeVine), Cambridge University Press, Cambridge, 1–24

Gersick C. J. G. (1991) Revolutionary change theories: a multilevel exploration of the punctuated equilibrium paradigm. *Academy of Management Review*, **16** (1), 10–36

Giddens A. (1979) *Central Problems in Social Theory. Action, Structure and Contradiction in Social Analysis*, Macmillan, London

Gilot F. and Lake C. (1964) *Life with Picasso*, McGraw-Hill, New York

Goffman E. (1974) *Frame Analysis. An Essay on the Organization of Experience*, Penguin, Harmondsworth

Gorbachev M. (1987) *Perestroika. New Thinking for our Country and the World*, Collins, London

Gray B., Bougon M. G. and Donnellon A. (1985) Organizations as constructions and destructions of meaning. *Journal of Management*, **11** (2), 83–98

Green S. (1988) Strategy, organizational culture and symbolism. *Long Range Planning*, **21** (4), 121–9

Griffiths P. (1978) *A Concise History of Modern Music. From Debussy to Boulez*. Thames and Hudson, London

Grinyer P. H. and Spender J. C. (1979) Recipes, crises and adaptation in mature businesses. *International Studies of Management and Organization*, **ix**, 113–23

Harris S. G. (1990) A schema-based perspective on organization culture. Revision of a paper presented to Organization and Management Theory Division at the annual meeting of the Academy of Management, Washington DC

Harvey-Jones J. (1989) *Making it Happen. Reflections on Leadership*, Fontana, an imprint of HarperCollins, London

Hassard J. and Sharifi S. (1989) Corporate culture and strategic change. *Journal of General Management*, **15** (2), 4–19

Heller R. (1967) British Railways after Beeching. *Management Today*, June, 64–136

Helms L. (1988) Tides change at Seafirst. *ABA Banking Journal*, November, 69–74

Hennestad B. W. (1991) Reframing organizations. Towards a model. Unpublished manuscript, Norwegian School of Management, Sandvika

Hesse H. (1984 [1943]) *The Glass Bead Game*, Penguin, Harmondsworth

Hochschild, A. R. (1983) *The Managed Heart. Commercialization of Human Feeling*, University of California Press, Berkeley, CA

Hollingsworth B. (1985) *An Illustrated Guide to Modern Trains*, Salamander, London

Huffington A. S. (1988) *Picasso. Creator and Destroyer*, Weidenfeld and Nicolson, London

Hughes M. (1988) *Rail 300. The World High Speed Train Race*, David and Charles, Newton Abbot

Hurst D. K. (1984) Of boxes, bubbles, and effective management. *Harvard Business Review*, May/June, 78–88

Hutchins E. (1983) Understanding Micronesian navigation. In *Mental Models* (eds D. Gentner and A. L. Stevens), Lawrence Erlbaum, New Jersey, 191–225

The Independent on Sunday (1992) Mighty mouse of the movies, 23 February, 13

Inzerelli G. (1980) Some notes on culture and organizational control. Centre for the Study of Organizational Innovation, University of Pennsylvania, Discussion Paper 84, September

Johnson G. (1984) Managing strategic change – a frames and formulae approach. Paper presented to the Strategic Management Society Conference, Philadelphia, USA, October

Johnson G. (1990) Managing strategic change: the role of symbolic action. *British Journal of Management*, **1**, 183–200

Kanter R. M. (1983) *The Change Masters. Corporate Entrepreneurs at Work*, Unwin, London

Kanter R. M. (1988) When a thousand flowers bloom: structural, collective, and social conditions for innovation in organization. In *Research in Organizational*

Behaviour, **10** (eds B. M. Staw and L. L. Cummings), JAI Press, Greenwich, CT, 169–211

Kelly J. (1990) Big brother, big blue, apple, yummies and the music of the spheres. Paper presented to the 7th International SCOS Conference on Organizational Symbolism and Corporate Culture, Saarbrücken, Germany, 6–9 June

Kennedy A. A. (1985) Ruminations on change: the incredible value of human beings in getting things done. In *The Planning of Change*, 4th edn (eds W. G. Bennis, K. D. Benne and R. Chin), Holt, Rinehart and Winston, London, 325–35

Kenny A. (1989) Ludwig Wittgenstein: why do philosophy if it is only useful against philosophers? *The Times Higher Educational Supplement*, 19 May

Kerr C. (1964) *Labour and Management in Industrial Society*, Doubleday, New York

Kirkbride P. S. (1983) Power in the workplace. An investigation of the phenomenon in industrial relations utilizing data from an engineering company. PhD dissertation, School of Management, University of Bath

Kluckhohn F. R. (1963) Some reflections on the nature of cultural integration and change. In *Sociological Theory, Values and Sociocultural Change: Essays in Honor of Pitirim A. Sorokin* (ed. E. A. Tiryakian), Free Press of Glencoe, New York, pp. 217–47

Koestler A. (1937) *Spanish Testament*, Victor Gollancz, London

Koestler A. (1983) *Dialogue with Death*, Macmillan Papermac, London

Krantz J. (1990) Lessons from the field: an essay on the crisis of leadership in contemporary organizations. *The Journal of Applied Behavioural Science*, **26** (1), 49–64

Kundera M. (1980) *The Book of Laughter and Forgetting*, Faber and Faber, London

Laing R. D. (1971) *Self and Others*, Penguin, Harmondsworth

Langer S. K. (1953) *Feeling and Form*, Routledge and Kegan Paul, London

Laurent A. (1989) A cultural view of organizational change. In *Human Resource Management in International Firms. Change, Globalization, Innovation* (eds P. Evans, Y. Doz and A. Laurent), Macmillan, London, 83–94

Lawrence P. A. (1976) *Georg Simmel: Sociologist and European*, Nelson, Middlesex

Leapman M. (1986) *The Last Days of the Beeb*, Allen and Unwin, London

Lévi-Strauss C. (1972) *Mythologiques II. Du Miel aux Cendres*, Plon, Paris

LeVine R. A. (1984) Properties of culture. An ethnographic view. In *Culture Theory. Essays on Mind, Self, and Emotion* (eds R. A. Shweder and R. A. LeVine), Cambridge University Press, Cambridge, 67–87

Levy A. and Merry U. (1986) *Organizational Transformation*, Praeger, New York

Logan A. and Stuart R. (1986) Action-based 'learning': are activity and experience the same? *Stirrings, Association of Teachers of Management*, **2**

Louis M. R. (1985) An investigator's guide to workplace culture. In *Organizational Culture* (eds P. J. Frost, L. F. Moore, M. R. Louis et al.), Sage, Beverly Hills, CA, 73–94

Louis M. R (1989) Newcomers as lay ethnographers: acculturation during organizational socialization. Working Paper, Boston University. (Also in *Organizational Climate and Culture* (ed. B. Schneider), Jossey-Bass, San Francisco, CA

Louis M. R. and Sutton R. I. (1989) Switching cognitive gears: from habits of mind to active thinking. Working paper 89-1, Boston University, Center for

Applied Social Science, and Stanford University, Department of Industrial Engineering and Engineering Management

Luchins A. S. (1940) Mechanization in problem solving: the effect of Einstellung. *Psychological Monographs*, **54**, 248

Lundberg C. (1985) On the feasibility of cultural interventions in organizations. In *Organizational Culture* (eds P. J. Frost, L. F. Moore, M. R. Louis et al.), Sage, Beverly Hills, 169–85

Malinowski B. (1945) *The Dynamics of Culture Change*, Yale University Press, New Haven, Conn

Mangham I. L. (1978) *Interactions and Interventions in Organizations*, Wiley, New York

Margulies N. and Raia A. P. (1978) *Conceptual Foundations of Organization Development*, McGraw-Hill, New York

Marshall C. (1988) Corporate culture: the role of top management. *Multinational Business*, Spring, 36–40

Marshall J. and McLean A. J. (1985) Exploring organization culture as a route to organizational change. Paper presented to Association of Teachers of Management Conference, with Ashridge Management College: Current Research in Management, Ashridge, January

Martin J. and Meyerson D. (1988) Organizational cultures and the denial, channeling and acknowledgement of ambiguity. In *Managing Ambiguity and Change* (eds L. R. Pondy et al.), Wiley, New York, 93–125

Masuch M. (1985) Vicious circles in organizations. *Administrative Science Quarterly*, **30**, 14–33

Mayo A. (1989) Business strategies and management development – the ICL experience. *Industrial and Commercial Training*, **21** (2), 17–23

McLean A. J. (1990) *Cultures at Work. How to Identify and Understand Them.* Bath Associates, Bath

Meek L. V. (1988) Organizational culture: origins and weaknesses. *Organization Studies*, **9** (4), 453–73

Meyer J. W. and Scott W. R. (eds) (1983) *Organizational Environments*, Sage, Beverly Hills, CA

Meyerson D. and Martin J. (1987) Cultural change: an integration of three different views. *Journal of Management Studies*, **24** (6), 623–47

Miller D. and Friesen P. H. (1980) Momentum and revolution in organizational adaptation. *Academy of Management Journal*, **23** (4), 591–614

Miller G. A. and Johnson-Laird P. N. (1976) *Language and Perception*, Cambridge University Press, Cambridge

Mintzberg H. (1978) Patterns in strategy formation. *Management Science*, **24** (9), 934–48

Mintzberg H. (1979) *The Structuring of Organizations. A Synthesis of the Research*, Prentice-Hall, Englewood Cliffs, NJ

Mintzberg H. (1990) The manager's job: folklore and fact; with a retrospective commentary. *Harvard Business Review*, **68**, March/April, 163–76

Mitroff I. I. and Kilmann R. H. (1985) Corporate taboos as the key to unlocking culture. In *Gaining Control of the Corporate Culture* (eds R. H. Kilmann, M. Saxton, R. Serpa et al.), Jossey-Bass, London, 184–99

Morgan G. (1986) *Images of Organization*, Sage, Beverly Hills, CA

Mueller R. K. (1987) Social networks and corporate culture. *The Corporate Board*, September/October, 10–13

Murphy P. E. (1989) Creating ethical corporate structures. *Sloan Management Review*, **30** (Winter), 81–7

Nakajo T. and Kono T. (1989) Success through culture change in a Japanese brewery. *Long Range Planning*, **22** (6), 29–37

Nichols R. (1992) *Debussy Remembered*, Faber and Faber, London

Nicoll D. (1984) Consulting to organizational transformations. In *Transforming Work* (ed. J. D. Adams), Miles River Press, Alexandria, 157–69

Nicolson N. (ed.) (1977) *A Change of Perspective. The Letters of Virginia Woolf*, vol. III: 1923–1928, The Hogarth Press, London

Nock O. S. (1983) *Two Miles a Minute*, Stephens, Cambridge

O'Farrell P. N., Hitchens D. M. and Moffat L. A. (1991) The competitive advantage of business service firms: a matched pairs analysis of the relationship between generic strategy and performance. Paper presented to the British Academy of Management Conference, University of Bath, September

Oakes G. (ed. and trans.) (1980) *Essays on Interpretation in Social Science. Georg Simmel*, Manchester University Press, Manchester

Ochs E. and Schieffelin B. B. (1984) Language acquisition and socialization. Three developmental stories and their implications. In *Culture Theory. Essays on Mind, Self and Emotion* (eds R. A. Shweder and R. A. LeVine), Cambridge University Press, Cambridge, 276–320

Ogbonna E. and Wilkinson B. (1988) Corporate strategy and corporate culture: the management of change in the UK supermarket industry. *Personnel Review*, **17** (6), 10–14

Ogburn W. F. (1922) *Social Change*, The Viking Press, New York

Ohmae K. (1983) *The Mind of the Strategist*, Penguin, Harmondsworth

Ott, K. (1984) Two problems that threaten organizational culture research . . . Paper presented at the 1st International SCOS Conference on Organizational Symbolism and Corporate Culture, Lund, Sweden, 26–30 June

Parrett H. (1987) Common sense: from certainty to happiness. In *Common Sense* (eds F. Van Holthoon and D. R. Olson), University Press of America, Lanham, MD, 17–34

Pascale R. T. (1990) *Managing on the Edge. Companies that Use Conflict to Stay Ahead*, Simon and Schuster, New York

Peckham M. (1970) *The Triumph of Romanticism. Collected Essays*, University of South Carolina Press, Columbia

Peckham M. (1976) *Romanticism and Behaviour. Collected Essays II*, University of South Carolina Press, Columbia, SC

Peckham M. (1981) *Beyond the Tragic Vision. The Quest for Identity in the Nineteenth Century*, Cambridge University Press, Cambridge

Peckham M. (1985) *Romanticism and Ideology*, Penkevill Publishing, Greenwood, Fl

Perrow C. (1972) *Complex Organizations. A Critical Essay*. Scott Foreman, Glenview, Ill.

Peters T. J. and Austin N. (1985) *A Passion for Excellence. The Leadership Difference*, Collins, London

Peters T. J. and Waterman R. H., Jr (1982) *In Search of Excellence*, Harper and Row, New York

Pettigrew A. M. (1985) *The Awakening Giant. Continuity and Change in Imperial Chemical Industries*, Blackwell, Oxford

Pettigrew A. and Whipp R. (1991) *Managing Change for Competitive Success*, Blackwell, Oxford

Piercy N. and Peattie K. J. (1988) Matching marketing strategies to corporate culture: the parcel and the wall. *Journal of General Management*, **13** (4), 33–44

Polanyi M. and Prosch H. (1975) *Meaning*, University of Chicago Press, Chicago

Pollner M. (1987) *Mundane Reason. Reality in Everyday and Sociological Discourse*, Cambridge University Press, Cambridge

Polsby N. W. (1963) *Community Power and Political Theory*, Yale University Press, New Haven, Conn.

Pondy L. (1978) Leadership is a language game. In *Leadership: Where Else Can We Go?* (eds M. W. McCall, Jr and M. M. Lombardo), Duke University Press, Durham, NC, 87–99

Pondy L. R. and Huff A. S. (1985) Achieving routine in organizational change. *Journal of Management*, **11** (2), 103–16

Potter S. (1987) *On the Right Lines? The Limits of Technological Innovation*, Pinter, London

Poulet R. and Moult G. (1987) Putting values into evaluation. *Training and Development Journal*, July, 62–6

Quick T. L. (1989) *Unconventional Wisdom. Irreverent Solutions for Tough Problems at Work*, Jossey-Bass, Oxford

Quinn J. B. (1980) *Strategies for Change: Logical Incrementalism*, Irwin, Homewood, Ill.

Quinn J. B. (1982) Managing strategies incrementally. *OMEGA*, **10** (6), 613–27

Quinn J. B. (1985) Managing innovation: controlled chaos. *Harvard Business Review*, **63**, May/June, 73–84

Quinn R. E. and McGrath M. R. (1985) The transformation of organizational cultures. A competing values perspective. In *Organization Culture* (eds P. J. Frost, L. F. Moore, M. R. Louis et al.), Sage, Beverly Hills, 315–34

Ray C. A. (1986) Corporate culture: the last frontier of control. *Journal of Management Studies*, **23** (3), 287–98

Renfrew C. (1979) Transformations. In *Transformations. Mathematical Approaches to Culture Change* (eds C. Renfrew and K. L. Cooke), Academic Press, London, 3–44

Richards I. A. (1936) *The Philosophy of Rhetoric*, Oxford University Press, Oxford

Ricoeur P. (1970) *Freud and Philosophy. An Essay on Interpretation*, Yale University Press, New Haven, Conn.

Roddick A. (1991) *Body and Soul*, Ebury Press, London

Rose G. (1988) *The Romantic Garden*, Frances Lincoln, London

Rose R. A. (1988) Organizations as multiple cultures: a rules theory analysis. *Human Relations*, **41** (February), 139–71

Rosen C. and Zerner H. (1984) *Romanticism and Realism. The Mythology of Nineteenth-Century Art*, The Viking Press, New York

Rosen M. (1991) Scholars, travellers and thieves: on concept, method and cunning in organizational ethnography. Paper presented to the 8th International SCOS Conference on Organizational Symbolism and Corporate Culture, Copenhagen, Denmark, 26–28 June

Saussure F. de (1974) *A Course in General Linguistics*, Fontana, London

Schein E. H. (1983) The role of the founder in creating organizational cultures. *Organizational Dynamics*, Summer, 13–29

Schein E. H. (1985) *Organizational Culture and Leadership: A Dynamic View*, Jossey-Bass, CA

Schiemann W. A. (1989) Strategy-culture-communication: three keys to success. *Executive Excellence*, August, 2–3

Scholefield M. (1989) Mentoring: an exciting way to fast track women? *Training Officer*, August, 238–9

Schon D. A. (1973) *Beyond the Stable State*, Pelican, London

Schutz A. (1967) *Collected Papers I. The Problem of Social Reality*, Martinus Nijhoff, The Hague

Scott W. R. (1987) The adolescence of institutional theory. *Administrative Science Quarterly*, **32**, 493–511

Sheldon A. (1980) Organizational paradigms: a theory of organizational change. *Organizational Dynamics*, Winter 61–80

Shelley J. H. (1980) Introduction. In *Structure in Science and Art*. Proceedings of the Third C. H. Boehringer Sohn Symposium held at Kronberg, Taunus, 2–5 May 1979 (eds Sir P. Medawar and J. H. Shelley), Excerpta Medica, Oxford

Shweder R. A. (1984) Anthropology's romantic rebellion against the enlightenment, or there's more to thinking than reason and evidence. In *Culture Theory. Essays on Mind, Self, and Emotion* (eds R. A. Shweder and R. A. LeVine), Cambridge University Press, Cambridge, 27–66

Silverman D. (1970) *The Theory of Organizations. A Sociological Framework*, Heinemann, London

Silverman D. and Torode B. (1980) *The Material World. Some Theories of Language and its Limits*, Routledge and Kegan Paul, London

Simmel G. (1921) *Der Konflict der Modernen Kultur*, 2nd edn, Duncker and Humblot, Leipzig. In *Georg Simmel: Sociologist and European* (1976) (trans. P. A. Lawrence), Nelson, Middlesex, 223–42

Simmel G. (1922) *Lebensanschauung. Vier Metaphysische Kapitel*, 2nd edn, Duncker and Humblot, Munich and Leipzig

Simmel G. (1955) *Conflict*, The Free Press, New York

Slater, P. (1974) *Earthwalk*, Doubleday, New York

Smircich L. (1983) Concepts of culture and organizational analysis. *Administrative Science Quarterly*, **28** (3), 339–58

Smircich L. and Morgan G. (1982) Leadership: the management of meaning. *The Journal of Applied Behavioural Science*, **18** (3), 257–73

Smith K. K. (1984) Rabbits, lynxes, and organizational transitions. In *Managing Organizational Transitions* (eds J. R. Kimberley and R. E. Quinn), Irwin, Homewood, Ill, 267–94

Smith R. C. and Eisenberg E. M. (1987) Conflict in Disneyland: A root metaphor analysis. *Communication Monographs*, **54**, 367–80

Solomon R. C. (1976) *The Passions*, Anchor Press/Doubleday, New York

Sorokin P. A. (1966) *Sociological Theories of Today*, Harper and Row, New York

Stebbins M. W. and Shani A. B. (1989) Organization design: beyond the 'mafia' model. *Organizational Dynamics*, Winter, 18–30

Stephens C. and Eisen S. (1984) Myth, transformation, and the change agent. In *Transforming Work* (ed. J. D. Adams), Miles River Press, Alexandria, Va, 186–90

Steward J. H. (1955) *Theory of Culture Change. The Methodology of Multilinear Evolution*, University of Illinois Press, Urbana, Ill.

Strauss A. (1978) *Negotiations. Varieties, Contexts, Processes, and Social Order*, Jossey-Bass, CA

Stravinsky I. and Craft R. (1979 [1959]) *Conversations with Igor Stravinsky*, Faber and Faber, London

Sturrock J. (1986) *Structuralism*, Paladin, London

Talman J. L. (1967) *Romanticism and Revolt. Europe 1815–1848*, Thames and Hudson, London

Thomas M. (1985) In search of culture: holy grail or gravy train? *Personnel Management*, September, 24–7

Timasheff N. S. (1965) *Sociological Theory. Its Nature and Growth*, Random House, New York

Toch E. (1977) *The Shaping Forces in Music*, Dover Publications, New York

Toynbee P. (ed.) (1976) *The Distant Drum. Reflections on the Spanish Civil War*, Sidgwick and Jackson, London

Trice H. M. and Beyer J. M. (1985) Using six organizational rites to change culture. In *Gaining Control of the Corporate Culture* (eds R. Kilmann, M. J. Saxton, R. Serpa et al.), Jossey-Bass, CA, 370–99

Tushman M. L. and Romanelli E. (1985) Organizational evolution: a metamorphosis model of convergence and reorientation. In *Research in Organizational Behaviour* (eds B. M. Staw and L. L. Cummings), JAI Press, Greenwich, CT, 171–222

Tyler S. A. (1986) Post-modern ethnography: from document of the occult to occult document. In *Writing Culture: The Poetics and Politics of Ethnography* (eds J. Clifford and G. E. Marcus), University of California Press, Berkeley, CA, 122–40

Vaill P. B. (1989) *Managing as a Performing Art*, Jossey-Bass, San Francisco, CA

Van Buskirk W. (1989) Symbolically embedded emotion in organizations: some implications for culturally based O.D. interventions. Paper presented to the Organizational Development Division at the annual meeting of the Academy of Management, Washington DC

Van Holthoon F. and Olson D. R. (eds) (1987) *Common Sense*, University Press of America, Lanham, MD

Van Maanen J. (1978) People processing: strategies of organizational socialization. *Organizational Dynamics*, Summer, 18–36

Van Maanen J. (1988) *Tales of the Field. On Writing Ethnography*, University of Chicago Press, Chicago

Van Maanen J. (1991) The smile factory. Work at Disneyland. In *Reframing Organizational Culture* (eds P. J. Frost, L. F. Moore, M. R. Louis et al.), Sage, London, 58–76

Van Maanen J. and Schein E. H. (1979) Toward a theory of organizational socialization. In *Research in Organization Behavior*, 1 (eds B. M. Staw and L. L. Cummings), JAI Press, Greenwich, Conn, 209–69

Watzlawick P., Weakland J. H. and Fisch R. (1974) *Change. Principles of Problem Formation and Problem Resolution*, W. W. Norton, New York

Webber R. A. (1977) Convergence or divergence? In *Culture and Management* (ed. T. D. Weinshall), Penguin, Harmondsworth, 39–55

Weick K. E. (1979) *The Social Psychology of Organizing*, Addison-Wesley, Reading, Mass.

Weick K. E. (1981) Managerial thought in the context of action. In *The Executive Mind: New Insights on Managerial Thought and Action* (eds S. Srivastva et al.), Jossey-Bass, San Francisco, CA, 221–42

Weick K. E. (1985) The significance of corporate culture. In *Organizational Culture* (eds P. J. Frost, L. F. Moore, M. R. Louis et al.), Sage, Beverly Hills, CA, 381–9

Weick K. E. and Browning L. D. (1986) Argument and narration in organizational communication. In *1986 Yearly Review of Management of the Journal of Management* (eds J. G. Hunt and J. D. Blair), **12** (2), 243–59

Wheeler J. (1980) First session. Thought and brain. In *Structure in Science and Art*. Proceedings of the Third C. H. Boehringer Sohn Symposium held at Kronberg, Taunus, 2–5 May, 1979 (eds S. P. Medawar and J. H. Shelley), Excerpta Medica, Oxford, 3–51

Whittle S., Smith S., Tranfield D. and Foster M. (1991) Implementing total quality: erecting tents or building palaces. Working Paper, Change Management Research Unit, Sheffield Business School, UK

Wilkins A. L. (1983) Organizational stories as symbols. In *Organizational Symbolism. Monographs in Organizational Behaviour and Industrial Relations*, vol. I (eds L. R. Pondy, P. J. Frost, G. Morgan and T. C. Dandridge), JAI Press, Greenwich, Conn, 81–92

Wilkins A. L. (1989) *Developing Corporate Character. How to Successfully Change an Organization without Destroying it*, Jossey-Bass, San Francisco, CA

Wilkins A. L. and Dyer W. G. (1988) Toward culturally sensitive theories of culture change. *Academy of Management Review*, **13** (4), 522–33

Williams R. (1965) *The Long Revolution*, Pelican, Harmondsworth

Williams R (1973) *The Country and the City*, Oxford University Press, Oxford

Willmott H. (1991a) Postmodernism and excellence: the de-differentiation of economy and culture. Working Paper, Manchester School of Management, UMIST, Manchester, England

Willmott H. (1991b) Strength is ignorance; slavery is freedom: managing culture in modern organizations. Revision of paper presented to 8th International SCOS Conference on Organizational Symbolism and Corporate Culture, Copenhagen, Denmark, 26–28 June

Wood P. A. (1991) Whitbread Inns; to investigate the impact and effectiveness of the 'service standards and value' programme. MBA Project Report, University of Bath, School of Management

Young E. (1989) On the naming of the rose: interests and multiple meanings as elements of organizational culture. *Organization Studies*, **10** (2), 187–206

Zijderveld A. C. (1982) *Reality in a Looking-Glass. Rationality through an Analysis of Traditional Folly*, Routledge and Kegan Paul, London

Zucker L. G. (1987) Institutional theories of organization. *Annual Review of Sociology*, **13**, 443–64

Zucker L. G. (1988) *Institutional Patterns and Organizations: Culture and Environment*, Ballinger, Cambridge, Mass.

Index

Name index

Subject Index